'This is a stunningly beautiful story of one woman's relentless campaign to save an iconic bird. And like her campaign, which caught the imagination of millions, Hannah's writing is elegant and engaging. The campaign should never have been needed, but it was and the swifts are lucky to have Hannah fighting their corner.'
Zac Goldsmith

'I applaud Hannah's book; her inner steel and her sassy take on conservation are inspiring. I am so heartened that there are courage-driven young women holding nature in the light so that it WILL be seen by the powerful.'
Mary Colwell, author of *Curlew Moon*

'This book might make you scream. It is the story of a fight that started with a promise to a small bird. It is about bird spirit and the spirit of a very singular human. Hannah Bourne-Taylor has a searing eye for both truth and charlatans. Hannah is a hero of our times who pitted herself against giants.'
Keggie Carew, author of *Beastly*

'Throughout *Nature Needs You*, Bourne-Taylor's elegant, impassioned and personal prose highlights in detail the challenges facing twenty-first-century conservation, and the innovative and dedicated campaigning required to achieve success.'
Nicholas Gates, naturalist, film maker and author of *Orchard*

'Swifts have found a superb champion, whose sheer passion and commitment shine through the pages of this wonderful book.'
Stephen Moss, author of *The Starling*

'Told from the biggest heart, this book will make you laugh and cry, will fill you with love and make you gasp at how one person could be so determined to save birds. Every word she writes makes me want to get up and do more for our beautiful natural world. Hannah Bourne-Taylor is a force of nature, and we need more like her – could that be you?'

Kate Bradbury, conservationist
and author of *One Garden Against the World*

'A compelling and powerful story of magnificent determination and love for the natural world. We need more people like Hannah.'

Lev Parikian, author of *Taking Flight*

'A wonderful book that will make you furious, hopeful and inspired by turns. Buy it, read it and then become an activist yourself.'

Roger Morgan-Grenville, author of *Shearwater*

'An inspirational book that screams with urgency, bravery, heartache and hope. By the end you'll be flocking to take swift action of your own to protect a world that needs us as much as we need it.'

Matt Gaw, author of *In All Weathers*

'*Nature Needs You* is a brave and brilliant book: a manifesto for change fired by love and resolve.'

Julian Hoffman, author of *Lifelines*

'Clever, fierce, funny and searingly clear-sighted, Hannah is an absolute inspiration.'

Nicola Chester, author of *On Gallows Down*

'After making a promise to two swift chicks, Hannah embarks on a seemingly impossible campaign journey. Heartfelt and full of passion, her story shows just how much one person can achieve when they have the courage and determination to stand up for what they love.'

Nic Wilson, *Land Beneath the Waves*

NATURE NEEDS YOU

NATURE NEEDS YOU

The Fight to Save Our Swifts

HANNAH BOURNE-TAYLOR

Elliott&Thompson

First published 2025 by
Elliott and Thompson Limited
2 John Street
London WC1N 2ES
www.eandtbooks.com

Represented by:
Authorised Rep Compliance Ltd.
Ground Floor, 71 Lower Baggot Street
Dublin, D02 P593
Ireland
www.arccompliance.com

ISBN: 978-1-78396-868-8

9 8 7 6 5 4 3 2 1

A catalogue record for this book is available from the British Library.

Typesetting by Marie Doherty

Printed by CPI Group (UK) Ltd,
Croydon, CR0 4YY

For

my natterjack Daddy, Dr Simon Gates

Lord of the Birds, Zac Goldsmith

the Golden Pillar, Jemma

and 109,896 strangers

Contents

'It's not the critic who counts; not the man who points out how the strong man stumbles or where the doer of deeds could have done them better. The credit belongs to the man who is actually in the arena, whose face is marred by dust and sweat and blood; who strives valiantly; who errs, who comes short again and again ... who knows great enthusiasms, the great devotions; who spends himself in a worthy cause; who at the best knows in the end the triumph of high achievement, and who at the worst, if he fails, at least fails while daring greatly, so that his place shall never be with those cold and timid souls who neither know victory nor defeat.'

– PRESIDENT TEDDY ROOSEVELT

Prologue
The Feather Speech

5 November 2022

On a cold November noon tinged by the electric yellow light of a grey autumn day, I stepped out of a black cab on the edge of Hyde Park, *almost* naked. Painted from neck to toe in inked feathers, wearing only a thong and ankle boots, I was a stark contrast to the anorak-clad passers-by whose shocked stares cemented the fact that what I was doing was extreme, radical even.

I walked through a waiting crowd, bum flashing, grateful that my waist-long hair covered my chest when the wind wasn't blowing. Stepping up onto an upturned apple crate decorated with the words 'The Feather Speech', I took my place as the newest 'speaker' at Speakers' Corner.

Speakers' Corner has the same diminished impression as meeting a celebrity – it's much smaller and less distinctive in real life. The legendary space, known for hosting a history of free speeches, is just an ordinary bit of Hyde Park, edged by black railings, where joggers, commuters and tourists file past. But here, the twentieth-century feminist words of Christabel Pankhurst once hung in the air, along with speeches from George Orwell, Karl Marx and William Morris. Among other topics, women's rights, the Spanish Civil War, communism and socialism have been passionately voiced here, and now here I was, about to make a five-minute speech . . . about birds.

Birds. Those feathered ancient creatures who witness our lives whether we notice them or not, so intertwined, so adapted, yet prehistoric. Archosaurs, they are the only remaining dinosaurs. Such a part of our daily lives, it would be unnerving to encounter a day without birds. Some live so close to us in the nooks and crannies of our walls, they sleep inches away from where we rest our heads.

In Britain, several birds nest in our buildings, including house sparrows, common starlings, house martins and common swifts. Each one is a beady-eyed companion living alongside us, reliant on nesting in our buildings to breed. For common swifts in Britain, this dependence is almost 100 per cent, with the exception of a small number who nest in the old Caledonian Forest in Scotland. Belonging to one of the most ancient orders of birds, swifts have existed, screaming their iconic screams, since Britain was a tropical shallow sea, their bloodline one of the longest in the avian world. About the same age as the Rocky Mountains, they evolved seven epochs ago in the Palaeogene period. For the 60 million years since, swifts have reigned the skies. One of their superpowers is to stay airborne for longer than any other bird on Earth. For nine months every year, they live in a single flight lasting around 6,500 hours, yet when they come home, they come home to us. Used to sleeping in the sky 18,000 feet up, above the clouds, the only ground swifts will ever intentionally know are the nesting holes in our buildings. Every year in August adult swifts leave our villages and towns, and fly to the Congo rainforests, following coastlines and crossing the Sahara, the largest desert on Earth. Every May, the same swifts return to Britain, right down to the exact nook they left nine months before. Able to live for twenty years, swifts often call our houses home longer than we do.

Historically, swifts bred in the high holes of trees in primal forests. When, in the seventeenth century, the diminishing forests of Britain and Europe, felled for timber and ships, disappeared, swifts adapted to nesting within man-made structures. Now they are on the brink of extinction, together with the other birds who share our walls, united in their plight by the loss of their nesting habitat. There are other factors contributing to their decline but if they can't breed in Britain, they can't exist here. This threat was what propelled me that naked day, trying not to shiver, standing on a box, speaking to a small audience made up of half supporters, half press.

My words rang out into the cold air: 'I stand here as a go-between for swifts to ask for your comradery because they need our help. Today I open a petition and invite you to sign it to make swift bricks compulsory in new housing across Britain. Together we can try to stop these remarkable British birds passing into legend . . .'

My voice was surprisingly steady and clear, loud enough to be heard but not quite a shout. Determined to learn my speech off by heart, I had been practising it, wearing just my pants, in a field near my house in Oxfordshire. My husband, Robin, had faithfully been my audience of one, holding a huge coat, ready to wrap me up to hide me from unsuspecting dog walkers. Now I was aware that Britain's press was recording it all and I was half wondering whether one of my legs shaking uncontrollably would be picked up on film. I had no idea whether the photos would be printed and my campaign launch would engage the nation with the plight of our feathered neighbours in a desperate bid to save them.

My five-minute speech attempted to distil their existence, outlining why these birds need our help, and presenting the solution of a simple brick. Alongside external wooden swift nest boxes, 'swift bricks' were invented decades ago. A swift brick is a brick that sits flush to the wall with a deliberate cavity that provides a nesting site not just for swifts but for all other urban birds who nest in holes in our buildings. Sustainable, requiring zero maintenance and as cheap as £34, they have been proven to work well, implemented in Gibraltar in the 1990s where swift populations have stabilised as a result. Critically, without swift bricks, there is no guaranteed safe, permanent nesting habitat for swifts or any birds reliant on building cavities in Britain. They are the answer to loss of nesting habitat for all cavity-nesting urban birds, but in 2021 the RSPB estimated that fewer than 20,000 swift bricks had been installed by developers. A start, but nowhere near enough to counter the national-scale loss of natural cavities, especially when theoretically hundreds of thousands of swift bricks could be installed each year thanks to the government's annual quota for new housing.

The speech was followed by a two-and-a-half-mile march. I walked under Wellington Arch, outside the gates of Buckingham Palace and down Birdcage Walk until I was next to the Cenotaph, the Houses of Parliament and finally Downing Street. The march that day, which happened to fall on Bonfire Night, was my tiny twenty-first-century version of outrage at the government's inaction. Instead of trying to blow up the Houses of Parliament, I was simply trying to spark a national conversation to help birds.

As I walked, I distracted myself from the odd looks, reminding myself that The Feather Speech was an accumulation of many elements. It was months of consulting with expert ornithologists and thirty-six years of the sheer delight I felt on seeing the first swifts arriving home to Britain each May. But as I marched, eyes forward, trying to ignore the rain that fell harder and harder, wetting my hair so it stuck to my shoulders, one underlining thought was roaring in the back of my mind: How the hell had it come to this? Why was anyone having to do this for birds?

And how come it was me?

Chapter 1

Mayday

May, 2021

The grass is singing. I lie on my back among the fast-growing blades, the May sun warm on my face for the first time this year. Next to me, a grasshopper flings its green body onto mine, looking at me with a roving eye.

We loll in the sunshine.

It feels like a perfect encapsulation of the word 'estivate' – derived from the Latin word for summer, *aestus* – meaning 'to spend summer in a torpid state', a wonderful warm trance of *being*, but it's not quite here yet. One crucial element is missing and we are lying in wait. The weather is just right: blue sky, bright sunshine and no wind over the landscape of green, studded with the white lace of cow parsley and hawthorn frothing along the hedgerows. When will they arrive? Hurtling effortlessly, soaring through the air, cascading over continents, they are coming, headed straight for where I am lying with the grasshopper. Any minute now, they will return all the way from Africa and bring the feeling of summer with them.

We scan the sky, ears ready to hear their screams.

Then we see one.

That unmistakable sickle shape, that black-feathered anchor, suddenly there in the patch of sky above us. The arrival summons a scream as I stagger up, jumping in the air with the grasshopper.

'Welcome home!!!!!!!!!!!!!!!!!!' I cry, arching up towards the sky. The meadow and the grasshopper and I are laughing with joy. All over the country, other grown women and men were holding their breath, staring up in wait, leaping into the air too, crying, whooping, rejoicing as their feathered neighbours return. That is the effect of a single 45-gram bird, loved so much that Brits have collectively dubbed them our icons of summer: swifts.

An hour later I was pedalling my bike as fast as I could go, through the dappled light and lilac back lanes of Oxford, throwing it down in excited abandon as I arrived at the Museum of Natural History. The museum is an imposing Victorian neo-Gothic building on the inner edge of the city. Both its design and contents are shaped by the natural world. Under a glass roof with wrought ironwork and column capitals carved into plants representing all the botanical orders is a vast collection of millions of objects, including 30,000 zoological specimens. Among them is the only surviving soft tissue of a dodo in the world and the 195-million-year-old ichthyosaur discovered by Mary Anning in the nineteenth century. But within the museum, there are things that, to me, trump the whole collection: the swifts living in the tower.

Under the roof cowls in the tower there are 147 swift nests, the entrance holes visible from the lawn in front. The tower is home to a colony of swifts, studied by the Edward Grey Institute since 1948 in what is the world's longest study of a single species of bird. I glanced up at the holes. Every May, the swifts arrive in waves, following isobars somewhere south of Europe, lurking where the insects are high up, until the weather gives clear passage. First the vanguards, then the adult pairs who reunite once back here, and finally the juveniles, who won't land but return to prospect for their own future nesting sites. I rushed up the great stone steps, to find George Candelin waiting for me. George is special. He is the

'Keeper of the Swifts'. Since 1995, every May he has embarked on a weekly monitoring of the colony, noting each bird, each egg, every chick and recording the precious new generation's development as well as ringing them when they are old enough, all in the dark so as not to disturb the birds. I had contacted him to ask him about swifts and he invited me to visit the tower, quickly taking me under his wing, allowing me to bombard him with questions. He was naturally calm, measured and never overstated, but didn't mind my high-energy enthusiasm.

Slipping through the discreet tower door, I followed George up the stone spiral staircase into a large room at the base of the tower. From there, up another spiral staircase into the dark tower, lit only by red lamps. I love this place. It is dark, quiet, still, like a great old ship that creaks in the wind, and it is full of swifts. Inside the tower there are three levels, with the nesting boxes on all four sides, but the southern-facing wall is almost empty of swifts who instinctively know the risk of summer sun overheating their chicks. Site loyal, each adult swift returns to the exact hole each year.

'They're back!' George whispered as he opened the first flap of the first nest box.

'Ah, my favourite,' I said, in awe, gazing at her dark velvet body, her big eyes, closed in the first proper sleep she'd had since she had last been here. For the nine months between, she'd slept on the wing, shutting off half her brain at a time so she could rest but remain airborne. Now she was in a blissfully sheltered, dark bedroom.

'She's as good as new despite her long journey,' I whispered.

'Just being a swift, doing what swifts do,' George said softly, careful not to humanise the birds, but I could hear in his voice he was smiling too.

We shuffled round the narrow walkways in the tower, George whispering swifts' secrets as we moved around in the dark. My favourite was one that connects the colony to the city in which they live: a nest dotted with little bits of tiny round coloured paper.

'Well, it's May, isn't it?' George explained. 'And during May, as the swifts return, university students are doing their exams. Traditionally, fellow students greet their friends outside the exam halls and celebrate by throwing confetti.' He pointed to the dots of colour. 'Little do they know that some of the confetti ends up in the tower as the swifts use it to build their nests.'

It was a wonderful thought. Swifts catch nest materials in the air: leaves, mown grass, scraps of tracing paper, rose petals, string, pigeon feathers and, in Oxford, confetti. Their beds, just like their homes in buildings, are interwoven with our own lives. The confetti had been thrown to celebrate the academic achievement of young minds who have the world at their feet. Now it was cradling eggs, marking the beginning of lives that would have the run of the sky.

'But since they were last here, they've been added to the Red List of highest conservation concern, together with house martins,' he said. 'That's seventy species of British birds on the Red List.'

'Maybe being on the Red List will help them. Maybe the government will stop allowing the dousing of the countryside with chemicals killing all the insects, maybe fully engage and invest in nature restoration, and protect the birds' nesting habitat,' I said, clutching at the potential silver lining.

'You mean, maybe the government will start caring?' George replied. 'British wildlife is condemned unless a lot of things change, otherwise there won't be anything left and swifts are in the middle of it all, hit every which way. They're poster children for biodiversity and they're plummeting.'

'Well, if the government won't act, maybe I'll make them,' I said, my heart suddenly starting to beat hard in my chest.

'How?' George asked.

'I have absolutely no idea,' I replied.

My mind pocketed this threat to do something, making a small bulge of thought while summer grew around me as I walked through my village territory each day. Between where the grasshoppers hopped and my house, the meadow had built itself high in bursting colour. Thistles and foxgloves towered over me as I leaned into the flower heads, listening to the scrabble of bumblebee feet as they ventured into the petals. Down the single-track lane framed by stone cottages, little yellow domes of pineapple weed grew through the cracks, drenching the tarmac with their pineapple scent at footstep level. Every time I passed, I paused, crouching to breathe it in. Above me, the invisible lines of blackbird melody flowed back to my stone cottage, which stands unfortunately close to the A road that slices through the village like a guillotine. Despite the constant nearby death threat of cars, my small garden, tucked away behind the house, was full of life. Like a maquette of a meadow, it is a refuge that, left uncut and unhindered, is home to iridescent beetles, bright pink moths, and wrens who sing, gram for gram, ten times louder than a cockerel.

I liked knowing my home by the map of wild territories, instead of human. I didn't know the name of my neighbour opposite who vacuumed up the dandelions on his buzz-cut lawn, but I had watched the colony of sparrows grow, living out their lives between his garden and mine, thanks to the tree he had decided to keep. When neighbours made their morning pilgrimage to the village shop, the rooks swirled above, whirling in a dance of voices to the fields that stretched out into the Cotswolds. During the summer, the swifts bound the landscape together, sleeping and nesting in the walls. My husband, Robin, would find me staring at gable ends in the village, trying to encourage me to walk on, knowing I was waiting to see if a swift would fly in or out of a hole under the eaves.

'Doesn't it just blow your mind?' I said to him as a swift flew right above our heads, its speed fast enough to rush the air that made a sound in its wake. 'They sleep here, right next to us, and then they make a journey to the Congo Basin – a place I've always dreamed of going – and they don't land until they're back here. Right there, in that little hole in this village nine months later?'

Robin smiled at my little speech, one I made at least once a week, gently dragging me away. He did love them, but partly because he loved me and I *love* birds.

Birds are not just feather and bone. They are go-betweens, shrinking the boundaries that separate wild and tame. All are connected to us, some existing so close that their lives are intertwined with ours. As a child, my parents nicknamed me Spadge after the sparrows and how wide-eyed they made me. As an adult, two individual birds redefined my life while living in the rural grasslands of Ghana. I rescued, hand raised and rewilded a finch whom I found abandoned after a storm blew down his grass nest. He spent hours weaving nests out of my hair, earnestly attacking the mole on my face and demanding the smallest of strokes under his tiny chin. After three months, the effort of spending every day in the grasslands with him so he could learn how to be wild paid off, and he rejoined his flock. The other bird was a swift, two weeks away from fledging, with eyes like polished planets. Raising the swift was intense, hunting insects for it, knowing it had to be a precise weight and size before it could fly. Every time I fed the swift, I was awestruck by the fallen feathered star in the palm of my hand. But the close-up view of the bird was jarring. I had only ever seen swifts diving and spiralling over the roofs in fluid motion above me. These two birds are two pieces of the wild who connected me to the rest of it, who broke down the concept of 'nature' and 'wildlife' into hearts that beat alongside mine. Only when I returned to England from Africa did I learn the nightmare unfolding on my doorstep: that beating wild hearts were stopping, one after the other, in their *millions*. Threatened with extinction, the swifts' screams turned into cries for help.

Since George had told me swifts and house martins had been added to the Red List, I had not skewered the mounting feeling of dread and concern into a tangible plan. I was used to assuming someone else with more expertise and authority would do something, or that perhaps nothing could be done so there was no point in tearing myself apart worrying about all the ways in which we were destroying the natural world and the systems that keep us alive. In contrast, one wild creature suffering is impossible for me to ignore. I am the person who will harbour a fly caught on a train until I can safely release it, scoop drowning insects from puddles, move snails off the path and turn my whole life upside down if a creature needs my help. On my honeymoon, I tucked an injured bird into my bra and delivered it to a rehab centre. Last winter, I found a hypothermic wood mouse on the road, put him in my glove and housed him over the cold snap. Within a month of moving back to England, Robin's and my life revolved around crows.

On a cold March morning, we found a small black mass lying in a frosted field near the house, bouncing away, unable to fly. Grounded, the crow flung itself into the air, trying desperately to launch. Each time it tumbled down quickly in a small, frustrated, frightened ball of black feathers. Robin caught the bird while two other crows tried hard to protect it, launching diving attacks, cawing their haunting cries. Smaller than them but almost fully grown, the disabled bird was a yearling, so we guessed the two others were its parents. Crows are famously loyal, and from the parents' point of view we were kidnapping their child, wrenching it from its family and holding it hostage.

Back home, I held the crow in my hands and felt for breaks in its bones but there were none. The damage was on the outside, the feathers ripped, possibly a victim of a Larsen trap, where game-keepers deliberately cut corvids' feathers to use them as live decoys, knowing their loyal family will try to rescue them, making them easy targets to shoot. Many of the young bird's wing feathers and tail were missing, leaving it unable to fly, but its eyes were burning bright. Its stare was sure – this was a bird that was trying to live.

We didn't know whether we would look after the crow until it grew new feathers and could be released somehow or whether we would have a pet crow until we were in our sixties.

'I think we should name it,' Robin said. 'We might have it for decades.' Convinced she was a female, we called her Constance, which derives from Latin 'to stand with'. The name went beyond the surface commitment we made. It was linked to principle. Despite the natural habitat and food sources decreasing, crows have successfully adapted to our changes, moving into urban areas that we consider ours. Crows plan ahead, hiding food in caches in nooks and crannies, saving for a day when food is scarce. They work together to mob predators and are highly territorial, pro-tecting their families, known as a 'murder'. This collective noun feels harsh, negatively steeped in human history: on *our* past bloody battlefields, near *our* medieval hospitals and at *our* gallows sites, crows were regular visitors, seen picking apart the dead. This associ-ation wove superstitions and folklore into the perceived lives of crows, people not seeing their part in the scenes, not understand-ing crows to be useful rubbish collectors, cleaning away scraps that would otherwise spread disease. Because of this mislabelled encroachment on 'our' land, these birds are considered a pest: vermin, a collective noun and generalised label on anything that humans consider inconvenient, often leading to their painful demise. We have defined this living, breathing creature by how it negatively impacts us, not for its own inherent qualities.

Constance was mesmerising mostly because she was clearly actively thinking. Suspicious to start with, she had to be force-fed, which she hated, crouching, her feathers flattened, hissing at me. Gradually we got into a routine that, although it worked, was bizarre. If I offered her a ramekin of mince and live mealworms, standing with my head down, eyes low, face down as though I was bowing to a goddess, she began to eat. She would snap the worms from the ramekin I held in my outstretched hand. This became our dynamic: we held her captive but she dictated the rules.

Until her feathers moulted and regrew she couldn't fly, and only when she could would she be free. The timescale for this process was at least one season, maybe more. A guilt attached itself to me immediately, as I sat with Constance. I knew she was lonely but I would never be enough. Crows need crows. Eventually, after weeks of searching, we found her company. In the end we fostered five crows, the other four having been rescued by a corvid sanctuary and, for various reasons, also needing long rehab to allow their feathers to grow.

The little murder lived in our shed for two years until all became strong enough to return to the wild, finally free. This was a huge commitment. Robin and I couldn't leave our house for more than one night together because the crows would be spooked by someone else coming to feed them and change their water or check on them in any way. While we deliberately didn't try to tame them, for the weeks Constance had been alone, we had played catch with her. It was Robin who had discovered this was possible. Using a cork tied onto a piece of rope, he had swung the cork towards her and she would snatch it. Then, with force, tilting her head back, she threw it back. We played it with her regularly, and in return Constance had taught me a lesson that resonated through how she looked at me. Intelligent and disdainful, Constance's stare was intense. When I looked at her, she looked away, unconfrontational, afraid, but as soon as I moved my glance, I could see her fixing her eyes back to me. I could feel her stare. Occasionally our eyes would meet and I would see the faint difference between her pupils and her iris, the colour of her eyes not black but brown, just like her feathers were tinted with a glimmering iridescent navy in sunlight. She was a wealth of secrets, of life waiting to be lived. But most of all, she was an active consciousness staring at me, wanting to know what was happening and what I was doing about it.

Looking into the eyes of a wild creature, rendered helpless because of human hands, felt like looking into a stark, brutal mirror of truth. There was no hiding or skirting around the facts, finding excuses, displacing blame. There was no bullshit. In her dark, piercing eyes, all crows were represented, and through the crows, all birds and all wildlife. She was precious, not only because she was unique, but on principle. Constance represented the adaptable, resilient wild that was being crippled and destroyed by us. As she tried to fly, flapping her shredded wings, wobbling as she lost her balance, she gave me both responsibility and power to rectify her life. A life that disliked me and everything I stood for, and this felt honest because Constance was wild, her stare holding me accountable for being human.

Chapter 2

The Promise

The swifts spurred me on to get to know some of the people in the area. In a nearby village, there was an active wildlife group with posters going up for talks and events that led me to a local Swift Conservation Society. I arrived in the village hall for their first meeting of the year. The three retired women who had started it were full of gumption. In her soft Scottish accent, Sylvia opened the meeting, addressing the small crowd of all ages in the room.

'We have gathered because the swifts have started to arrive here in Oxfordshire and across the country. With this joy comes a nightmare. As you all know too well, many swifts will return after their perilous journeys to find their homes in people's walls and roofs blocked off by soffits, reroofing, repointing or demolition. It is our job to try to ensure their homes are protected, unblocked, or that nest boxes are erected as quickly as possible.'

The other two founders, Margaret and Julie, nodded in agreement.

Sylvia continued. 'For any newcomers, let's remind ourselves what happens when some unfortunate swifts return.'

'The poor buggers fly at the wall over and over, trying to get into their home until they often break their wings or necks and die,' Margaret added, her voice clipped with anger.

'Yes. Indeed. The "poor buggers",' Sylvia said. 'Swifts return to the same nook or cranny year on year which, considering they

can live to be over twenty, makes them long-standing members of
our community.'

The small crowd nodded as she carried on. 'We are here to
help. Some don't die but get gravely injured, needing intensive care.
Many give up, and then with decreasing nesting options, struggle
to find new sites in time to breed. So, we have made swift business
our business.' Sylvia paused, letting the information sink in to those
new to the group, staring over her spectacles.

'Please familiarise yourselves with the rota so you know
when you're on call. You know the drill: if you see swifts trying
to get into a blocked nesting site or scaffolding being erected,
knock on the door, and *politely* explain to the occupant. Resist
raising your voice. We don't want to get ourselves a reputation
for bullying.'

'They'll think we're missionaries!' Margaret said.

'Someone thought I was a Jehovah's Witness last season,' a
teenager replied, giggling.

'If they decline to help, you can explain that blocking an active
nesting site breaches the Wildlife and Countryside Act and is therefore a wildlife crime. Problem is, to enforce it, a wildlife crime
officer or the police have to firstly be available, and secondly, be
willing to follow through, which doesn't always happen and then
there is not much we can do, so use all the skills you possess, please.
Charm, wits, what God gave you,' Sylvia added.

Margaret made a lewd expression and gestured to her bosom,
which was a surprise given she was a seventy-year-old wearing a
mauve cagoule.

'This is a matter of life and death, but we do need to operate
with decorum,' Sylvia said in response to the high-spirited conversations that had begun to fill the room, raising her hands to quieten
us down.

'If you see swifts trying to get into blocked nesting sites, send a message to the group with the words "code red", with the location,' Sylvia said, ending the meeting.

And so the summer started, and with it, all across the country, volunteer-led swift conservation groups began their local campaigns to protect their local swifts. One hundred and nineteen small groups and counting were part of the Swifts Local Network (SLN), a collection of people and groups actively raising awareness about these birds, trying to protect swifts from building changes. Founded by dedicated leaders of different swift groups around the UK, the SLN was formed in 2017 to enable everyone to keep connected and for new people like me to learn from those who had spent years committed to swift and house martin conservation. Linked to Action for Swifts, a resource created by Dick Newall to enable people to help swifts, there was an abundance of supportive information available.

I joined the SLN and was instantly plugged into an evening digest email that circulated news. Through the SLN I found out about the extent of effort across the country: groups such as Bolton and Bury Swifts, led by Louise Bentley, and Wolverton Swifts, led by Emma Rix, raise awareness locally. A builder from Kent with a soft spot for swifts, Nik Mitchell, has set up a club trying to change the culture of tradesmen in his area to look out for wildlife. Paul Wren, a builder in Oxfordshire, spends every spare hour going from village to village, keeping a watchful guard over existing nest sites and putting up swift boxes, for free. Helen Lucy paints beautiful pamphlets, delivering them to developers and councils asking them to install swift bricks and boxes. Graham Knight spends his spare time contacting local developers and councils, protecting nesting sites across Hertfordshire. Volunteers check for grounded birds, who either need just a helping hand to return them to the sky or full-time intensive care. Groups coordinating taxi services for grounded swifts operate all over the country, to ensure each patient gets to a rehabber in time. Volunteers rehab those swifts who survive, dedicating whole summers to care for them, falling in love with each one, their lives revolving around theirs until they release them into the sky.

Sheffield Swift Network, a fiercely loyal group, has successfully saved whole colonies of swifts from being displaced. One of their leaders is Chet Cunago, who leaps to the swifts' defence whenever scaffolding goes up in the area, knowing renovations risk blocking swift homes. She made the national news when she safeguarded one colony in Sheffield after frantic calls to the council that managed to get scaffold boards removed. Assembling a band of volunteers, they searched for overlooked swift nests in all the council houses scheduled for renovation in the area. The more they looked, the more they noticed the extent of the threat of renovations for swifts, surveying 1,500 council homes.

Chris Swaine, who set up Wakefield Swifts, protects existing nesting sites through collaborative innovation. Wakefield has a large number of social houses and pit houses, built post-war, that now belong to Wakefield Council, run by Wakefield District Housing (WDH). Wakefield's swifts favour these buildings, so whole colonies reside in lines of council houses. Reroofing had led to the destruction of several colonies in one afternoon, an action repeated all over the county. When Chris and the Wakefield group found out, they reacted, managing to hold an emergency conference call with the sustainability manager. Passionately explaining the need to help the swifts by saving the nesting sites scheduled to be blocked by further reroofing projects, the group proposed a solution of cutting small holes in the soffits to unblock each swift home and supplying wooden concave nests. The WDH agreed, inspired by

Chris. Thanks to citizen science, love and a practical solution, as the WDH have reroofed, they continue to install and leave little holes for the birds, protecting and mitigating hundreds of swift homes.

Witnessing swifts trying to get into their blocked homes is the main motivating factor for the members of the SLN, because to see it just once is to have the horror etched on your mind forever. I had been innocently walking round my village when I first saw it happen. It was early May and a swift whooshed right past my head on a flight path into its home, perhaps returning for the first time that season. I expected the bird to shoot through the hole and disappear, but instead it hit the stone wall and managed to correct itself, faltering, clutching to the wall. Its claws, the same colour and sheen as pencil lead, kept it there while it peered up and down. Then it sprung off the stone wall and flew back along its invisible flight path, hurtling past my head. I spun around, keeping my eyes on it as it circled back round and flew at the wall again. I braced myself for the collision, although fortunately this one carefully clung once more, looking again, as if perplexed. It had left here last August after having gone in and out of its home countless times, knowing exactly how to curve past the other rooftops and the telephone wires.

There was nothing I could do in the moment but to stand there, filling up with a wretched sense of numbed horror. I desperately knocked on the door of the house, but no one was in. I scrawled a note begging for the hole to be unblocked, pushing it through the letterbox. A day later I got the number of the owner and rang it, feeling awkward before they answered. They agreed to unblock the hole, the man coming the following evening, but it was too late. The swift had gone, nowhere to be seen. I watched the hole for days, but no swift returned. That single nest wasn't just important for the pair of swifts who were anticipating a proper rest after nine months in the sky, reuniting at home, but because as a breeding pair they could create two or even three more swifts, from egg to flying machines in just six weeks. While two or three chicks might not sound like very many, each of those birds could also go on to have two or three chicks every year; the potential lost in a line of ghosts. It was a bitter lesson of how wild lives can be compromised or ruined by the small, ordinary decisions we make, often without us even knowing, and it happens all across the country, every May.

This awareness mounted thanks to the SLN, but it was the heatwave that turned me into a campaigner, summoned by the flames that burned 19 July 2022 into the record books as the hottest day noted in Britain. The day was captured in headlines like it was straight from hell: 'Tinderbox Britain'; 'Wildfires destroy houses'; 'Day of 40°C shocks scientists'; 'Fields and buildings ablaze on the outskirts of London'. For a few days, Britain lived a nightmare that we had been warned about for decades. After months without rain, the days had steadily got hotter, the Met Office issuing its first-ever extreme heat warning.

In my village, some of the farmland I walked in every day was licked by flames. Tractors sped down the main road to the fields, the brave and desperate farmers attempting to put fires out by driving head on into them. Apart from the sirens and the line of fire on the outskirts of the village, there was no movement or sound. It was eerie, a sudden ghost town, as people hid from the sun. I stood in the empty road, recognising that I was witnessing a turning point, a historic shift in the wrong direction. People remembered where they were when JFK was shot, I remembered where I was at the news of Princess Diana's death and when the twin towers were hit on 9/11, and I knew as I stood on the road, I would never forget 19 July 2022. Stuck to the spot in a silent village edged in flames, I witnessed the sun bringing climate change to my doorstep. The sirens of the fire engines were the embodiment of the alarms whistle-blowers had been sounding for decades. It was as though we were being shaken violently awake. I could decide to return to my house and stand with my fridge door open, sucking an ice lolly, or I could *do* something. This was the decisive moment. The emergency situation justified me to do something that I had been gearing up to do for a while: panic. The idle game, 'if your house was on fire, what would you save?' became a question on a loop in my mind, extended to the village territory. The answer was conjured by the strongest instinct we all possess: the instinct to protect what we love. And what I love, more than anything, are birds.

Within half an hour of standing in numb panic on the road, I was walking down a hedgerow having ransacked my cupboards of oven dishes so I could create makeshift water stations for the birds and other creatures whose small paws and feet would struggle to get anywhere near the river. This small act went against what I had been taught to believe: that we should let wild things be wild, that human intervention was silly, unnecessary and wrong. This stance had been ingrained in me as a West Country girl surrounded by farming relatives. The attitude was a mixture of British stiff upper lip and practicality, where caring was tutted away as being sentimental, costly, a waste of time or counterproductive, to the point where even suggesting doing something differently in the countryside seemed very much out of bounds. I knew truths now that countered that traditional dismissal. It might seem like a small thing to do – to provide water to creatures who were thirsty – but under the extreme circumstances of the heatwave and the undisputable destruction of habitats on a national scale, it was necessary. According to the charity Froglife, 70 per cent of small bodies of water in the British countryside have disappeared in the last fifty years thanks to being filled in or because they've dried up.

One blackbird didn't even wait until I had left, rushing to the water to take long sips as I watched from a metre away. Then the others came. A dozen yellowhammers and chaffinches splashed into the water dishes. Some sat down, while others shimmied and all of them drank. I sighed at their obvious relief, acknowledging I would have to return with more water and bigger dishes and, once the ground wasn't rock hard, seek permission to dig a pond.

By the afternoon, I walked past a neighbour's to discover newly erected scaffolding was blocking swifts getting in and out of their home and accessing their young. I knocked on the door and explained the situation, politely asking for just the top of the scaffold to be removed immediately.

'But can't they just get round the pole like other birds?' the neighbour replied.

'No. They're not like other birds. They can't perch or hop – they whizz in and out and need a clear flight path to do it, like a Spitfire taking off,' I said, trying to hold my cool, realising it wasn't dissimilar to a hostage situation. If the scaffold wasn't removed at the top under the eaves where the nests were, the chicks would die, starving to death while their parents were rendered helpless, but I could not lead with anger or judgement. I had to be polite and friendly; after all, the man had only inadvertently blocked them. He had no idea he even had swifts nesting in his eaves and his response was completely reasonable.

'It was a real pain to put up,' he said, 'so I think I shall just let nature take its course.'

'I bet it was in this heat, but the thing is, it's not nature taking its course – it's actually a wildlife crime.'

The neighbour buckled at the word 'crime' and changed his mind.

As I thanked him profusely, in under five minutes, the man had removed the top poles, agreeing to put them back once the swifts had gone. Almost immediately, the swifts returned to their nesting hole, arriving with mouths full of insects. The neighbour was gobsmacked as he watched the birds disappear into his wall.

I stayed there, watching too. In the silence of the day, I heard the faint winnowing of the chicks as the parents fed them, their family life rectified in an instant, but only because I had happened to pass by. Only because I knew. Only because I had the nerve to bother the homeowner and only because the homeowner had agreed. For many swifts, scaffolding would block them from their chicks, the law unknown or ignored, or their homes would be blocked when they were on migration, perfectly legally. I stared up at the hole, the faces of the two chicks just peeping out. Given half a chance, these chicks would go from being quiet and unmoving to suddenly living in the sky for up to three years before they touched ground again. As I looked at their little faces, everything changed.

Until that moment, although I had made long-term commitments to help individual birds, the seed of political action lay underneath the surface, dormant even, as I became increasingly aware of biodiversity loss. The term 'biodiversity' happened to be coined the month I was born – September 1986 – for the very reason of communicating the collective and increasing decline of the natural world, thanks to us, the new kids on the block. The Biodiversity Forum, co-created by the leading American conservation scientist E. O. Wilson, was launched to bring attention to 'a most urgent, global problem: the rapidly accelerating loss of plant and animal species'. Twenty years later, in 2006, he together with scientists across the world were declaring the first stages of the sixth mass-extinction event, caused solely as the result of human activity. Ever since, the statistics have got worse. Globally, according to the United Nations, 1 million species face extinction. The most critically endangered species on Earth that hasn't gone extinct yet is the Javan rhino with only sixty-seven currently remaining, who live with a 24/7 armed guard. Another rhinoceros – the western black rhino – became extinct in 2011 along with millions more lost forever, each year the list growing. Gone. Closer to home, our seemingly ordinary animals are perishing too. Biodiversity loss is happening right on our British doorstep. The UK has destroyed more biodiversity than any of the other G7 countries, making our 'green and pleasant land' one of the most nature-deprived corners of the world.

Mirroring the alarming statistics is human concern, equating to millions of people navigating a feeling of utter despair. One in six Brits suffer from eco-anxiety (that's over 11 million of us). The term was coined in 2005 by Glenn Albrecht, a professor of Environmental Studies. Eco-anxiety is categorised by psychologists as rational, often described as a form of grief. In 2021, 43 per cent of adults in Britain reported having been 'very' or 'somewhat' anxious about the future of the environment. A scientific paper published the same year shared that a study of 10,000 sixteen- to twenty-five-year-olds around the world resulted in almost 60 per cent saying they felt 'very' or 'extremely' worried about climate change, raising concerns about a whole generation's mental health in relation to the environmental crisis. I am the one in six, and every fact I learn lodges as a splinter of worry. I have become used to living in a state of almost constant, numbed anxiety. I might be doing the most mundane things like putting bread in the toaster or washing up, and the radio will announce another nail in the coffin in between songs: casual grenades that roll towards us announced but mainly unnoticed. I don't know what to do with the information that scientists have spotted warning signs of Gulf Stream collapse or that the global fishing by-catch totals 38 million tonnes every year, made up of tallies including 300,000 dead dolphins, sharks and whales, and 300,000 dead seabirds, or that an estimated 1 billion birds die every single year from building collisions, normally on their migrations where cities have been built in their flight paths – often in ways that can be prevented relatively easily. How do you know where to start? Every time I hear another dreadful fact, I feel helpless.

But that day, my worry turned into a fuel.

As I looked at the two young swifts, I saw my happiest memories spanning a lifetime of watching these birds: wide-eyed as they raced over the roofs of each childhood garden, whizzing round me with so much energy I wondered whether they would lift me off the ground, standing on my tiptoes in eager hope. As an adult, my heart leapt as I watched them in Ghana, spinning and diving between the coconut palms, round the enormous studded trunks of the kapok trees and cresting the baobabs that stood like silver skyscrapers in the African grassland. I had watched them swoop over the spires and cupolas of Oxford. A bird immortalised in poetry the way the city's skyline has been, they have also been symbols of adventure and discovery since medieval times, the whole world in front of them, yet half an hour before, the lives of the babes in the wall were about to end, living on a knife edge of existence because of sharing their home with us. The little horror scene was a vignette of the global biodiversity loss. Suddenly the two swiftlets became poster children for the whole of the nature crisis and, in combination with the panic-inducing heatwave, these two birds finally gave me my political agency. All the years of worrying and inaction condensed into one intent. I looked at the swifts and said out loud, 'I promise I will do everything I can to save you.'

Once I had made the promise, I idly unpicked what I had just sworn, realising that if I were to keep my word to the birds, I would have to do a lot more than save them from scaffolding. I could see their lives play out, and with their future came challenges only humans could overcome. For them, only political intervention would safeguard them. Knowing that stopped me from being able to look away.

I knew that these swift chicks would find it even harder to seek out their own home in three years' time. This gave a natural timeline to my promise: I had three years to secure their homes. Three years to ensure, somehow, that swift bricks were installed industry-wide to create a nation full of permanent nesting habitat, a step to recovery.

I sat with this thought for a while. It was abstract. Unreal. Unrealistic. Silly. How arrogant of me to think that I would be the saviour who stepped in when others had been doing so much for so long. How foolish of me to think that I would be capable of attempting to keep this promise. The ignorance too. The childlike ignorance of telling a bird in a language it couldn't understand, that I, Hannah Bourne-Taylor, was going to make a promise I had absolutely no idea how to keep. I was a writer, not an ornithologist. I had no contacts in the building industry and I knew absolutely nothing about politics. I was about the least-connected champion these birds could ever wish for. I had spent the bulk of my adult life roaming the African grasslands, not legally allowed to work, but that was why I had made the promise. I had spent time with birds, observed them on a second-by-second basis for months on end. I had raised a finch in my hair, a swift in my hand and revolved my life around five crows. As a result, I was hook, line and sinker in love with them.

I hadn't woken up that morning as a campaigner, but at some point during that afternoon, it occurred to me that I had just become one. In order to achieve the national installation of swift bricks which I had just promised the two swifts in the wall, somehow I needed to bring about a change in the law for birds.

Chapter 3

Feather-brained

The huge promise I made didn't alter my life to start with, but a weevil in the meadow reminded me that the whole is greater than the sum of its parts.

Did you know weevils play dead? If disturbed, they go limp until they think it's safe, like possums. I know this because during the dawns that summer, I collected wildflower seeds from a neighbouring farmer's meadow to enrich the grass in my garden, while I worked out how I could keep my promise to the swifts. The seeds were fascinating in their varied functional creations. Sainfoin seeds are big and patterned with craters, like little fragments of the moon. Others are so small, they kept catching under my fingernails, stowaways I found later in my bed and my shoes. Orchid seeds are even smaller, like specks of dust made to be blown in the wind. Other seeds were like torpedoes, falling into the nearby earth or fitted snugly into pods that spiral open and scatter. Some journeyed in the bodies of birds and mammals, being deposited miles away, some dormant for centuries in natural seed banks.

As I decanted the hay rattle seeds into my hand, so too came weevils, who pretended they weren't there, hiding in plain sight. A fleck of life that represented a whole collection of creatures on which the rest of nature depends: one tiny insignificance and yet, everything. These weevils were one of 500 weevil species in the

UK, part of the precious collection of 24,000 species of insects the UK is home to.

My hand was enormous in proportion to the beetle within it. Lying on its back with its eyes closed, it waited a few moments before peeping around and striding off over my fingers. Each stem housed another weevil or a smart green-and-white-striped spider who performed abseiling escapes. Violet ground beetles tumbled across the earth, carrying snails as their prey. I peered up at the sky from their point of view and at the blades of grass punctuated by the bright yellow hay rattle flowers among dots of purple vetch and blue-mauve cranesbill. A whole world lay here, I, a giant within it, cumbersome and transfixed.

Insects make up over half the species in the world, our planet's health dependent on them along with insect-eating creatures such as swifts. In the UK, the conservation charity Buglife conducted the Bugs Matter Citizen Science Survey, counting bug splats on vehicle number plates, revealing a 58.8 per cent reduction in the abundance of actively flying insects in the UK between 2004 and 2021, a pattern of decline mirrored across the world, described by entomologists as 'apocalyptic'. A 'Warning to Humanity' was issued by the Union of Concerned Scientists in 1992 and reissued in 2017, signed by over 15,000 scientists who claim humans are 'pushing Earth's ecosystems beyond their capacities to support the web of life'.

Ever since I was a child I had known about the decline in insects because of my dad. His bookcases were stuffed with manuals and pamphlets about the state of the environment published in the 1970s and 1980s, amassing like a pile of evidence against humanity. One, by Friends of the Earth, had etched into my memory, entitled *Paradise Lost? The Destruction of Britain's Wildlife Habitats*. On the first page there was a photo of the botanist David Bellamy wearing a T-shirt with the words 'EXTINCTION IS FOREVER'. 'Conservation must begin at home,' his foreword said, before the rest of the pamphlet detailed and quantified the loss of habitats, stating that the amount of money allocated to nature conservation every year was, per person, the equivalent cost of a Mars bar.

Part of the ecology team that first highlighted the importance of roadside verges in the early nineties, my father compiled and edited a manual for the Department of Transport called *The Good Roads Guide* to try to ensure the slices of remaining ground became untouched oases for wildlife, especially insects. Whenever we drove anywhere, Dad would excitedly point out particularly successful or important motorway verges. Tiny triumphs in a nation obsessed with lawns, where the cultural norm of mowing the grass became a symbol of 'tidiness' and 'respect'. Now, according to Plantlife, there are over 313,000 miles of rural road verge in the UK, which equates to half of the country's remaining flower-rich grasslands and meadows. If we cherished these strips of green space, we could nurture an estimated 400 billion more wildflowers. With even one mile of flower-rich verge producing 20 kilograms of nectar sugar per year, verges represent an opportunity for communities to make a difference.

As I collected the seeds, I thought about insect decline versus nesting-habitat loss. Both were critical for the swifts' survival, but one was a complex problem that to be resolved would mean changing a fundamental element in the very fabric of how our human societies currently function, linked to our economy as well as the biggest corporations in the world. The other was just a brick in a wall. The attempt to reverse insect decline is ongoing but with cavities in buildings becoming a thing of the past, no swifts would be able to breed anywhere in Britain even if there were insects galore. Loss of nesting habitat has been cited as a factor in the decline of four species since 2002, when house sparrows and starlings were added to the Red List. Scientific studies since then show a clear correlation between loss of cavities and continued urban population decline. This is an empirical truth but one that was being almost completely ignored.

The natural nooks and crannies in our walls and roofs are being destroyed through demolition (an annual tally of 50,000 old buildings), renovations and the nationwide, government-funded push for insulation. New-build designs have strict climate mitigation measures and modern materials that deliberately prevent cavities.

Surely birds who are site loyal, returning to the same hole year on year, should be given special protection of their homes, formally guarded by ecologists, so that if building work is done, the birds can be considered like bats are. Especially if they are endangered. Especially if scientific data links nesting habitat loss to their declines. But no such protection exists. Securing cavity-nesting habitat for the sake of rapidly declining birds reliant on buildings to survive was not part of the Environment Act 2021 or any other law or policy regarding nature and nature restoration in the UK, despite its critical importance. Even the government's new biodiversity scheme – biodiversity net gain, created to incorporate nature within development – misses cavity-nesting habitat. Legislation was focused on vegetated habitat, which would directly support swifts through the ecosystems the habitat would sustain, but their nesting habitat had fallen through the gap. With this blind spot came an opportunity.

As I thought about this, because I was in the meadow surrounded by the tiny seeds and the mini beasts, what I saw changed. Every flower head was multiplied by its seeds, one meadow an entire bank of life: a future held in capsules, ready to conquer.

Each seed countered the diggers and machinery from the construction site of the new development on the village outskirts and the chemicals that had industrialised nearby farmland. Each seed linked to the life of an insect, which linked directly to the life of a bird and, indirectly, to us. Each seed represented necessary change, each one in the palm of my hand reminding me that everything starts somewhere, and that we instinctively plan for the future. I was the seed. I was the weevil. I was the bird. I was a tiny insignificance who could tap into a whole much, much greater than just me.

Reluctantly, I became a parish councillor in order to raise awareness about local nature recovery in general and swift bricks in particular. Along with lengthy discussions about potholes, parking and antisocial disputes, we discussed grass verges, hedgehog road signs, bumblebee-friendly gardens, and every planning application reviewed had my swift-filtered eyes scanning the details. My swift-brick focus steadily rubbed off on the council as a whole and by extension raised awareness to the district council, which was yet to add swift bricks as a condition to their local plan, just like almost all of the other local planning authorities in the country. Local planning authorities (LPAs) *can* add a swift-brick planning condition to their local plans, something suggested in the National Planning Policy Framework since 2019, but the uptake had been minimal: out of all the LPAs, which totalled over 400, only nine had included swift bricks, with a further forty or so including weaker general guidance about various biodiversity measures that may or may not be followed. Surveys carried out by swift groups on new developments that had been told to include swift bricks by their LPAs had shown over 60 per cent non-compliance, the councils not having the resources to check or enforce. But it was still better than nothing. At the end of one of the parish council meetings, I went up to one of the district councillors and asked him why there was such a small uptake.

'Problem is, there would need to be a district champion successfully advocating for swift bricks in the first place and I hadn't heard of them until I met you, but the action then runs the risk of being dismissed by the government inspectorate because it's not a government directive,' he said. 'The biggest obstacle though is the five-year review cycle of local plans because even if a council is willing to include swift bricks, if they've just completed their review, they wouldn't be able to add it for another five years.'

When I did some further digging, contacting the vice chair of the Association of Local Government Ecologists, he confirmed how unviable local government action was: 'Leaving swift bricks to planning authorities to implement through planning conditions, local planning policies or supplementary guidance, is neither an effective nor efficient way to implement an urgent conservation measure.'

Clearly, someone needed to tell the government this, and my promise had made that person me. I searched online for options. With no budget, no organisation of people and no profile, only one option was viable: a petition. For a member of the public to formally propose a change in legislation, the strongest chance, in theory, is to open a government petition in an attempt to prove that your proposal or concern is mirrored by the public. Together, we the people could rise up for swifts if enough of us clubbed together through a petition. We could turn from being insignificant individuals to a collective that couldn't be ignored. For the government to even consider a parliamentary debate, they invite members of the public to gather 100,000 signatures in a petition that only stays open for six months. 'One hundred thousand signatures in six months,' I said out loud in disbelief, laughing at my computer screen in despair. The invitation read like a dare. I had about twelve friends. My mind raced. Sylvia, Margaret and Julie and everyone in the local swift group would sign and knock on every door in the vicinity but even if we and the rest of the SLN canvassed our communities and rallied our families and friends to knock on every door in theirs, the petition might manage a few hundred, maybe a few thousand signatures. Maybe if I got on local radio or the regional news, I'd get five or ten thousand, perhaps double that if I managed to get any traction on social media. I found my head was in my hands, my finger and thumb rubbing my forehead in a subconscious attempt to make my mind come up with a better solution. I looked at the other petition options that would generate far more signatures through payment schemes, but they were not the official democratic route. There was no promise from the government attached to these to 'consider parliamentary debate', so I would have to play by their rules: six months, 100,000 signatures.

I looked at the limited petition word count given by the government, which, including the title, is 148 words. The government offered a couple of paragraphs that in this case could make the difference between life and death for swifts. My lips thinned, my eyes narrowed as I reread the petition instructions. 'Fine. So be it. You're on,' I said out loud, already sizing up my opponent, and myself. It wasn't an even match. The inconvenient truth to a petition is that it is a plea to both the public and the government. Without public support, I'd get it nowhere near the government. It would be like having to convince both judge and jury, and I was just a random woman who loved birds.

'You can do it!' members of the local Swift Conservation Society said, Margaret patting me on the back vigorously, but I knew sheer passion alone would not translate into the target.

I was not the first ordinary person to decide to take responsibility for trying to protect birds. In the late nineteenth century, the co-founding women of the RSPB took on a far bigger challenge from a far weaker position. In their day, many species of birds were in rapid decline because of the plumage trade: the morbid, cruel and disgusting fashion of hats adorned with often whole, often multiple, dead birds. The fashion trend began in the 1870s, its popularity quantified by the vast numbers of birds being killed. By 1886, 5 million birds were being slaughtered every year, many facing extinction as a result. The declines were sped up by killing the adult birds during the nesting period because that was when they were smartest with spring plumage, leaving orphaned chicks to die.

Feathers were used as part of the British army uniforms and the suffragettes wore egret plumes, the feather a distinctive mark of women activists, but the vast majority were used on women's hats. They were so popular that by 1915 feathers were more valuable than gold. Britain, Europe and the USA bustled with women accompanied by dead birds atop their heads, many strolling into salons with a handful of hummingbirds slumped around their hair. Egrets, grebes and birds of paradise were targeted more than others, with hunters killing a thousand birds a day, shiploads arriving for auction houses that sold lots of 26,000 pairs of wings at a time, met with delight by women.

There were some women, albeit in the minority to begin with, who were appalled by the trade. In 1889 the English woman Emily Williamson created The Society for the Protection of Birds to try to reverse the fashion. Meanwhile another woman, Eliza Phillips, had set up a similar organisation called Fur, Fin and Feather Folk. These groups of women pledged not to wear feathers from any birds unless they had been killed for their meat, or they were ostrich tail feathers, which could at least be harvested leaving the bird alive. The two organisations merged in 1891.

Opposition to restricting the trade was huge. Its continuation had a direct impact on not just fashion but the economy. To start with, the society did a lot of letter writing, communicating their views to ornithologists who had a tendency to dismiss and belittle the women's efforts, but a few men became key allies. They also wrote to fellow women, passing notes in church objecting to their Sunday hats, and printed articles in newspapers and pamphlets in local towns. In response to the society's efforts, lies were printed by the media claiming that feathers were harvested from farmed egrets without cruelty or death, when the opposite was true. Milliners began relabelling real feathers as 'artificial' and gender-focused propaganda was fed to the public, branding the likes of Emily Williamson as 'feather-brained'. The society hit back, printing factual information. Despite the smear campaigns, it grew in popularity. By 1904 the society was awarded a Royal Charter, making it the Royal Society for the Protection of Birds, with the Duchess of Portland as the patron.

Eventually they succeeded in stopping the plumage trade with the Plumage Act, which, although drawn up in 1908, wasn't implemented until 1921. It took them thirty years. *Thirty years.* But they did it. What is remarkable is that these women had the gumption to even try. Second-class citizens, they didn't have the vote and yet they clubbed together to confront one of the most lucrative trades of the day. What's more, over thirty years they did not give up. The RSPB began with one woman with exactly the same profile as me: a married thirty-six-year-old without children. Thirty years later she claimed victory and her legacy along with the others is now 130 years old with a membership of 1.2 million people. Their legacy was instilled in me by the author Tessa Boase, who discovered and then celebrated their story in her book *Etta Lemon: The Woman Who Saved the Birds.*

I contacted the RSPB, speaking first to its designated 'swift champion' who then put me in touch with several colleagues.

I soon realised that this giant organisation was full of people who were positive and refreshingly combative, ready and willing to fight for swifts. The RSPB's leading women were the formal twenty-first-century version of the co-founding women. I liked them very much, and the birds were lucky to have them.

I was starting to play the game: I wasn't credible, but others were. Ornithologists were, conservation organisations were, collectively the SLN was. I spent hours reading scientific papers trying to suss out what the best 'ask' to the petition was. I had long phone calls with one of the original swift campaigners in the UK, Stephen Fritt, who had engaged councils and developers for decades, and spoke to Dick Newall, who had invented different types of swift bricks, and Mike Priaulx, the SLN's planning expert, whose encyclopaedic knowledge of local planning authorities was immeasurably valuable. I threw questions at them: should the petition be asking the government to make swifts and other Red-Listed cavity-nesting urban birds 'protected species' like bats, so that whenever renovations took place, there was formal red tape for ecologists and developers? Or should the provision of swift bricks be added to the new development metric 'biodiversity net gain', which instructed developments to enhance biodiversity by 10 per cent or more? Or should I ask for swift bricks to simply be made compulsory? And if so, should I ask that they be compulsory in all new builds, or just new housing?

It became an active discussion between dozens of people, the answer reshaping with every opinion. I emailed strangers from Britain and abroad: scientists I had seen credited for papers, government officials, policymakers, housebuilders, ecologists, my MP, other MPs known for green initiatives, such as former leader of the Green Party Caroline Lucas, a shining link between conservation and politics. Caroline Lucas had delivered an impassioned speech about swifts in the House of Commons, and I realised I wanted to be someone making an impassioned speech about swifts to the government too.

I had conversations with dozens of members of the SLN, and swift-brick manufacturers. Many people never replied and some made scathing comments, but dozens came back to me, each with their own advice, often completely contradicting each other. One thing was unanimous: every single person, whatever their background, loved swifts. The general consensus, though, was a total lack of faith in the government, accompanied by low expectations about a petition making any difference at all. 'You'll never do it,' one expert said in an email. 'It's naive of you to try,' said another.

'I don't understand this sentiment,' I said, despairing to Robin when we walked the dogs, telling him about the feedback I was getting. 'If people who care about swifts and know their plight think it's not worth trying, surely that is a self-fulfilling prophecy? Surely unless we collectively try, we will ensure these birds we say we love will have no future?'

Robin nodded. 'You've never been like everyone else. You think for yourself, so think for yourself,' he said, only now beginning to understand that my idea – my promise – was creeping into reality, and that I really meant it.

One summer evening in Bicester allowed me to ignore the nay-sayers. Local swift conservationist Chris Mason tells Oxfordshire communities about the resident swifts by taking people on evening walks to places where there are large performing colonies. Skulking at the edge of the group in a back street of Bicester, I listened to Chris's gentle voice introducing the wonder of swifts to the small group. As they flew over right on cue, everyone looked up and gasped like they were watching fireworks. The ordinary cul-de-sac was transformed by the swifts, a connection to the natural world among parked cars and pavements. A palpable sense of community sprang up. Passers-by stopped, looking up in awe, joining the crowd in delighting in the whoosh of wings overhead. People who were neighbours but had never spoken, chatted, bonding over their mutual wonder.

Next to me, an elderly woman who hadn't taken her eyes off the swifts suddenly started talking. 'All my life I have been too busy to notice, my mind wrapped around how I was going to get the kids to school on time, get to work, get home, make ends meet. But now,' she said, 'I feel like finally I am living at sixty-nine. My old body is slow, my mind is getting on a bit, but I see these birds and they give me energy. They remind me I'm still ticking.'

'Me too,' a middle-aged man said, joining in. 'I always thought birdwatching was for oddballs but come on, I mean, just look at them!' He smiled up as about twenty birds shot past us in a formation that looked like a Red Arrow flyover. 'They're blooming magnificent!'

'They were the first thing my daughter smiled at after her accident,' said one woman, quietly, just to me. 'We've been told she's unlikely to ever be able to walk again and she's only nine, but little things like this take her mind off it.' Her daughter was transfixed, her arms waving as her brothers ran, weaving through people with their arms out, copying, half boys, half birds.

More and more people chatted, asking endless questions to Chris because the more they saw the birds wheel and dive and scream, the more unbelievable they became. 'So they really don't land? They really fly all the way from here to Africa and back, the same birds?' a man was asking Chris.

I smiled behind them, listening to Chris explain, and the people's eyes widening, mouths opening in awe. The collective reaction was like giving your favourite book to someone who hadn't read it, knowing the feeling they would get once they had finished. It was a gift. As I watched the way everyone came together, I realised this was the birds' best chance. I just needed to harness this gift and amplify it to the scale of 100,000.

'If anyone can do it, Hannah, it's you,' Chris said with his signature kindness.

Harnessing the emotional connection had worked for another English woman, Rebecca Hosking. In 2007, Rebecca launched a campaign on behalf of the albatross: birds who wander oceans with their 11-foot wings, like feathered sails, enabling these gliding giants to travel thousands of miles and live for seventy years. Rebecca was filming a documentary for the BBC about the marine wildlife crisis of Midway, the remote Hawaiian island which is the main breeding ground for Laysan albatross. There, the adult albatross soar above the waves and court on land, but the reason Rebecca was there surrounded her on the beach: thousands of dead and dying albatross chicks, dying because of our collective use of plastic, thousands of miles away. Eighty per cent of marine litter comes from land and 90 per cent of it is plastic. It takes 300 million years for crude oil to form and we use much of the plastic made from that oil for just a few moments before discarding it: twenty seconds to down a plastic bottle of juice; a minute to scoff a chocolate bar; two seconds to unwrap a greetings card . . . and 400 to 1,000 years for that plastic to degrade back into the environment. As Rebecca says, 'Is that not utter madness?'

Adult albatross fly over the sea for thousands of miles looking for brightly coloured squid to feed on, and to feed their chicks. Where the albatross breed in the North Pacific, the currents move in a huge circular motion, which makes for an excellent feeding ground. But the same currents that bring the fish suck in all the rubbish from the surrounding continents too. Much of that plastic is brightly coloured and does such a good impression of albatross food that the birds frequently mistake it for breakfast, lunch and dinner.

The scale of this devastation had not been documented until Rebecca and the film crew arrived. They filmed people wading knee-high in plastic as they walked along the beach. Close-ups of the cups, keyboards, DVDs, plates, combs, knives, forks, babies' dummies, children's toys, TVs, drink bottles, sandwich wrappers, lipsticks, hairbrushes, pens, shoes, plugs and clocks showcased what had become of the albatross nesting ground. Even the sand wasn't sand but tiny fragments of plastic: trillions of minute plastic pieces, small enough to be eaten by animals right at the bottom of the food chain. This plastic was, and still is, killing the birds. The plastic fills the chicks' stomachs, so they die from either dehydration or starvation. Strewn across the beach carcasses rot, disintegrating to reveal the fatal plastic inside – bags, cigarette lighters, toothbrushes and toys.

Fledglings still alive tried to fly but many were too weak and fell into the waves, only to drown, the water as full of dead and dying chicks as the beach. What Rebecca witnessed, she found unbearable. When she returned home to Modbury, a small town in South Devon, she explained what she had seen to a friend who happened to own one of the shops. She told him how scientific studies showed that bits of plastic in the ocean absorb chemicals such as pesticides and retardants that we have leaked into the oceans. These chemicals cling to the surface of the plastic, creating countless poison pills. When these are eaten by sea creatures, the chemicals move up the food chain and end up in us. There are no winners. Rebecca's friend's reaction was to voluntarily commit to stopping using plastic bags in his shop. Then another shop owner had the same reaction.

These two reactions – of traders saying they could still trade without the use of plastic bags – were what gifted Rebecca her agency. With it, Rebecca became the global spokesperson for the banning of plastic bags, almost overnight.

First, she gathered her town's traders, told them what she had seen and what she knew, and invited them to vote. Every hand went up in favour of banning plastic bags. She thought it would stop there, a seemingly small but earnest achievement thanks to the trust and respect of her neighbours. Actually, what they had collectively agreed was revolutionary. Over the following month, national and international press turned up with reporters from as far afield as China and Russia. The little Devon town of Modbury made it to the world news because Modbury wasn't just the first town in Britain to ban plastic bags, it was the first town in Europe to do so. Six months after the ban of plastic bags in Modbury, the traders had saved half a million bags from being issued. Movements on banning single-use plastic began, the ripple effect ongoing. Awareness and collective pressure from the public have continued to achieve change. 'I'm not a plastic bag' caught on, people carrying cotton shopping bags instead, but so did flasks instead of plastic cups, and paper straws instead of plastic ones. Thanks to Rebecca Hosking, the idea of taking on a national, political cause felt, at least theoretically, doable. If she could do it, I could do it.

*

It was the factual evidence that became my absolute focus. I knew the facts were what would be respected first and foremost even if it was the emotion that in some ways counted more than anything. Data would allow me to campaign for swift bricks because it meant scientists were able to officially recommend the measure. The data proved they worked.

Knowledge of uptake of swift boxes and bricks has been well documented. Dick Newall, who founded Action for Swifts, invented the S brick and has championed swifts for decades, has strongholds of swifts to show for it. In his home county of Cambridgeshire, Dick has overseen the installation of over 1,300 swift bricks and boxes. The boxes adorn gables of houses and churches in dozens of villages and towns. In the village of Milton, just three houses have a total of thirty-two nest boxes between them, home to twenty-four pairs of swifts and four pairs of starlings. Each time a colony or a pair of swifts has been helped directly, the success has turned into a statistic that has helped the population as a whole. Data was not dry and theoretical but the silver thread of hope. It was the very foundation of both the nightmare and the opportunity to intervene.

It was the partnership between the RSPB and the Duchy estate that had achieved the most data on swift bricks. Under the guidance of His Majesty The King (then Duke of Cornwall), in 2015 the Duchy estate started installing 'integrated nest bricks' into its new developments. The King loves swifts and has been recorded saying so by the BBC: 'I admire them and I love them; for me, the world would come to an end if the swallows, swifts and house martins didn't come back.'

This love was perhaps inherited from Prince Philip, who also loved swifts, watching them scream through the Mediterranean as a young man and delighting in the colony that calls Windsor Castle home, boosting their numbers by adding swift boxes. Following suit, the swift bricks included in the Duchy developments in the West Country set a precedent for other developers to follow across the country. Many new homeowners took part in the RSPB surveys of swift-brick occupancy led by ornithologist and urban bird consultant Dr Thais Martins. The survey results delighted her because the swift bricks have been, and continue to be, used by several species. As well as swifts, house sparrows, starlings and other urban species such as great tit, blue tit and nuthatch, the greatest surprise was that house martins have moved into the swift bricks.

On the village hall of my parents' Somerset village and so many others across the country, house martins' mud nests line the eaves, their faces peeping out in a friendly manner. They, too, desperately need swift bricks. While their population baseline is far higher than swifts (at an estimated 480,000 pairs according to the British Trust for Ornithology), their breeding population has declined by 52 per cent. Citizen science has helped raise the alarm for house martins. The British Trust for Ornithology conducted a large-scale citizen-science survey in 2016–17 to assess how their breeding performance, measured by the number of attempted broods and nest success, is being influenced by nest landscape. The study found that nests built on plastic soffits of buildings were less likely to sustain multiple broods and less likely to be successful compared with other materials. Informal observation has seen many people watching house martins try and fail to get any mud to stick on soffits, the plastic being an incompatible surface. Suggested conservation measures therefore include discouraging the removal of old nests, especially since house martins are also site loyal, and encouraging the installation of artificial nests, particularly on buildings with plastic soffits. The conclusion was that nest-building success is a contributing factor to the house martins' national decline. Although they make their natural nests out of mud, using an average of 1,000 mouthfuls, the Duchy surveys show that they would also use swift bricks. This also means that the time and energy saved due to not having to find the mud and build the nest was likely beneficial to these birds. The risk of the nest falling due to heatwaves drying it out or there being no mud to start with, or due to human destruction, also vanishes.

The problem was that the statistics alone weren't enough to make people act. Among others, Stephen Fritt and Mike Priaulx have doggedly worked on approaching local planning authorities with the aim of persuading them to impose a planning condition around swift bricks. Michael Oxford, a government ecologist who worked with Stephen Fritt, went on to create the British Standard for integrated bird nest boxes. The whole point of a British Standard is that they are created in order to help a measure or instruction be applied industry- and country-wide. The brilliant thing about our campaign was that its foundation of facts and guidance was the result of the combined effort of people who had championed swifts steadily for decades. Propping up the swift population was a whole collection of dedicated people. All I had to do was get the 100,000 signatures so we could use it as a step in the right direction, building on the life work of countless others.

The 148 words of the petition were a group effort, involving people I had never met, led by the SLN's planning expert, Mike Priaulx. Measured, precise and knowledgeable, Mike carefully judged each option as he steadily shaped the plea. I added the end sentence, 'The RSPB supports this petition', which was approved by the RSPB. I was proud of these five words backing me as a brand-new campaigner. However, on submitting the wording to the petition committee for approval, the petition clerk emailed telling me he had deleted the final sentence, giving no reason.

'That sentence is staying,' I muttered to myself as I scowled at the screen. Half an hour later, the RSPB directors had contacted the committee personally, securing the wording.

'Clearly, this whole thing is going to be fought inch by inch,' I said to Margaret over a cup of tea.

'Yes, and I suppose if you think about it, every single signature will count, just like every nesting site and every bird counts,' Margaret replied.

The petition lay in secret wait, because once it was opened, the six-month countdown would begin, and I knew a petition on its own wouldn't be enough to reach the target. It was this sense of urgency that both plagued and fuelled me. According to the British Trust for Ornithology, between 1995 and 2020, the breeding population of swifts in the UK declined by 60 per cent. The estimate for their population after this decline is 59,000 pairs, based on density estimates derived from the BTO/RSPB/JNCC Breeding Bird Survey (BBS). The smoothed BBS trend indicates the population has declined by a further 24 per cent since, leaving it in the region of 45,000 pairs. Since 2007, the annual rate of decline measured by the BBS has been between 3 and 7 per cent (average 4.8 per cent), suggesting that by 2025 the numbers may be below 40,000 pairs. In contrast, across Europe, according to BirdLife International, common swifts' populations were stable. Here in Britain, the birds' numbers were plummeting as fast as their skydives and it was like watching a parachutist jump from a plane, knowing their parachute will fail.

Chapter 4

Lady Godiva

In the summer evenings I watched the swifts play tag, rushing in and out of the small gaps between the houses, screaming as they flung themselves through the gaps. As I watched the birds, my mind focused on the need for a highly strategic plan to win the hearts and minds of the British public. I rolled my eyes. How the hell would I achieve that? What were the modern-day success stories of the co-founding women of the RSPB? As a pair of swifts rushed past almost close enough to touch, a name surfaced from the depths of my memory: Julia Butterfly Hill.

The American activist Julia Butterfly Hill was twenty-three when she climbed a 180-foot, 1,000-year-old redwood tree in California, later named Luna, in order to protect the tree from being felled in 1997, and in a broader protest to stop the redwood forests from being clear-cut. Vowing her feet would not touch the ground until the authorities agreed not to chop Luna down, Julia climbed up onto two 6-by-4-foot platforms. She deliberately stopped washing her feet so they had a better grip when climbing, and weathered freezing conditions and hurricanes in solitude. Despite threats in the form of helicopter harassment, a ten-day siege by company security guards, and attempted intimidation by angry loggers, she refused to leave Luna. In the end Julia lived in Luna for 738 days, only climbing down when a resolution was reached in 1999. Eventually the Pacific Lumber Company agreed to preserve Luna and all trees within a

200-foot buffer. Today Luna still stands, under the stewardship of the nonprofit Sanctuary Forest. All because of Julia, a barefoot twenty-three-year-old woman who had refused to give Luna up.

The personal sacrifice from Julia was not only enduring just over two years living in challenging circumstances, but also breaking the law. Would I have to do that? There had recently been a surge of environmental protesters taking this disruptive, law-breaking route. Was I about to copy them, and break the law for swifts? It was something that, as a bystander, I had always felt uncomfortable with, aware that for many, it put them off environmental causes, making it counterproductive. I felt deterred by disruptive action, despite agreeing with their reasons to act. Protesters had hung off bridges, stuck their hands to tarmac, conducted slow marches to stop traffic, but it took the infamous attacks on priceless public art to engage me in a different way. Specifically, the attack carried out by two Just Stop Oil activists on a painting in the Courtauld Gallery in June 2022. It was the painting choice that engaged me because it was Van Gogh's *Peach Trees in Blossom* hung in a gallery I loved. The two activists, Emily Brocklebank and Louis McKechnie, caused just under £2,000 of damage to the frame and went on to be charged. Brocklebank received a twenty-one-day sentence, suspended for six months, and was electronically monitored for six weeks. McKechnie was jailed for three weeks. People were outraged because it was a precious Van Gogh. Yet what they were protesting against was the war man is waging on nature. It has got so bad that real fruit-tree crops in parts of China have to be pollinated by hand, each flower dabbed with pollen by workers often using their children to climb to the tallest blooms, putting their lives at risk, because insecticide use has decimated bee populations.

The outrage to the painting damage emphasised the lack of outrage, and ignorance, towards global insect decline. One out of every three mouthfuls of our food depends on pollinators. As the charity Buglife states, 'It is almost impossible to over-emphasise the importance of the service pollinators perform for us.' It is estimated that 84 per cent of EU crops (valued at £12.6 billion) and 80 per cent of wildflowers rely on insect pollination. Yet, the current global agriculture chemicals market size is estimated at $250 billion, with projections indicating a rise to $350 billion by 2027. The people destroying ecosystems fundamental to our own survival aren't being held accountable or stopped. They aren't being put in jail. They're making billions and we are giving it to them through our consumption.

Once framed like this, it made the whole story a modern-day fable, considering Van Gogh's work when he was alive had not been popular at all. Only in death did his paintings become among the most valuable in the world. Maybe bees are overlooked, striped, priceless Van Goghs?

The evening sky streaked in pink, the swifts spiralling higher and higher around the church tower in the distance. I did not want to break the law. That was my line, not least because the chances of the government agreeing to debate my petition would be nil if I promoted it by criminal activity, but the antics of Just Stop Oil and XR stuck in my mind. While their stunts were criticised for being a gimmick, there was a lack of understanding in how this big ugly game works. I had never thought about it until I was trying to work out how to engage the whole of Britain with something most people would know nothing about. For a nobody's voice to be heard, or that of an organisation, an attention-seeking stunt seemed to be the only effective way to engage the media, and the media was the only realistic way to engage the public. If I wanted to have a chance in hell of collecting 100,000 signatures, I needed to court the media. How was I going to do that?

I lay on the hallway floor, where I go to think and mope, the dogs sprawled out next to me.

'I have no assets and no contacts,' I said to Robin as he carefully stepped over me to get back to work.

'That's not true. You are *obsessed* with birds, Hannah. You care more than anyone else I know.'

I twisted the thought around in my head, inspecting it like a magpie would a coin. He was right. Caring about nature, born from noticing, came from my father. From as early as I could walk, Dad had shown me the world through his eyes. He had taught me that if you peer into a hedge, what you find is a whole world in miniature. A world full of dark corners and patches of sunlight, of tiny spaces guarded by dozens of criss-crossing, often thorny, branches. Living lines that run past us all, down the length of Britain in unseen secrets waiting to be discovered.

When I was seven, he took me and my sister to a stretch of hazel hedge in Dartmoor in search of nuts. It was 1993 and we were taking part in the biggest-ever nationwide voluntary wildlife survey to check up on the endangered dormice population. By examining the nibble marks on the hazelnuts, Dad showed me how to decipher whether they had been made by dormice. Each nut we found – smooth and pale brown – had a big hole in it, but the holes were ever so slightly different. Hazelnuts eaten by birds and squirrels have crack marks, the shell partially shattered. Vole-chewed nuts have tiny grooves made by their teeth, while wood mice leave toothmarks that run straight upwards from the hole. But dormice-nibbled nuts have toothmarks that swirl around the rim. These carvings became obvious with practised eyes. It was impossible not to get excited because each marked nut I held in my hands told me that somewhere nearby there was a little butterscotch-coloured dormouse with a long furry tail who was probably curled tightly in a ball, fast asleep. Surrounded by snoozing dormice, we searched. In turn, the outside world of school, people, pavements and lawns vanished. It was just me and my dad and the sleeping mice.

Dad didn't stop at dormice or hedgerows. He took me all over the country, on expeditions that normally involved anoraks and bribes of chocolate. My mum and sister often came too, Mum pointing out barn owls quartering, and the wrens and song thrushes she loves so much in the hedgerows. I also went with Dad to collect data on otters by going in search of their spraint, giggling as I huddled with a group of adults who delighted in peering at the black, shining turds lying along the edge of the river. At the end of every trip I would return home bursting with a story about how I found a snake skin or we had come across a strange kind of fungus or a dead bat. Whatever I found crammed me full of new facts to reel off to anybody who would listen – that the skin of a great crested newt contains glands that secrete a poisonous substance to deter predators or that shield bugs turn from green to brown as they near hibernation to blend in with the leaves. Each time I found an animal and learned about it, their wild lives embedded themselves inside me. The trips had no rules or boundaries – I witnessed adults erupt with the sort of excitement normally only expected of children; I was allowed out after bedtime; and I felt free because we were always outside.

In the spring my dad and I would lie on our tummies in bluebell woods at dusk, watching badgers, and tramp across moors in search of adders and grass snakes. In the summer he would wake me up and take me outside to listen to the nightingales that sang loudly from the thicket outside my bedroom window. Come winter, when the beaches were free of tourists, we went to the Jurassic Coast. Taking off his shoes and socks and rolling up his trousers, Dad would paddle in and around the rock pools. I followed him, watching as the world at his feet consumed him. Crouching down, he would beckon me over and share his findings: common blennies – fish that look like polished gargoyles and, when we dangled our fingers into the shallow water, darted up to nibble; translucent prawns tiptoeing up the rock below the water's surface; yellow periwinkles among the seaweed that flowed back and forth as little waves stumbled in and out between the rocks. Rock pools, like hedgerows, are places that can be easily overlooked as part of the scenery within a much bigger landscape, existing lower than human eye level and on a much smaller scale. But by rock-pooling and hedgerow peering, Dad taught me, through example, to look. To focus on small patches and really inspect, because if you stare at something, sooner or later it reveals itself. To glance is to see a shape of a plant or an animal – something labelled with a word that you either know or don't. But to invest time in looking transfers into discovering complete worlds that are otherwise hidden in plain sight, regardless of whether or not you know exactly what you're looking at.

It was this careful inspection that for many, including my father, had turned into a deep connection and, ultimately, protective action. As a twelve-year-old, Dad spent every spare minute in the salt marshes and dunes around Hilbre Island at the mouth of the Dee estuary, a sheltered place that sucks the River Dee into Liverpool Bay. It is a strip of shallow sea, dunes and salt marshes that act as a vital home for wintering waterfowl populations as well as the perfect habitat for natterjack toads. Barefoot, his trousers rolled up, he'd walk in the shallows surrounded by stingrays and, with the backdrop of Liverpool's lights twinkling in the dark, he discovered the spellbinding glow of bioluminescence. At night he'd listen to the curlews' calls, slipping out of the house and down to the dunes at the bottom of the garden to hear them, whistling back.

He kept watch over the shelduck ducklings and became fond of the other inhabitants of the salt marshes: natterjack toads. Although uncommon, they were thriving there and he would sit and watch them congregate in the shallow pools. One spring, when teachers needing frogs for dissection classes came trying to take bucket loads of the toads away – because they were easy targets and free – he began patrolling the dunes, physically guarding the toads from being caught. He stood up to the adults, with his voice loud and his hands in fists, for days on end, grabbing the buckets from the teachers until they gave up and went away. He made such a song and dance about the toads to the staff at the museum where he volunteered that eventually the staff campaigned, and the natterjack toads were granted protection as the estuary became a Special Protection Area (SPA).

I rang my dad to tell him about my vague plan to help swifts. Full of boundless enthusiasm, he suggested we went on a pilgrimage so he could show me the toads he had helped save. Over sixty years had passed since he was a boy, but his love for the toads and his rage for the people lingered. On the outside he was an old man walking the path of his childhood – a path along the edge of the salt marshes weaving between the dunes, that he had not been to for years, with the sand sloping down on one side and the estuary on the other. But on the inside, he was alive with memories, busy reliving his youth. The water glistened silver, the sand stretching out for miles as I listened to my father whistling to the waders, the sound like water fizzing in your ears. A happy, peaceful sound that was simultaneously all-encompassing yet distant – a persistent tinkling that hung in the air in an acoustic haze. Dad showed me the exact place that he had guarded the toads – in the salt-marsh pools beyond the sand-dune slacks, the preferred breeding spot for the toads because the shallow water is quickly warmed by the sun.

There should have been natterjacks, ridged and mottled and covered in sand, little friendly monsters sitting by our feet. But the natterjacks were no longer there. They had ceased to exist in this spot. My father hadn't known, and his face shifted in an instant, his expression falling in shock. He had driven 250 miles with me so he could show me the toads after decades of telling me all about them. Crestfallen, I saw how his memories and everything he held dear were snatched away from him the moment he realised the toads were gone.

'This is where the toads used to hibernate in the winter,' he said, walking over to holes in the dunes that rabbits had burrowed. 'I never told anyone where they overwintered – or that they hibernated at all. People didn't seem to know and I thought it was best to keep it a secret – safer for the toads. This was *their* patch,' he said defiantly, looking back at the shallow pools, now stagnant with a veneer of rainbow stains, and the line of dogs splashing through them, their owners ignoring the signs to keep out. The Royal Liverpool Golf Club that ran into the nature reserve had been allowed to destroy one dune to make way for another prized hole. Management of the site had fallen into complete disarray and there was no living memory of shelducks or natterjacks at all.

We stayed in the dunes as the sun went down, the evening warm and still, and watched the waders sprawled out in flocks along the sand. The oystercatchers in front of us suddenly took flight. Smart in their black and white plumage, the urgency of their wing-beats made each bird look like a toppling domino, except instead of falling, they ascended into the vast sky, in a wave of movement emphasising the linear stillness of the water below. The sky turned blue-grey and the light started pixelating as it dimmed.

'What should be happening now, at dusk, is the call of the toads,' Dad said, listening in vain, just in case. 'A spirited call that gets louder and louder and gives them their name: "natter" referring to their constant chat and "jack" referring to men because it was the males who were calling, trying to attract the females.'

I looked at the sand, thick with phantom toads, imagining dozens of small dark shapes grouped together. Their lively nattering call is similar to how my father had chattered in the car about the toads on the way to the estuary, not knowing he wouldn't find them, that they were no longer there. Now he was quiet, his attention held by the silence that fell on every grain of sand.

As well as the natterjacks, the curlews who were still there had become critically endangered. Startling truths, such as only six curlew chicks being reported to have fledged across all of southern England in 2018, have led to dramatic conservation efforts. 'Headstarting' programmes now run every year, raising and releasing curlew chicks into the wild to try to boost their numbers to stabilise their population.

Dad looked out at the bay. 'I brought you here to show you this place, to give you hope. Now I'm showing you a landscape full of ghosts. And people don't know they were ever here.'

The silence rang like an alarm. It represented the loss of a colony of toads and their endangered status as a species, but also how quickly the connection between person and place can be severed. For my father, these toads, along with the shelducks who once nested in the sand dune that itself had been destroyed, were the root of his understanding and connection with nature. Without it, there was a void. This robbing of connection conjured a surge of despair inside me. A fear. A desperation, my mind lurching forward to my niece and nephew and their generation, worrying about what they would never know.

We stood together without speaking. My father looked at the horizon, head tilted up, tuning into the sounds that did still exist, putting on a brave face. I tuned in to *him*, picturing him as a boy, standing right here. As I looked at him, what I saw was a lifetime of connection. He looked in pain, and I felt wretched for him, but my mind settled not on the toads' absence and my father's sorrow, but on this connection and the deep value he placed on it. I held tight to this alliance. His childhood actions of physically protecting the toads showed me that one person can make a difference, teaching me what passion really is. Passion is a word that has crept into daily vocabulary as a way to describe people's enthusiasm for anything, from frothy coffee to power walking, but the definition of the word is 'strong and barely controllable emotion'. From the Latin *pati* meaning 'to suffer', it is also defined as 'a feeling of intense enthusiasm towards or compelling desire for someone or something'. Known through its use as a descriptor in the Bible documenting the final period of Jesus's life, it has been traditionally used to cement the idea that if you love something enough, you will do anything for it, even if it causes you pain or anguish. Its meaning feels, regardless of religious views, like the epitome of faith. And what is rooted in this word that I had seen as a tangible characteristic of my father is the essence of standing up for what you believe in. Of standing up for what you care about and actually doing something. Once back home, what I remembered was not the anguish, but the power of connection. It lit a fire inside me.

As July turned to August, I thought about options, feeling pressured by the seasonal shift that would provoke the swifts to leave, their departure starting an invisible stopwatch. The days were tinged with autumn, the air smelled different. A thicker, earthier smell than the freshness of pollen or grass. Sunlight was tinted subtly, too, into a greyish yellow and all along the hedgerows there were the first signs that summer was beginning to dwindle. Small, hard green haws and blackberries, goosegrass burrs stuck to the dogs' fur and the bottoms of my trousers as we walked down the edge of the field. Grasses slanted together in a block of dark yellow. In the evenings I walked around the village and into the fields behind the houses, eyes glued to the sky, following the swifts. I watched as the clouds gradually took over the blue with bright white towering sculptures, the swifts, high-up black dots of life effortlessly speeding across the vastness before launching into head-first dives, hurtling to Earth.

There were fewer swifts in the air now, and the screaming parties had stopped. I visited the tower to say goodbye to them, looking in each nest box with George Candelin, gazing at the chicks. In just a few weeks, they had turned from bald and blind to drop-dead gorgeous, their sleek primary wing feathers soon to be just the right length to propel them into a life in the sky. As each chick got ready to go, they spread their wings out and performed press-ups, strengthening their flight muscles. Then, in the final prep, they shuffled into position like aircraft waiting on a runway, sometimes for several hours or even days. From being huddled together, each would inch nearer to the exit hole. I looked into one nest where one was ready to go, its head looking out, its body still. In silence, suddenly, the swift took off. There was a slight kerfuffle of feet and claws, then a whoosh.

'There it goes,' George whispered.

The people below were just having normal days, oblivious to this feathered rocket launching from the heart of Oxford.

The village swifts began to leave too. Eleven of them stayed in the skies, wheeling within the big grey clouds. Every now and then they'd fly near enough for me to hear their calls, but mostly they were tiny black anchors in the sky. Every time I saw them, I thought it would be the last time. I began to feel restless, distracted by their imminent journey. Every night I did the rounds of the village territories, the swifts reduced. Occasionally, I heard a faint screech above that cut through the heavy traffic of the road right next to me. By the end of the week, there were four left, including the precious babes in the wall I'd saved from the scaffolding. By 8 August, I saw my last swifts of the season. There were just two, sweeping through the sky within a flock of martins. The following evening I went out again, not knowing they wouldn't be there. I searched the skies around the village and the fields behind the houses and further, up the hill to the next village, up to the top meadow to the edge of the beech wood, but they were not there. They had gone.

Clouds rushed in the sky, wind rustling the trees. Grasshoppers still sang within the blades of grass. Traffic on the main road flowed in a low, rushing roar. But even with all these sounds, I heard the silence that had not been there before. The quietness of a sky empty of swifts, their absence, a loud loss that dominated and drowned out the other sounds. The loud silence and the sense of grief encapsulated the idea of the nightmare I feared the most: of the first summer in England without swifts, of a May where the swifts did not return.

October came and with it the smell of woodsmoke, the rosy sheen of apples and nights during which I did not sleep, thinking instead about how I could create a campaign around the petition. At night, I paced round the village, passing boxes of apples neighbours had put on their doorsteps with signs saying, 'Please, take me'. Most of the apples remained, turning slowly brown, the sorry piles slumping as they began to rot. I started to take them, popping some in my coat pocket and half a dozen in the fold of my jumper. Down the lane I went, rotund with apples, decanting them along the hedgerows, because while I was walking around the village thinking about a petition for swifts, winter migrants were arriving.

During the last few wet nights, feathered travellers were making their way to Britain in their thousands: redwings. The smallest UK thrush, redwings are smartly dressed in their stripy dashes of fawn and rufous. Gathering in flocks along the coast of Scandinavia during autumn dusks, they embarked on a 500-mile journey across the North Sea to the UK. It is a perilous journey in wet weather – many drown, pinned down by the rain, crashing into the waves. Sometimes I looked at the live radar maps of them flying – little green dots inching across a screen, each representing a 60-gram bird confronted by churning waves. Those who survive are hungry and exhausted. The first ones had arrived a few days before, their soft, gentle 'peeping' call alerting me to their presence as they flew over the village, towards the old hedgerows on its outskirts, hoping to find berries and apples. Their arrival seemed to have gone mostly unnoticed, and the connection between the village's wasting apples and the redwings' dire need for them went unlinked. There were some people who had noticed though, acting on a far greater scale than me, including one birder in Dorset, who took carloads of apples to the coast, sprinkling them in the brash nearest the shingle beaches for the grateful travellers. He had scooped one thrush from the waves just in time, gently carrying it to land, food and shelter.

Every time I saw the rotting apples, this innocent ignorance, this lack of united opportunity, made me embrace the petition and the need to make a big statement. A statement where I could show I was willing to put my whole self on the line for birds because then maybe it would make others notice. Maybe if I showed how much I cared, then others would care with me and wake up to our closest wild neighbours and engage in the crisis faced by the birds who share our walls.

As I loaded more apples into my jumper and waddled into the dark field, I hit on a thought: to court the media, there seemed to really only be two choices for a member of the public to get national attention – break the law or get naked. I'd already dismissed the first option, so by the process of elimination, I was left with getting naked.

'Naked in public,' I said out loud, inadvertently frightening a cat who rushed away, processing the idea, wracking my brain in case there were other options I had somehow not thought of and I was just being dramatic. Sure, if I was a celebrity I could have perhaps got on TV and radio or been interviewed in a magazine or newspaper about my concern for birds. If I was Taylor Swift I could post one statement about my namesake and I'd get 100,000 signatures in a minute. But I wasn't.

What I was left with was either one very long plan of trying to build community engagement from scratch, without funding, or finding a way to harness the link between nude pictures and tabloids. The vulnerability of being a woman combined with the historic obsession with objectifying and sexualising women could now work in my favour. It had worked for Lady Godiva, the eleventh-century noblewoman who rode through Coventry naked, covered by her long hair. The medieval stunt was a protest against the oppressive taxes her own husband, the Earl of Mercia, had imposed on his tenants, and a thousand years later her name is still legendary.

I happened to have waist-long hair. I beamed, scheming as I hoarded more apples, lugging them down the lane. I wouldn't ride a horse like Godiva and I didn't want to sexualise my body. If getting naked was my route of securing media, then I would utilise my body as a canvas to secure my message. By the time I had moved all the apples, I had formed the whole idea: I'd (somehow) get a renowned body painter to paint me from neck to toe in feathers to represent the Red-Listed cavity-nesting birds the petition was for, and paint swifts on my back. On my hands there would be one swift painted that came together with a movement. I would launch the campaign and the petition by giving a speech at Speakers' Corner in Hyde Park and then walk to Downing Street, hopefully with a crowd of supporters.

I returned home, soaking, to tell Robin my plan.

'Are you sure?' Robin asked.

'What do you mean?' I replied, standing in the sitting room, the raindrops from my anorak dripping loudly onto the floor.

'Well, it's quite a big deal. It will be hard to pull off and it might not be effective,' he said, reasoned as ever. He didn't flinch at the idea, just the chances of it working.

I scowled, walking out of the house again and round the village to think. The rain splatted on the tarmac, the redwings arriving out of sight, the change in guard between summer and winter migrants almost complete. These birds risked their lives to get here, swifts would risk their lives coming home.

I went back inside.

'I'm sure. I don't know whether it will work but the point is it *could* work. More than that, logically, it seems like the only option that might lead me to reaching the 100,000 target,' I said, taking my dripping anorak off, wondering whether he would try to talk me out of it.

He hugged me in a gesture of support that meant so much. 'OK, let's do this. Let's save the swifts!' His sentiment was spot on, but spoken in our sitting room, it sounded so feeble.

The next day, instead of carrying on editing and ghostwriting books, I started writing a 'to-do list'. Through someone I knew, I had been put in touch with Paul Goodenough, the founder of the charity Rewriting Extinction. We spoke via Zoom and he offered to contact a body painter he had heard of called Guido Daniele.

Guido was famous for painting a chimpanzee on Dr Jane Goodall's hand, going all over the world transforming bodies with paint to resemble creatures. To my amazement, when Paul asked on my behalf, Guido agreed immediately. The condition was that he would do it for free (generous considering his commissions normally commanded several thousands of pounds) but I would have to pay for his accommodation. I thought about it, discussed it with Robin, failed to find alternatives, and we agreed together. 'Well, go big or go home,' Robin said. 'The value of the media you'll get if it all works out will be far higher than the expenses and if you're going to commit the next six months to the petition, you need to give it the best chance of working.'

'We'll just have to keep an eye on money,' I said, worrying about how much it would end up costing, and how we would pay the bills.

The nudity itself didn't faze me that much, perhaps because my first job was as a model. At nineteen, I was signed to Models 1, Europe's biggest modelling agency, and I spent days modelling, mostly lingerie, when I should have been in university lectures about photography. I found myself in peculiar set-ups, such as modelling luxury underwear outside, with a whole crew of people waiting to wrap me up in coats between shots. Once, during a racy Agent Provocateur shoot, I accidentally flashed a family, who were shocked when they bumped into me posing in suspenders in a field. I stood for several days in a vast room wearing only my knickers in front of the fashion icon Tom Ford while he fitted his entire debut women's collection to me. The only major difference was that I was now in my mid-thirties and I would have to put a huge amount of effort into toning my body, boosting my self-belief with intense physical training. No carbs. No sugar. No butter. No booze. A gruelling hour on the rowing machine every day.

I didn't tell friends or family about the plan to start with, because until I had secured all the elements, it wasn't real. In fact, it sounded very silly. As well as Guido, I needed a photographer who would take my campaign portrait which could then be used for all comms and provide a backup if the launch flopped. I had my heart set on one photographer: Tim Flach. A world-renowned wildlife portrait photographer, Tim was, hands down, my favourite. His images are spellbinding. Not only are they aesthetically perfect photographs, but he approaches his animal subjects in a unique way. He photographs animals, normally individually, as though he is taking a human portrait. As a viewer, you find yourself staring into the eyes of a tiger, a monkey, a frog, who is looking directly at you. Collaborating with scientists, he contributed to a pioneering study entitled *Using Animal Portraiture to Activate Emotional Affect*, comparing how individuals respond to traditional wildlife photography and to animal portraiture. Those who were exposed to animal portraits reported increased empathy along with positive and relaxed emotions. By engaging critical anthropomorphism, the research conclusion was that it is an essential tool to encourage conservation efforts and that animal portraiture may be an ideal 'attention grabber', after which wildlife images can serve as 'educators'. In other words, the right portrait of a wild animal is compelling enough to help them.

I emailed him, wondering how best to compose a message out of the blue. I already knew him, but from fifteen years earlier and I hadn't been in touch since. Would he remember being my mentor when I was in my final year studying photography at London College of Fashion? Would he remember coming to see my photographs hanging in the Royal Academy fourteen years before? 'Hi Tim, I need your help to save birds,' is what I went for, asking him if he could photograph me to create a campaign portrait I could tempt newspapers with and use as a way to drum up petition signatures. For free. He said yes.

With Tim on board, the date was set. I rang up an old university friend, another photographer, Rachel Louise Brown, who was the photography director for *Harper's Bazaar* and a lecturer at the London College of Communication. With her trademark flair for creativity and excitement, she agreed to set her students a brief to photograph me when I launched the petition, in return for Tim and me coming to give talks at the university. Suddenly, I had gathered leading creatives who had all said yes immediately, trusting that what I had concocted out of thin air would work.

Chapter 5

The Petition Launch

A t the next meeting of the Swift Conservation Society, my idea
felt like a confession.

'Bloody hell, girl! That's the way to do it!' Margaret said,
spontaneously standing up and clapping while the others looked
slightly shocked.

The SLN had a similar reaction – some email replies came in
enthusiastic capital letters while others did not comment, many
queried it, wondering whether I was off my rocker. When I told
my parents and sister, they gulped down the telephone and were
simultaneously apprehensive and not surprised.

'Darling, do you think it will work?' my mother asked, her voice
laced with worry.

'I really don't know. I won't know until I've done it,' I replied.

I got the impression that most people I told secretly thought
it was very unlikely even to make the news. This led to a protective
stance from my parents, but I had worked through all the different
scenarios – of a creep assaulting me, of passers-by booing me, of
no one turning up, of it being so cold I got hypothermia – but I
couldn't control any of that. I had made my decision, which was
unwavering: I was doing it.

I sat in my kitchen and marked Saturday 5 November 2022
on the calendar, the day I would open my petition. I had chosen it
because it marked the year anniversary of swifts and house martins

being added to the Red List. It was also the week of the United Nations Climate Change Conference, COP27, which I hoped meant the media might be more inclined to cover an environmental story.

There was a buzz during the Swift Conservation Society meeting before the petition launch. Excitedly, Sylvia told me they were hiring a minibus so they could all come up together while we painted signs with the words 'The Feather Speech' and 'Save Our Swifts!' and 'Passion is a Superpower'.

I was unusually quiet with nerves, a sense of guilt creeping up on me at the idea of potentially letting these people down. Once the signs were finished, still with flecks of paint on our hands, we gathered in the pub.

'This will settle any nerves, love!' Sylvia said, ordering me a glass of wine.

'Na, THIS will settle your nerves, love!' Margaret said, handing me a shot of tequila.

The pub landlord asked us what the fuss was about.

'Our Hannah is going to walk naked for swifts in London on Saturday!' Julie said.

There was a flicker of pride in her voice that was immediately stamped out by the landlord's response.

'What a godawful idea. When did lawless passion ever help anything?' he replied.

'Firstly, it's not lawless passion. It's highly strategic passion,' said Julie, her eyes narrowed and angry as she leaned her small frame over the bar, 'and secondly, you mean to say that someone with her amount of passion shouldn't be the one with the best chance of saving them?' She stared at the landlord without blinking.

'Well, she's a nobody,' the landlord said, shrugging his shoulders, and walked off.

His words stung because they were true.

Julie rolled her eyes, clinked my tequila shot with hers and shouted, 'Passion is a superpower!'

The day before the launch, as I arrived at Tim's studio in East London, I still had no press and I worried whether the landlord was right.

Tim's studio is a serene white space, light years away from the Shoreditch high street immediately outside. There's a hive-like energy that Tim emits and his team takes on, busy but often working in silence, dwarfed by the enormous portraits of animals and birds. These images, printed on paper that glistens, are not images that hang in the background but stare, compelling you to stare back. As Tim set up a test shoot, I posed fully clothed so he could get the light ready for the following morning, his Hasselblad camera clicking every time he took a shot.

Early the next morning, I returned ready to welcome Guido, a seventy-something Italian stranger, who within five minutes of arriving was painting me as I stood in just my knickers. He started at 8 a.m., his careful brushstrokes becoming a rhythm played out on my body for ten hours. My back steadily turned into a mural of flying swifts while my arms were adorned with house sparrow feathers. My torso and neck were painted turquoise and purple to represent starlings, little flecks of white like freckles all over my body. Somewhere in the mix, the dark feathers of house martins were added so that my body became a symbol of all the endangered birds who would be helped by swift bricks. Everyone in the studio stared, and when I caught myself in the reflection of one of Tim's framed photographs, I realised the visual transformation was arresting. I looked avatar-like, innocently bold, otherworldly and nothing like anyone printed on page 3 of the *Sun*.

All the while, I rang news desks but couldn't get through, the phones endlessly ringing. It was only when Guido had finished that

I tried the Press Association, desperate. It was a big deal, this cold call, because if PA media covered it, they would send the images to all the picture desks of all the newspapers.

Standing in just a black thong, in Tim's bright white photographic studio, I rang the number, Guido next to me holding his breath. A man with a thick cockney accent answered the phone, 'PA media. Make it quick,' he said, his manner intimidating.

'Tomorrow at noon, I'm going to launch a petition for birds, wearing only paint, in Hyde Park,' I said.

'If you're covered in paint, you won't be naked then, will you?' the guy said, unimpressed.

'Well, can I show you right now on video call?' I suggested. 'Because I feel pretty naked.' It was an odd concept, to ring an unknown man at work and invite him to look at my painted, but naked, body. The only thing overcoming my inhibitions was the risk of the media not turning up.

'Go on then,' he said, intrigued.

So I did.

'Ah, gotcha. You're basically naked!' he said. 'Just in Adam and the Ants,' he chuckled, speaking in cockney slang that I knew meant 'pants'.

'Why are you doing it, what did you say about birds?' he asked.

I explained about swifts, the other birds, the swift bricks, the petition.

'Ah swifts, always in a Bob Murray,' he said.

'Excuse me?' I replied, not understanding.

'Bob Murray, you know, "hurry". I love birds. My father used to take me down on the Essex marshes every Sunday when I was a nipper,' he said, pausing. 'You're on, you've got yourself a jellied eel. Do you have a name for the campaign?'

'The Feather Speech,' I replied, grinning at Guido who by this point was waving his hands around in confusion mouthing 'jellied eel', not understanding it meant 'deal', but smiled when I smiled, both thumbs going up.

I told the man the timings and thanked him. Before I hung up I asked, 'Do you think it will get the coverage then?'

He replied, 'If we're covering it, it will likely be in every single newspaper.'

I gulped.

That night, I slept in Tim's studio on a sofa bed covered in a sheet, lying still on my back, trying not to smudge the paint, staring at the ceiling, worrying.

'Get some rest. You have to switch off, Hannah,' Robin said, but I couldn't, worrying about the route from Speakers' Corner to Downing Street, about the 6-degree temperature and the rain forecast. I worried about whether anyone would turn up to support me. Most of all, I worried about my speech and whether I would get it right. I had never made a speech before and this one was going to be recorded by the nation's press. As a writer, my words were my bread and butter. All the naked, painted, strategic fuss was to get the word out, for my words to give a voice to the birds. Messing up the speech would be the worst omen.

By the next morning, the quiet nerves had been replaced by action. A friend of mine, Jemma, who worked as a parliamentary researcher, had managed to get me on GB News for a live interview with two Conservative MPs, Esther McVey and Philip Davies. Naked. By 11 a.m. I was in the TV news green room surrounded by producers who were fretting.

'Where should I put the mic?' one producer said to another. 'There's nowhere to put it and she's on air in ninety seconds.'

Broadcasters and C-list celebrities huddled round, troubleshooting, suggesting the mic could be stuck to one of my nipples before I realised I could just hang it round my neck like a necklace. Twenty seconds later, I was on live television, sitting on a high stool at a counter next to Esther McVey MP and Philip Davies MP, the first politicians I had ever met. They introduced the story as 'The Bottom Line', with Philip Davies reading the cue card cautiously and with clear surprise about me walking unclothed to Downing Street. What could have been a silly, sensationalist interview, they made sure was serious. For three minutes, we chatted about scientific data on swift decline, government schemes such as biodiversity net gain, and building regulations.

An hour later, I left the studio to go to Speakers' Corner with my sister and a friend, who hailed a cab. While my father had stayed behind to look after the dogs, my mum had arrived in Hyde Park with a minibus full of family friends. Together with Margaret, Sylvia and Julie, they were busy with Robin, setting up, handing out placards and making sure anyone who was arriving to show support knew where to go. The cab ride was cold as we sat in silence, nervous glances flashing between us as we became increasingly aware of how surreal the situation was. 'No pressure,' I muttered, and they smiled back at me, not entirely sure what to say. There was a moment where I stared, unblinking, at the cab floor, transfixed by the chance of it all failing. I was acutely aware of the risk of making a total fool out of myself, but then I reminded myself that the real failure would be if this country lost these birds. I was irrelevant, merely a vehicle for the desperation of the swifts.

The small crowd, made up of friends, family and members of the SLN, waited for me to arrive. I could see many familiar faces holding placards, waiting for me.

The journalist and political commentator Matt Stadlen had agreed to introduce me. We had met only once, when he had interviewed me at Hay Festival, and had instantly got on through our mutual love for birds. He had a seemingly unflappable demeanour, and I felt he was a trusted ally. As he stood in a duffle coat waiting for me, I looked at him wondering whether I was about to regret the whole thing. He smiled, behaving as if what I was doing was totally normal, helping me embrace the moment. After he generously bigged me up, I walked through the crowd, got up on an upturned apple crate and began.

'I stand here today as a go-between for swifts . . .'

The small crowd stared, but I looked through them, speaking to everyone in London and beyond, not just to those who were present. There was an automatic shift in my mentality similar to any performance, whether it is sporting or theatrical, and with it, I stepped into a frame of mind that stopped me from being nervous or thinking too far ahead, focused on the words I had chosen that would only be heard at all because I was standing there unclothed.

'Swifts are awe-inspiring and every bird counts. Small enough to fit in the palms of our hands, swifts spend more time airborne than any other bird on Earth. They eat, bathe, court and sleep on the wing, flying millions of miles in their lifetimes, living in the sky. They are adventurers, travelling from Britain to southern Africa, crossing the Sahara Desert twice every year, not landing like other birds – until they come home to us. Adults return to the exact holes in our walls: to cul-de-sacs and terraces, old houses and wherever there is a space for them to rest their heads and have their feathered children. By sharing our walls with swifts, birds whose agility and speed inspired fighter-jet design, we share our homes with feathered patriots, who bring summer with them and fill our skies with joy.'

I paused, the word 'joy' ringing out as joggers weaved past, some jogging on the spot to hear what I said next.

'But these iconic birds have been on the Red List of highest conservation concern for one year. They face national extinction, their population plummeting, hindered further by their homes being inadvertently blocked off by us,' I said, remembering every single home I knew to have been blocked. Then I began the section of the speech that was really more of a song for swifts, an ode for their survival.

'If swifts could fight for their existence with words, they might say this:

'You have not seen what I have seen. I have spiralled above clouds cloaked in the setting sun, spun through the eyes of ferocious storms, crossed deserts, oceans, continents. For generations my kind has existed, our bloodline unbroken for millions of years. And we have screamed in delight at your creativity, innovation, progression. But now we are screaming for you to help us. To look up. To remember you share your home with other kinds. Feathered, furred, finned, scaled, winged. Our shared home is becoming parched of life, destroyed, flooded, licked by flames, ABLAZE. Through these shared struggles, we only ask for one thing. A safe place to rest after our perilous journey home. You can help us. You can remember your walls also belong to adventurers. You can unblock the holes and make new ones. You can sign the petition to help us and we will be forever grateful. We will scream in delight at your creativity, innovation, progression.'

Defiant now, I spoke louder. 'The Feather Speech is not just a campaign aimed at the government or the people of Britain. It is an alliance with our wild neighbours. Let the records show we care. We are connected and we will unite on behalf of the nature on our doorsteps, starting with swifts, who watch over us all. As we prepare to welcome our feathered patriots home in the spring, let us recognise the power of our own voices. Let us recognise we can make a difference. When the environmental crisis feels overwhelming, let us come together and show that passion is a superpower.'

Pausing, I looked around, finally catching the eye of some of the people in the crowd, of family, friends and strangers alike, before my final words gave the instruction to sign the petition. 'This petition has six months to gather 100,000 signatures to help swifts, starlings, house martins and house sparrows, to help these irreplaceable British birds. Don't sign because I ask. Sign because swifts can't. Sign because every bird counts.'

As I stepped down from my upturned apple crate, everyone cheered, tears in their eyes, clapping. 'Passion is a superpower!' I heard Margaret yell.

I didn't react externally but their energy flowed through me. I walked, headstrong, towards Downing Street, chaperoned by several policemen. To conduct the march, I had had to alert the Met Police as protocol. Worried they would say public nudity was illegal, I was surprised when the email response said, 'Oh no, Madam, it's fine. We help organise a naked cycle ride every year. You're golden.'

The police officer next to me grinned and rolled up his sleeve. On his arm, he had a tattoo of a swift. He looked at me and said, 'Thank you.'

The gratitude of a stranger was completely unexpected. As I walked, passers-by joined the march. By the time I got to Buckingham Palace, the crowd was bigger. It felt surreal. I felt a streak of glee as if I was doing something a bit naughty but not harmful, like eating some icing off a cake before it has been served. There was a 'I cannot believe I am doing this' track on repeat in my head – after all, London is a city of almost 9 million people, with an extra 200,000 tourists visiting each day, and I was (probably) the only person walking through Central London in my pants. Every now and then I found a tear rolling down my cheek as my thoughts flocked to the swifts. This emotion held the heaviest weight of all, feeling like a prayer, clashing with the passers-by who stared in

utter shock, doing comic double takes. More people started photographing and videoing me. I got a couple of people glaring at
me in disgust, but then a ten-year-old girl came up to me, walking
as fast as she could to catch up. I didn't know her or her mother
but they were part of the SLN. 'You're my hero,' the girl said in an
embarrassed whisper. 'You're really brave.'

Her words, the policeman's, and the fact people had turned up
in support, validated and empowered me. I had already become
more than just me. By the end of the two-and-half-mile march,
I was no longer made up of just my own hopes for birds. I had
become a physical representative of a passionate group of people
whose love for swifts was unwavering.

I finished my march outside 10 Downing Street. By now the
rain was falling hard and I was shivering, the afternoon slipping
into teatime. A big crowd gathered, the press huddled around me
asking questions, but I began to come out of the performance.
I was hungry, tired and wet, beginning to shiver uncontrollably. I
didn't realise that I should stop, wanting to squeeze every last
opportunity out of the spectacle, but on seeing I needed to get
dry and warm and, perhaps most importantly, away from everyone,
Robin and my sister took me round the corner, thanking the press
and the crowd for coming. In a fortunate and random coincidence,
Robin's former military regiment, the Household Cavalry, had
stables and a museum right there. It was a place I knew well from
my early twenties when I had spent time photographing the horses.
Within a few minutes, we were in the little museum next to the
stables, the horses offering immediate comfort with their familiar
smell and gentleness. Robin handed me his old military training
trousers and coat from his bag, which were far too big for me
but thermal and therefore immediately snug. I hadn't worn clothes
by then for thirty-six hours.

By bedtime, unable to scrape all the body paint off, I went to sleep half bird, half woman, Robin whispering he was proud of me. The next morning, I walked to the corner shop. The newspaper stand was full of naked pictures of me – almost every national newspaper had covered the campaign. 'Nearly-nude Painted-bird Ruffles Feathers'; 'Lady Godiva Goes Nude for Birds'; 'Near-naked Bird Lover in Protest March to Save Her Feathered Friends'; 'Activist Marches Through Central London in a Bid to Save Birds'.

I stood on the street staring at the newsstand. It was a surreal moment. Exhausted, I felt a wave of relief that didn't summon excitement, just a dulled, odd reality.

'I did it. I actually did it,' I said flatly to the newspaper man, who looked at me as though I was still drunk from the night before, not realising the papers he was selling were adorned with my naked body.

I walked back to the B&B, greeted by Robin, who was grinning. 'You've already got 20,000 signatures, Hannah!' he said, handing me his phone to show me the petition. A single tear rolled down my face. 'There's a chance, then,' I said.

I thought I would be ecstatic, jumping around, hyperactive, but I just wanted to sit on the bed, quiet for a moment, processing the Pandora's box I had just opened for myself, realising that starting the petition meant I would be held captive to the goal of 80,000 more people signing it. Robin handed me a croissant. 'You need food,' he said. I hadn't eaten carbs for months and I ate ravenously, slowly starting to feel revived, a smile creeping on my face as it all began to sink in. The fight to convince the government had begun, and I wasn't alone anymore. I had the support of 20,000 strangers and counting.

Chapter 6

The Trolls

By the afternoon I was sitting in a quiet pub in Kew, being interviewed for an exclusive with the *Mail on Sunday*, which I picked over the others because it has the largest readership, and because they'd agreed to include a big QR code linking to the petition. By the evening I was in another television studio the other side of London about to be interviewed live by Piers Morgan, world famous for being ruthless. As I was repainted in a dressing room, ready to go on live TV naked for the second time, I tried to give myself a pep talk and feel ready to defend myself against someone known for tearing environmental protesters apart.

'You're up next, Hannah,' one of the producers said, popping his head round the dressing-room door and beckoning me to follow him down the corridor to the studio floor.

'I wonder if this is a bad idea,' I said to Robin.

'You'll be fine. Just trust your gut, it's got you this far,' he answered.

I waved nervously as I made my way past the other guests, wondering what it was like for Robin to see his wife's bare bottom toddling off to go on TV. Again.

As I was ushered onto the dark studio floor, Piers Morgan got up from his usual place behind a long desk and walked to where I was. The interview was going to take place standing, because that way the cameras could show off my whole body.

Smiling broadly, he shook my hand. 'Well, you're impressive!' he said.

I wasn't expecting him to say that. I smiled back.

'Look, we don't have much time because my other interview overran, so make sure you just get your message out, OK,' Piers said.

I nodded, smiling, nervous and confused. He was so friendly, so nice and totally disarming.

'I've just got to make sure my eyeline stays on yours, otherwise I'll have hell to pay!' he joked.

'Well, you're not missing much. I don't have great tits,' I replied, poking fun at my own small boobs in a cheesy ornithological joke.

Piers threw his head back laughing in surprised delight and then quickly composed himself as the on-air red light went on and the interview began.

'You're on national television right now, barely wearing a stitch of clothing, this is mostly paint,' Piers said.

'I really love the birds!' I replied.

He laughed. 'This takes guts to do this.'

'Yeah, I'm pretty nervous right now, Piers, to be honest!'

He laughed again. 'Well, what are you thinking as you stand there?'

'I'm thinking, I'm doing this for the birds. I can be publicly ridiculed and judged but I'm doing it for the birds, I'm desperate for them,' I replied.

'What reaction have you had from people?' Piers asked, his tone more serious.

'Mixed. People are saying I'm brave. I'm not – I'm desperate. People are saying I'm stupid. Fine – I'm ridiculous, but I'm actually just trying to get this voice for the birds because they can't speak,' I said.

Changing the tone so it was light-hearted again, Piers said, 'I did go sort of naked once for a commercial and I am prepared to go back to this look,' as the screen broadcast a huge photo of Piers lying in front of a fire with only a burgundy velvet drape covering his modesty in a photoshoot that looked like it came right out of some 1980s soft porn magazine.

'What do you think?' Piers said, jokily.

'I think more feathers, and we're onto something!' I replied.

We both laughed.

'You could really help. You've got 8 million followers on Twitter. I need 100,000 signatures,' I said enthusiastically, half begging, half demanding.

'I'm going to get your numbers up for you, because I actually think it's a good cause. We don't want swifts to become extinct!' Piers said. 'What about the other birds?'

I started listing all the birds.

'And no problem with the tits?' he asked, a glint in his eye.

'Tits aren't really involved in this,' I said, unblinking, a smile creeping onto my face.

'How do people sign the petition?' he asked.

'They go on your Twitter,' I replied, laughing.

To my utter surprise, Piers Morgan was the first public figure to show support, and I was extremely grateful to him. Before I was even out of the studio, he had tweeted, 'Save the birds! I stand, over-clothed with naked bird lady @WriterHannahBT and her brilliant campaign. Sign her petition here.'

Then the negative comments started. The downside of the publicity, necessary to bring in the signatures, was the online trolling. I knew to expect it, but the first nasty comment — *You should not be allowed to go naked because of your shit tits* — took my breath away, and that was just the beginning. There were two categories of verbal abuse, both surreal because they came from strangers. One line of attack was to mock and criticise my body and the survey taken by arseholes showed my A cups are apparently not popular.

> *I can't tell whether she is a woman or a man.*
> *I think she is trans.*
> *To be honest, it would have been better if she had bigger tits. Just being honest.*
> *You're a joke of a woman.*

Every name under the sun that could go with the word 'tits' was spat at me in neat little sentences of mindless hate. Sticks and stones came with the territory of putting myself out there. Of course I was going to get judged. When I felt in a strong mood, I wanted to reply, 'God, can't you at least acknowledge my abs! I worked so hard on them!'

But there were other comments I read that made me feel immediately sick. For the most part, I didn't engage. Friends called me up, seeing the comments, checking to see if I was all right. When I arrived at the Swift Conservation Society meeting, Margaret didn't even wait to greet me, before saying, 'They're mainly men who have all probably failed in their achievements and have much smaller penises than they would like.' Sylvia joined in: 'As Einstein said, "Weak people revenge. Strong people forgive. Intelligent people ignore",' and put her arm round my shoulder.

'Or as Taylor Swift says, "Shake It Off",' Julie added, smiling.

It was easier said than done. Worse than the physical insults were the ones that targeted my state of mind and my motives.

> *You're a narcissistic bitch who is degrading birds.*
> *You're clearly mentally deranged.*

You attention-seeking whore.

Shame on you and your cause you skanky slut.

You deserve to get gang raped.

The comments smacked me between the eyes. Unpleasant to read in any circumstance, they were even more disturbing when I knew they were directed at me. Hundreds of strangers – human beings – had seen and judged me, and felt compelled to tell me horrible things, and one person with a beating heart and the ability to feel pain and suffering had decided to think *and* tell me, '*You deserve to get gang raped*'.

They had looked at me and reacted like that. Who were these people?

The comments on the *Daily Mail* and from Piers Morgan's fans were mostly physical insults, while the ones attacking my mental state of mind came from people reacting to the RSPB social media posts.

Attention-seeking idiot.

What a mentally deranged cow.

You should be locked up you're mental.

I would laugh if you got murdered you sick fuck.

You silly, silly woman.

You are degrading women and birds.

The RSPB's vice president personally contacted me to apologise and offer his own support. Robin told me to never look at any of the comments, confiscating my phone. 'Seriously. Don't. They will eat you up and it's just white noise. Social media is set up, governed and built on divisiveness.'

He was right, but every now and then I would spy a nasty comment and it would taunt me. The ones that affected me the most, though, were criticisms from nature lovers.

Lesson one, Hannah, you should focus on insect decline.

You should learn more about the housebuilding industry first.

Your efforts won't make a difference.

What you need to do is be more professional.

The government won't listen to you.

Do you really think the government will care?

You are wasting your time.

I don't agree with your methods. Put some clothes on!

You should get the government to stop using chemicals in farmland.

They mostly came from a profile that could be categorised as middle-aged white man. He (because I started to think of them as all the same) told me about insect decline as if I didn't know. He told me that *I* should be focusing on reversing the decline and stopping pesticide use. He instructed me like he knew better, despite having done nothing himself to try to help swifts in any capacity. This was the person I swore at, enraged. It was he who stuck in my head and made the campaign feel toxic.

Then there were the passive-aggressive comments that told me I should thank those who had said nice things, that I would get more out of it.

People will engage with you more if you bother to thank them.

It would be nice if you replied. We signed your petition.

You need to share our petition because we've just shared yours.

You need to care about all nature, not just swifts.

There were thousands and thousands of comments from people making wrong assumptions.

Shame on you for profiting!
I will sign as long as you give the proceeds to charity.
I've been trying to contact your team.

When I bumped into Julie on a dog walk, she gave me a hug.

'Let's see. You don't have a team, you're broke and people who you don't know from Adam are criticising every inch of you. I think you need a medal!' she said.

'It is beginning to feel like it will turn out to be the worst unpaid job ever,' I said, smiling, trying to make a joke out of it.

'Just remember that for every horrible comment, there are thousands and thousands of people who are learning about swifts thanks to you. We're all behind you,' Julie said, giving me another hug.

She was right. The positive comments flocked in too.

Queen of the swifts!
Warrior!
Swift saviour!
Goddess of the sky!
Hero!
Thank you!
Well done!
When I grow up I want to be like you.
Hannah Bourne-Taylor is a law-abiding great niece of the Birdman of Alcatraz!

Most importantly, given all the noise and my newfound fear of reading comments, the support was quantified in signatures.

Thousands of people had not commented at all, they had simply signed and shared. I got addicted to the green line of the government petition that got longer as it headed away from 0 to 100,000, refreshing it throughout the days to check the latest tally. Within less than three weeks of launching it, the petition had reached the quarter mark of 25,000 signatures.

'Go girl!' Margaret said, thumping me enthusiastically on the back as I bumped into her and Sylvia in the village shop.

I wanted to thank every single person who signed, hoping each one knew how grateful I was that they cared too. That WE cared. This sense of unity was the key ingredient to being a 'solo campaigner'. I was officially on my own but people were attaching themselves to me – to our common cause. A collection of both individuals and organisations was mounting and we were becoming a coalition for birds. One such proponent was Pete Barber, a businessman who had contacted me via my website to offer to help my campaign by making a short animation film called *A Swift Story* to raise awareness. After living in a house in Margate for several years, Pete had only realised that swifts had been there longer than he had when one of them became gravely grounded during the heatwave and was subsequently attacked by his cat. He explained via email that on finding the bird he didn't know what species it was, so had searched online. He had found a video on social media of me explaining about the dangers of the heat to birds who share our walls, with advice about what to do. Thanks to the video, his actions had saved the swift. Accompanying the email was a photograph of the front of his house and an enormous trampoline he had placed temporarily under the eaves blocking his bedroom window – a safety net should another swift chick fall. Gratefully,

I had accepted his offer and arrived near his office to be greeted by his entire production company. By the end of the morning they had filmed me and recorded my voice to go with their beautiful animation, complete with music composed specially for it. Pete's generosity was matched by his belief: 'Well done, Hannah, for starting a movement.'

I was bowled over by Pete – and the support kept coming. Channel 4 News invited me to do a feature-length news piece linked to their coverage of the United Nations Biodiversity Conference, COP15, that commenced after the climate conference. They used my campaign as a way to engage the public in Britain's biodiversity loss as a whole. Gathering on a cold December afternoon, we filmed at a starling roost because starlings are one of the four main endangered target birds who benefit from swift bricks. This was the first media coverage where my campaign, and I, were taken seriously. I wore clothes. It felt good.

All the while, at COP15, a landmark political deal was being negotiated, culminating in the adoption of the Kunming-Montreal Global Biodiversity Framework (GBF) in which almost 200 countries agreed to twenty-three targets, all set up to halt 30 per cent of biodiversity loss by 2030. One of those targets, Target 12, states 'ensure biodiversity-inclusive urban planning'. I read it full of hope.

A few days later I received an email from the government, which is obliged to respond formally to any government petition reaching the 10,000-signature mark. The response often gives an indication of how receptive the government will be should the petition reach the target and be granted a parliamentary debate. The initial response came from the Department for Environment, Food and Rural Affairs (Defra) and as I read it, my heart sank.

'We welcome actions by developers to provide "swift bricks", however government considers this a matter for local authorities depending upon the specific circumstances of each site.'

'They don't get it,' I said to Robin despairingly. 'The whole point is that local government has not taken responsibility. Local government has not acted. Even the former housing minister, Kit Malthouse, who included recommendations of swift bricks in the National Planning Policy guidance, said there had been almost no uptake.'

When I told the Swift Conservation Society at the next meeting, Margaret echoed Robin's sentiments. 'They're fobbing us off!' she said, her eyes screwed up in despair. Sylvia calmed everyone down and reminded us all to keep going. Quietly, I felt forlorn, constantly aware of being out of my depth in a game I had started and didn't know how to play other than to doggedly focus on the 75,000 more signatures necessary. 'We'll cross that bridge when we come to it,' I said in response to the questions.

Just before Christmas, Paul Goodenough, the founder of Rewriting Extinction, invited me to a parliamentary reception as his plus one, my first chance to properly engage with politicians.

Paul and I walked through Westminster Hall, where Queen Elizabeth II had lain in state three months before, and through the labyrinth of corridors of the never-ending green carpet that told us we were in the Commons, not the Lords. Parts of the palace looked regal – the gilded ceilings painted with stars – but a contrast was given by the smell of canteen food and strip lights.

When we arrived at the reception in a long permanent marquee off the back of Parliament, Paul wished me luck and we split up. My plan was to work the room: to go up to politicians and brazenly introduce myself and my cause in the hope of getting their support.

I had studied the members online, pinpointing about a dozen I thought were most likely to be interested, but the idea of going up to powerful strangers who did not want to speak to me filled me with horror. The reality would prove to be even worse.

The vibe was relaxed, the room full of little cliques of people holding glasses of wine that were drunk fairly quickly. I was relieved that I had to delay my mission when the secretary of state for Defra stood on a little stage and made a speech. Wearing a Father Christmas hat on her head at a jaunty angle, she made a quip about how she had been at a boozy Christmas lunch and then started a very positive speech about the environment in which she said in a booming declaration, 'We are the voice of the voiceless!'

I let out an involuntary squeak of anger and disbelief at her words. Only a fortnight before, her department had dismissed swifts with their response to my petition. That same week, her department had also reversed the ban on neotocite chemicals, the pesticides that decimate pollinators, which had been banned because of the ecosystem collapse they spark.

Once she had finished, the cliques reformed, like clams closing up, and I wanted to leave, to hide in the loo, to run away. 'There is no point in being here unless I do it,' I said to myself under my breath. Picking a group, I went up, put my hand out and said, 'Hello, I'm Hannah and I'm campaigning to help swifts.'

It didn't go well. The group visibly recoiled, then looked bemused, presumably because they didn't necessarily know what swifts were, and they certainly didn't know what a swift brick was. Most importantly, they did not want to know. I tried another group and the reaction was the same: a polite dismissal in the form of an apology that they weren't the right people for me. I felt like a street seller at a banquet. Wishing the ground would swallow me up, I carried on trying.

'I'm sure you don't want to speak to me but I'm trying to save birds. Twenty-five thousand people have signed my petition in just a month and I'm hoping to get your support,' I said, bulldozing a nearby conversation.

This opening line worked a bit better, leading to a few chats, but the outcome was the same. No one was interested. Only one man, the Tory peer Lord Robathan, was nice to me. For a start, he smiled at me, which was novel.

'Look, you need MPs not peers, so I'm not going to be much good, but come on, come with me, I will introduce you to a few.'

He tried. I was grateful. But the MPs he introduced me to were drunk to the point of hiccupping and his kindness was eclipsed by the last interaction I had that evening.

Motivated by his friendliness, I approached an MP who I recognised to be a lead on climate change. Next to him was a young man, distinctive in a three-piece tweed suit, doing an impression of a full-blown wannabe fogey, who was not an MP but an advisor. As I introduced myself and my cause, the MP stood silent, as though assuming the man next to him would field anything difficult away from him, and he did.

'Word of advice. You are far too passionate,' he said, cuttingly.

His words stung me like a slap in the face.

For a second, I was silenced. He looked at me like he thought he was a king and I was a peasant.

'Ironic you should say that, when my campaign's motto is Passion is a Superpower,' I said, feeling, appropriately, like a total tit.

The man didn't answer. The MP skulked away. I left, via the loo, avoiding looking in the mirror because I felt as small as he had intended me to feel, my motto feeling silly and childish and apparently untrue in sentiment. Being humiliated when already vulnerable was something that I realised would likely crop up repeatedly during the campaign. To be a campaigner, I kept learning, meant having such a thick skin it turned to scales. No wonder one of the RSPB's co-founding women, Etta Lemon, was dubbed 'the dragon'. Clearly, I, too, would have to breathe fire when all I really wanted to do was curl up on the sofa and watch trashy telly.

Chapter 7

Our Home Is Their Home

Christmas brought friends and family together, everyone asking how many signatures I had got. Drinks parties became like the real version of social media, where friends and relatives all gave me well-meant pieces of advice that I had, by now, heard hundreds of times.

'You just need to get on TV again,' someone would say in between scoffing vol-au-vents, as though it was as easy as filling out a form or ringing up a secretary.

'Your best bet is to contact Chris Packham or Taylor Swift,' another said as he knocked back mulled wine in a Rudolph Christmas jumper.

I smiled, trying hard not to clench my jaw, and found a way to remove myself from the conversation. Robin discovered me shivering outside, muttering to myself, bringing me a drink that I downed in one. 'I know everyone means well,' I hissed.

Having begun the campaign because I preferred birds to people, I was now trapped within the human world. People automatically offered advice but almost no one offered to help. I avoided the rest of the season's drinks parties and long lunches. Walking for hours in the damp, grey countryside, I sought out nature to balance me out, searching for the dose of wonder that acted like a balm to my anger and frustration.

As families slept off the twelve days of Christmas, napping in armchairs in front of the telly, there were others sleeping outside. Small collections of peach-furred, snoring dormice curled in tight balls in nests made of strips of bluebell and honeysuckle stems. Hibernacle caverns made from bracken banks where dozens of adders lay in a pile, hedgehogs under drifts of leaves in the hedges and gardens of Britain. But there were also wild ones who were awake and hungry, battling against the cold: birds. As I walked, I realised that for my entire life I had looked at the British countryside as a wild, natural landscape. Growing up, I had always been told, reassured, lectured, that the countryside was wild and that wild animals didn't need help. But that is not true. The situation in our farmland has been grave for decades, leaving farmland birds in dire need of help. I had had no idea about their plight until, over Christmas, I met an octogenarian, Louise Spicer, who lived in the next village. Louise, a retired childminder with a love of birds, had set up a local charity, Farmland Bird Aid Network (FBAN). She, too, had stumbled into helping in reaction to realising the seeds in the landscape – the food source for farmland birds – were depleted by midwinter. Twenty years ago she was walking with her botanist husband when they had come across a huge flock of linnets feeding on mustard seed in a disused quarry. Linnets are beautiful. Small brown farmland finches, the males have a crimson chest with a dab of crimson on their forehead like a little red cap.

'It was January when we noticed the linnets,' Louise explained when we met for a coffee. 'Spring was months away. When the mustard seed ran out, they would starve.' She looked at me with wide, worried eyes.

'What do you mean?' I asked, wondering how any birds were left.

'It's all because of the change in farming practices after the Second World War,' she said. 'Chemicals, monocrops, the decimation of 100,000 miles of hedges . . . there is no longer enough food for the birds to eat. Not enough wild space within the countryside. Sounds silly, doesn't it? I mean, most people think the whole of the countryside *is* wild,' Louise said, quieter now, sitting back in her chair, readjusting the blanket over her legs. 'Actually, much of it is not anymore. Many of the crops might as well be deserts.'

She told me about how the flock of linnets had spurred her into action.

'I organised bags and bags of oil-seed rape and millet, getting a big bin and storing the seed at the quarry after I'd got permission. Then I fed them, broadcasting the seed thinly across the ground near the hedgerow, to mimic how they would naturally feed and to stop pheasants and bigger, more common birds eating it,' she explained. 'Don't get me started on the pheasants and the game birds! I mean, for goodness' sake – did you know that according to the RSPB 40.6 million game birds are annually released into the UK countryside?'

We paused, both shaking our heads in disbelief.

'But the feeding of the linnets . . . it worked?' I asked.

'Yes,' she said. 'They kept coming, feeding together on the ground, but because of that one flock, I knew all the others needed help too, so I set up Farmland Bird Aid Network.'

Over the last twenty years Louise has worked with local farmers and landowners and galvanised volunteers to establish feeding sites across West Oxfordshire. Every morning from late November until April or May, depending on the spring temperatures, volunteers go out to these sites, on field margins near hedgerows, and feed flocks of farmland birds. Thanks to FBAN, 3,000 birds made up of twenty-eight different flocks are fed with seed grown by local farmers, ensuring that in West Oxfordshire there is a stronghold of farmland birds. Through one exemplary farmer, Mike Kettlewell, over forty local farmers from the North East Cotswold Farmer Cluster CIC (a group committed to landscape-scale regeneration, led by Tim Field) have followed suit, implementing supplementary feeding on their land, often taking their children with them, creating a new tradition. In 2023, the cluster produced almost 30 tonnes of seed to feed their flocks and FBAN's. Teaming up with WildCRU and Oxford's Department of Zoology, surveys have been conducted to provide an invaluable baseline for the right future habitat for farm birds. None of this would have happened without one woman who noticed, cared and acted, and managed to charismatically gather over sixty volunteers who change their winter plans every morning to feed birds.

'Is it a sticking plaster?' I asked Mike when I met him on his land to watch the bramblings feed, their bright orange breasts vivid against the grey landscape. 'Well, what needs to happen is a nationwide change in farming practices,' he replied. 'There are winter seed crops grown deliberately for these birds subsidised by the government, but they run out by midwinter. We feed the birds through the "hungry gap" because if we don't, these birds will vanish from our fields for good. Even here it has happened before my eyes. A decade ago there were tree sparrows, but no longer.'

The equation lay in the landscape and had been staring at me my whole life: there were half as many hedgerows as there had been in the 1940s; monocultural crops grew in bigger fields to maximise yield; advanced pesticides killed insects, and with their deaths came the starvation of any creatures whose diet was insects. Herbicides killed wildflowers that used to grow among crops, and with the death of the wildflowers came the starvation of creatures who relied on the seed. Linnets and other farmland birds have a diet of both insects and seed. Farmland had been made more efficient to produce the food we eat to support a growing population, with crops infringing on field margins, eking out every inch of space. In 1986, when I was born, 56.68 million people lived in the UK. In the same amount of space, 67.44 million people now lived, equating to over 10 million more mouths to feed. The cost seemed to be the decline of any creatures whose food was sacrificed for ours.

Mike explained how there are still ways for non-organic farmers like him to make room for wildlife that are often not practised by other farmers. He showed me the widest field margins I had seen, full of wildflowers and therefore wildlife. He showed me parts of his farm that were managed without chemicals such as hay meadows, and hedgerows that acted as both corridors and abundant natural larders for wildlife, the blossom and then the berries left unshorn. A measured and unpanicked man, Mike continued to state how bleak the national portrait is and would continue to be unless the bulk of farming practices changed.

After I met Mike, I went home and researched scientific papers, looking up information to double-check, to make sure my facts were straight, that the situation was really as bad as it seemed. It was worse. A recent study had been released by the RSPB sharing new data that revealed the death toll of birds across the UK and Europe since 1980 was 600 million birds. SIX HUNDRED MILLION. As I looked at the number, my chest tightened. For every year of my life, over 16 million birds had gone from the landscape I thought I knew.

'There is an urgent need to conserve birds associated with agriculture,' the report stated, reiterated by Anna Staneva, the head of conservation from BirdLife Europe. 'This report loudly and clearly shows that nature is sounding the alarm,' she said, concluding that

'the outputs could help the public as well as the responsible politicians, to realise that common birds might not be common forever
if we take no conservation actions.'

Nineteen species of British bird are dependent on farmland,
unable to thrive in other habitats. Overall, on average, they have
experienced a population decline of 48 per cent since 1970. Twelve
of these species are on the Red List, threatened with national
extinction: tree sparrow, corn bunting, turtle dove, grey partridge,
yellow wagtail, starling, linnet, lapwing, yellowhammer, skylark,
kestrel, reed bunting.

These statistics sent electric pulses into the tips of my fingers.
They revealed a portrait of death in a place I had noticed, the
wildlife right on my doorstep in ruins. It wasn't just birds. With
69 per cent of UK land being farmland, apart from the 3 per cent
of organic farms and the pockets of exemplary farming practices
among the landscape, it has become increasingly inhospitable
for wildlife. A study by scientists at the London Natural History
Museum in preparation for the 2021 UN Biodiversity Conference
showed that Britain sits among the worst global 10 per cent. Since
the 1970s, there has been a 41 per cent decline in species in the UK.
Contemplating the rest of nature from its collective perspective
makes it clear humans aren't good at sharing. It isn't convenient. We
have barged in and grabbed everything for ourselves. So much of
what is left of British wildlife lives within nature reserves or refuges.
Refuge: shelter from pursuit, danger, or difficulty; scaled, feathered, furred
refugees of the natural world.

In a knee-jerk reaction, I established my own farmland bird-
feeding site over Christmas, under the hedgerows of the old Salt
Way a few miles from my house. Not shared with other volunteers, this was a commitment that would mean me returning every
single morning until the spring, to feed a single flock of birds,

broadcasting seeds in the crisp dawns on the frosted ground. Until the end of April when the petition closed, every morning my day would begin with the reward of committing to helping birds.

I had chosen the site because of the high double hedges where I had seen yellowhammers in the summer. For a fortnight no birds came. I felt silly, wondering whether to stop putting the seed down. But then a few scouts found the food. Two turned to six turned to a dozen and then one morning there were fifty birds on the ground, huddled, feeding. I stood still, watching as the flock moved in tiny hops, as if they were performing a choreographed dance. Each morning, I continued to feed the farmland flock. They all needed 6 grams of food to survive – such a small amount individually, but collectively, a real burden. Each tiny body reminded me that even the smallest steps in the right direction were worth it – that small things add up. In the damp, grey stretch of hedgerow, the birds lit up the winter, swelling in numbers to 200, my morning pilgrimage the highlight of my day. By lying in the hedgerow, spying on the flock, the birds tied me to the village territory. Hares lolloped right past, gentle and slow. I lay uncomfortably on my back against the hawthorn, looking up at the flock as they zoomed past, hearing the gusts of wind their wings made just above me. As the flock grew in number, they illustrated the need to intervene, which was now, in this era of destruction, vital.

While I was personally committing to farmland birds, politically, I was solely focused on the birds who share our walls. I plied all my energy into social media, utilising all the photos and videos from the launch and an image bank of swifts, provided by artists, photographers and swift rehabbers from the SLN. It was working, my posts being seen hundreds of thousands of times, generating thousands more signatures. By the middle of February, 50,000 people had signed the petition. Fifty thousand strangers coming together for birds. The problem was, I needed 50,000 more, and I only had until 30 April to do it.

'Look, between us, we can ramp up signatures,' Margaret said over a cup of tea, but I knew the group had asked everyone within the local radius. They'd been knocking on doors, approaching people in the pub, stopping people in the shop, asking people on the bus. All over the country members of the SLN had been doing the same and you could tell: on the petition map that showed the hotspots, the whole of the country was covered in markers that represented signatures.

As spring neared, every dawn I walked through the fields streaked in silver moonlight, positioning myself in the hedge, waiting for audible signs of the season change. When the birds started their spring courting calls, they gave me the gift of melody, a language sung by individual birds who I had seen every day. They also gave me their clarity of purpose. Against the backdrop of uncertainty, of fatal statistics that spell out such loss, the dawn chorus is a mark of the future. Birds sing to claim new territories, to make bonds with new partners, to create life. As I lay in the hedgerow surrounded by colourful feathered bodies, their feet clutching to the branches so their bills could open wide with promises, the birds cocooned me in hope. Every bird represented a battle that had been won, every pair of tiny inky eyes looking forward, not back, embracing the light of spring. They savoured and utilised every minute, their lives revolving around the promise of better days to come. It was the skylarks who started singing first, high in the night sky, like a secret reward for feeding the flock every day. Out of the mixed flock, one male yellowhammer caught my eye, not because of his bright sunny plumage but because of his character. When the flock winced, constantly flying back into the hedgerow reacting to a potential threat, he remained on the ground: an individual who went against the flow, standing out from the crowd. His small stature emphasised his defiance, and he became my talisman. A David and Goliath story had played throughout the Anthropocene and he reminded me that, against all odds, David had won.

The male yellowhammer also reminded me that strength often comes from unexpected places, so I changed tack, going into schools to speak to the generation who would be the first to lose out on swifts if grown-ups didn't act now. Presenting to eco clubs, classes and whole-school assemblies, I used the campaign to educate and inspire children and teachers alike. Each time, the pupils reacted identically. They simply could not understand why the government hadn't already done it. One primary school in London was particularly high spirited. After the school assembly where I showed Pete's animation film, *A Swift Story*, a boy's hand shot up. 'Can we hold a protest like you did?' the boy said. 'I know we wouldn't be allowed to leave easily because it's school and everything but could we hold a protest here, right now?'

The teachers nodded.

'Right, you're in charge,' I said to the boy. 'You organise everyone, and I will do it with you.'

The boys huddled round.

'On the count of three,' I heard the leader whisper, his eyes fixed like they were about to go into battle or perhaps a competitive game of football or hide and seek.

'One, two three!' His command was followed by thirty boys shouting in unison, 'OUR HOME IS THEIR HOME! OUR HOME IS THEIR HOME! OUR HOME IS THEIR HOME!'

Oh, it was brilliant. Jumping up and down, they chanted. I joined in and for a few minutes, I let their united energy wash over me.

By mid-March, when there were six weeks left and the petition was still 20,000 signatures short, a new restlessness came because from then on, swifts began to make their journeys back to Britain. With their homebound journey, the final countdown started. As I was trying to get people to pause their busy lives for a matter of one or two minutes, these birds were embarking on a 4,000-mile journey. With no passports and no laws, the sky was theirs for as long as they could survive. From the green warmth of Equatorial African rainforests they'd set out, following rivers up Africa, crossing over grasslands, towns and the biggest desert on Earth. Navigating storms, oceans, bird catchers, aeroplanes, droughts, chemicals, air pollution, predators, each journey was a gauntlet to overcome. My favourite day of the year is the one in May when I see the first swift return, but this year it was a day I was now dreading, willing to delay it as I lay awake at night. I was plagued by a single thought: that the swifts would arrive at the same time as I failed to reach the signature target. Giving up on sleep, I embraced the nighttime world of a nocturnal summer migrant who is one of the first to arrive from Africa every spring: nightjars.

European nightjars fly between Europe and Africa, knowing both places in the same way swifts and house martins do. Hot and cold. Blustery and still. Back and forth. Home and home. During the day, whichever continent they are in, nightjars rest on the ground or perch on open branches, in partial shade, turning to face the sun to minimise their shadow. Their plumage is a portrait of their surroundings, a study of bark and scrub made from mottled feathers: rich brown of peat bog; grey of hawthorn and beech but also acacia. Accents of burnt-umber heather and African earth. Slithers of black mimicking dappled shade and flecks of white borrowed from the moon. Found on the heathlands, moorlands and in open woodland of Britain, they are ground-nesting birds. Currently on the Amber List, this is a hopeful status because it's an upgrade from being on the Red List for years. They are a species that has, with active help, managed to claw its way out of extinction. Thanks to scientific surveys, the restoration of heath reserves has ensured there is a variety of habitats for the birds, generated by herds of cattle, assisted by ponies, donkeys and pigs. Wilder grazing systems using animals constantly change the heath on a small scale, the grazing animals' hooves breaking up vegetation, creating bare ground as they pass through. This, together with their dung, attracts insects such as dung beetles, which are great nightjar food.

On a Saturday night in Dorset, not far from my parents' house, I went to a heathland high above the lights of Weymouth and Portland Bill twinkling below. A rugged island above the sea and the fields, the heath stands alone, stark and bracing, Hardy country; it breathes nostalgia into the landscape like conjuring a ghost. In the dimpsey light, the bleak terrain of the heath was softened by stars of deep yellow gorse flowers: a tamed beast that welcomed the wind and the sea frets. Without shelter, the gorse and heather stood gnarly and bruised in clumps of purplish-brown, darkening with the blue twilight.

I took my young niece and nephew with me, getting out of the car at dusk.

'Will we see them?' my niece asked.

'I don't know, but if we don't look, we won't find out,' I replied, trying to manage their expectations.

Walking together quietly down the chalk path that gave off a glow as the dusk sank deeper, we waited. Staring into the grey sky, the wind picked up, rushing at our faces, making the bent hawthorn trees squeak and rattle.

'What do they sound like?' my nephew asked.

'A churring hum,' I said, 'which is legendary because it used to get people a bit frightened.'

He was intrigued, squeezing my hand, wanting to know why, so I explained how nightjars had been misunderstood for centuries. Leading crepuscular and nocturnal lives, their disproportionally big mouths and their peculiar calls have left them shrouded in uneasy mystery. For centuries, they were called many things.

'They've got some cool nicknames. Like dew-hawk, nightchurrs and fern owls,' I said.

'Fern owls,' my niece repeated, looking around hopefully.

I told them how the names are attached to the habitats they were found in and their behaviour – seen on the ground among ferns; awaking when the dew is being made; making a sound like 'jar' or 'churr'.

'They're also nicknamed lich fowle and night raven and goat sucker,' I said, explaining the link to goats came from Aristotle's mention of them, believing that they sucked the milk from goats, when really they feed on insects that are flushed up by passing herds. That wrong assumption became so ingrained that the order in which they belong is Caprimulgiformes, from the Latin 'goat-milker'.

'Cooooooooooooool!' my nephew said. 'Goat sucker!' he repeated, chuckling. 'How big are they? Are they huge?'

'No, they're about the same size as a pigeon and are not at all scary,' I said.

Half an hour passed. I began to doubt they were here. Maybe they were yet to arrive. I looked out over the sea at the darkening sky and imagined nightjars approaching like a fleet of ships. Their migration has unveiled a revelation. Gabriel Norevik at Lund University in Sweden studied their flight patterns by attaching tracking devices to thirty-nine European nightjars, and the discoveries showed that they synchronise their flights with phases of the moon.

An itinerary dictated by the lunar cycle felt infinitely special. A crescent moon appeared as the clouds parted, a slither of glowing pale amber, giving me hope that they had already arrived.

We stood next to the edge of the conifer wood that sloped down the hill in a block of black. Moths flitted about the edges of the bushes like threads of silver weaving the sky to the land. A deer sprang up in a flash of roan, its footsteps on the flint path ringing long after it had disappeared from sight. Suddenly, from out of the dim light, came the noise of nightjars. I clutched my niece and nephew's hands and they squeezed back, gasping at the sound of the distinctive chirring – a call that sounded more like a chorus of amphibians or insects than of birds. A continuous undulation of sound. Not a song sung but a noise made. An almost constant hum that rippled, both frantic and peaceful. Stopping abruptly, it was replaced by a concoction of flicking, tapping, clipping sounds, like horseshoes on a road, and a series of squeaks strung together. A peculiar percussion instrument or wizened being-of-the-bushes whistling itself awake.

'Maybe the stories are true! Maybe they have magical powers,' my nephew said as we walked down the hill. There, a pair of nightjars flew straight up from the ground, appearing from among the gorse and the beginnings of bracken. My niece and nephew jumped, startled, and then giggled quietly. As we stood holding hands, one after another the nightjars flew over our heads in a darting flight as though they were puppets being jerked on their strings. Dark, jolting shapes against a glowing blue dusk, they then melted into the darkness of the ground, dropping out of the air. We heard a squeak behind us, and suddenly there was a nightjar, followed by three more. Four nightjars flew in jerks upwards from the ground before circling the air above us, curious about who and what we were. One flew across the path of the moon, its silhouette etched into my eyes forever before it flew straight and fast, hovering in a rush of focused energy before vanishing, back to the ground where night had already fallen. The children were stunned by the performance, and we stood in a silent standing ovation on the heath under a halo of dancing nightjars.

During the nights that followed, I lay awake worrying as the swifts followed the nightjars home from Africa, and I realised that so much of my fear was that this experience would be gone forever for me, and for younger and unborn generations.

This desperate narrative of loss was why people were signing the petition in their tens of thousands. Every week I was receiving hundreds of emails and comments from strangers who had signed it. They told me of their childhood love of swifts. Every year, just like me, they would watch open-mouthed, but as they had grown up, they had noticed fewer swifts returning. With this loss came not only sorrow but a fear that their children and grandchildren would be robbed of this wonder. The boys from the prep school and my niece and nephew haunted me in this way. By the time they were my age, it was more likely than not that there would be no more swifts. While nightjars on heathlands at nighttime aren't accessible to the majority of people, urban birds are. They are our nearest touchpoint to nature, right on our doorsteps, living alongside us. This was the thought that simultaneously plagued me and motivated me each night: swift bricks wouldn't only safeguard the existence of these remarkable birds, they would also protect our connection with them.

By mid-April, the countdown had created momentum on social media, my posts being viewed 100,000 times within twenty-four hours, and the signatures were beginning to flow. The campaigning organisation Wild Justice waded in to the campaign, Lucy Lapwing and Mark Avery appearing like brilliant knights in shining armour, wise to the battles of nature, calm but decisive in their demeanour. Lucy made beautiful and bold social media adverts, Mark wrote several blogs and newsletters to their thousands of followers and, together with Chris Packham, they posted on socials. Thanks to their concerted effort and active, generous support, the green line of the petition grew longer.

Motivated and desperate in equal measure, I created a huge gold ball gown in the style of a Disney-princess, covered with white shapes of cut-out swifts. Each swift had a message that had been written on social media or by schoolchildren. Now, instead of campaigning unclothed, I was wearing the love of a nation. I made a huge train and wrote 'Sign the Feather Speech Petition' on it. I rang all the media contacts telling them I was in the final throes of the petition. They all replied with one question: 'Are you going to be naked?' When I said no, they said they weren't interested in covering it.

Unpublicised, I went into Oxford and London, wearing my silly gold ball gown adorned with swifts, and approached everyone with new vigour. It was more embarrassing than walking naked, but it was better than failing. On the Underground people approached me, taking selfies. During commuting times, people politely asked what it was all about, and on weekend nights, the dress coaxed huddles of drunken friends who, like magpies, inspected me. Only the regional news was interested, but I took any coverage I could get, springing onto local radios at the crack of dawn, speaking enthusiastically, glad no one could see me banging on about swifts from bed.

Just before Easter, I looked at the green line as soon as I woke up, as I had done for almost six months, and saw it had reached a milestone. 'Ninety thousand signatures!' I yelled, waking Robin up, the dogs scattering off the bed.

'That's the capacity of Wembley Stadium,' Robin said sleepily.

Public figures in the conservation world and a few celebrities with big followings continued to share the petition, along with thousands and thousands of members of the public. On Easter Saturday, the national press became interested, my Twitter posts going viral, reaching half a million views. When I refreshed the petition's green line, it was picking up pace as the signatures rolled.

'Bloody hell, Hannah! Three hundred people an hour are signing the petition! As long as they don't stop, we can calculate the exact time that the petition will hit the 100,000 mark,' Robin said over breakfast.

'When?' I asked.

'3 p.m. on Easter Sunday.'

Margaret was banging on the door. 'Have you seen it? It's actually moving! It's a flowing river of signatures!' she shrieked. 'We're all going to pile in a car and go to Oxford with you if you want?'

Nodding excitedly, I raced around getting ready, hopping as I put one sock on and then the other, trying to find my shoes, my heart pumping loud in my chest. After five and a half months of watching the petition in silence, of worrying to the point of not sleeping, of begging strangers and celebrities and everyone to share the petition, to rally others to sign, suddenly, there was a rush of energy. Suddenly, it all felt real. Robin and I leapt into the car with Margaret, Sylvia and Julie, stuffing the skirt of my gown in as everyone patted it down.

Easter Sunday was the perfect day, with clear blue skies, no wind and bright sunshine lighting the Oxford stone so it shone golden. When we arrived, we were trailed by news cameras. Passers-by gaped at us – the little handful of people surrounding a woman in a silly pantomime-like dress. We all approached random people holding our phones out which had the petition QR code on, brazen in our invitation to sign the petition. 'Who wants to be the one hundred thousandth person to sign this petition?' Margaret was shouting. People were gathering round, intrigued, others were taking photos, wanting selfies. I was in a slight daze, overdosing on adrenaline, knowing I was about to experience a feeling not of happiness but of utter relief.

Under the Bridge of Sighs, a middle-aged woman named Sarah with her child in tow happened to be the one hundred thousandth signature. She was polite and friendly and hadn't known much about swifts but had wanted to help them.

'Thank you,' I said quietly. Then in sudden excitement I yelled up at the sky. 'WE DID IT!' I screamed, my voice ricocheting onto the Oxford colleges, bouncing skywards in sheer delight.

'WE DID IT!' I shouted again in disbelief.

I spoke to the news crews, while random kids danced around me. 'When the environmental crisis feels overwhelming, we have come together and *proved* that passion is a superpower!'

Margaret was running around whooping, clashing with the calm mood of passers-by. No other reaction would have matched the collective achievement. It was intense. I involuntarily let out a laugh, shaking my head, crouching down in shock. I had put my life on hold for this. I had launched The Feather Speech almost naked and almost alone. Now it was a campaign that belonged to 100,000 strangers, uniting for birds.

When I got home, I changed and walked to the village shop, thinking the excitement had peaked. Until I heard a noise. My favourite noise on Earth. A scream from the blue sky. I thought I was going mad. Disbelieving, I looked up and there one was. Three weeks earlier than normal, a single swift wheeled in the sky. 'WHOOOOOOOOOOOOOOOOOOOOOOOOOOOOOOOOP!!!!!!!'

I yelled, jumping in the street, tears streaming down my face. 'WELCOME HOME!!!!'

Arriving earlier than I had ever seen one in my life, the swift felt like a talisman just for me, like a single Red Arrow doing a fly-past as my personal reward.

By the time the petition closed, it had collected well over 100,000 signatures. In spite of all the hype, and the number of people involved in making it successful, the moment the petition closed played out in silence. I was alone in my kitchen. I looked at my phone on the final day and saw the final number under the green line: 109,896.

'One hundred and nine thousand, eight hundred and ninety-six signatures,' I said quietly. 'Thank you,' I whispered, acknowledging those signatories I'd never get to thank in person.

I walked round the precious gable wall that was home to the swifts. While the two swift babes from last year would be far away in another piece of sky over Africa, I watched their parents in the sky where they had begun their maiden flight. 'I'm one step closer to keeping my promise to you and your children,' I whispered.

Rushing up the steps of the Oxford Museum of Natural History, I flung myself into the arms of George, Keeper of the Swifts.

'Congratulations!' he said into my hair, as I clutched him in enthusiastic hope. Only a few swifts had returned, most still on their way. We crouched down next to one who was preening, its bill meticulously sliding down the sleek black primary feathers that made it such an elite flyer. I looked at its closed wings, like swords resting after a battle, and let out a sigh of relief.

Chapter 8

The Parliamentary Debate

The local swift group marched me to the pub, Margaret buying rounds of drinks just for me in blind-drunk enthusiasm.

'Never had any doubt!' she said loudly, half to me, half to the sceptical landlord as she slammed down the newspapers with images of me and swifts on them. 'Passion is a superpower!' she yelled, flinging her glass up. Everyone else followed suit, clashing with the genteel quietness of a rural pub on a Sunday. All over the country, the SLN celebrated in their own ways and on social media, the echo of strangers who had supported throughout the six months sung in streams of messages.

The relief of reaching the 100,000-signature target didn't last long. 'The petition committee will consider a parliamentary debate,' the government statement read.

'What the hell! You mean they might say no after all this effort? After all the public support and media coverage?' Margaret said, her mouth open in surprise.

When I enquired, the petition committee replied a few days later saying there was a backlog of petitions, reminding me no petition was ever guaranteed a debate, telling me they would hope to update me in a month.

'You're going to drive yourself nuts, Hannah. You need a break. You need to refuel like the swifts,' George said when we were in the tower as he monitored the swifts.

'This is the only place I feel at peace right now, where I live in the moment,' I admitted.

He understood. 'Birds always give me a sense of calm too.'

The first chicks were hatching out of eggs the size of half my thumb. Blind and bare and still, it was almost impossible to comprehend what lay ahead of them in a matter of weeks. Adults kept returning, banging as they arrived, surging into each nest box with mouthfuls of weevils, flea beetles, leafhoppers, dividing their bolus between their chicks before turning around like aircraft on a runway and launching out into the sky again. One after another they went, the demand for insects relentless, needing to feed each chick up to 20,000 small insects and spiders a day. All over the country, parent birds were feeding their young, some finding it increasingly difficult to do so thanks to limited food resources; swifts have been known to commute as far as Spain in their hunt for food.

Over the next nights I considered what George had said and when the opportunity to take a break and help a different kind of bird came up, I grabbed it. Two hundred and fifty miles south of my house in Oxfordshire lies St Agnes, the most southerly point of Britain. Blissfully, it might as well have been in another universe. Instead of obsessing over the campaign, I was living in a tent on a windswept cove. I was there to help survey the globally significant breeding population of seabirds on the Isles of Scilly: a collection of remarkable individuals, some of whom wander the ocean for decades, dive headfirst into the water at 60 miles per hour or make epic maiden 3,000-mile flights alone. The Isles of Scilly is home to 20,000 seabirds, made up of thirteen species, including a third of all the shags in England. The isles are the sole English breeding site for European storm petrels and one of only two breeding sites in England for Manx shearwaters that together with Lundy Island equate to 75 per cent of their entire global population. Mirroring the national decline, 25 per cent of Scilly's seabirds have died out since 1983, but some species, in particular the Manx shearwater, have made a remarkable comeback thanks to the Seabird Recovery Project, a partnership between the Isles of Scilly Wildlife Trust, Natural England, the Duchy of Cornwall and the Isles of Scilly Area of Outstanding Natural Beauty (AONB).

During the days, I jumped on a boat with a group of conservationists and ornithologists to venture to different uninhabited islands. The sole agenda was to count birds, their nests, eggs and chicks. The excitement for the task equated to a kids' birthday party at the post-cake, sugar-rush stage.

I saw the driftwood throne nests of cormorants, noting how each colony of shag adopts a different signature nest style, with some islands featuring plastic waste like bottle caps and wrappers, while others shaped their nests with old rope. One smaller island was covered with nests that had been buttressed with crab shells. I discovered gulls keep their chicks safe by nesting under tree mallow, their fluffy, spotted babes hidden under parasols of pink petals. I stared at the shags at close range, marvelling at their sea-green eyes, astonished to hear them growl. On islands made of boulders, I stood surrounded by razorbills and guillemots, mimicking and perfecting their calls, and caught glimpses of their private lives. Seeing the chicks raised so diligently, witnessing gannets who were on a 140-mile round trip to fish for their young, made me feel a tangible sense of duty to look out for them and their future. If only all politicians could make this pilgrimage.

It was the nights, though, that surely would have engaged Members of Parliament. Each night, just after midnight, I stood in the darkness facing the Celtic Sea. Steadily, my eyes adjusted to the starlight, the rocky outcrops looming behind me in rugged silhouettes. The June scent of honeysuckle and bracken carried in the wind that rushed in gusts at my face, picking up my hair. I waited. Over the watery pendulum of the waves coming and going, I heard what I'd woken up for. From the sea, eerie calls filled the air, conjuring myths and legends, whispering a soundscape of recovery. These strange calls belong to Manx shearwaters. Ocean banshees who beatboxed in shrieks, their calls lighting up the coast in a halo of sound, connecting each cove and the space between the islands.

Manx shearwaters are small black-and-white seabirds, their flight pattern of flapping rapidly on the surface of the sea 'shearing' the waves, inspiring their name. Every year on migration, they fly 3,000 miles across the Atlantic to South America and back, returning to the ground burrows of home. They do this journey, and live out their whole lives, during the night. The cover of darkness provides safety from predators, and they use sound to locate their burrows and their partners. The Isles of Scilly have been their stronghold since prehistoric times, but twenty years ago, Manx shearwaters were on the brink here, with just a handful of breeding pairs remaining. They were completely gone from St Agnes due to the predation of non-native animals: rats. Data collected over the years showing the decline of these extraordinary birds had resulted in conservation plans to eradicate rats from the islands. It had worked almost instantly. The Isles of Scilly Wildlife Trust teamed up with islanders implementing a rigorous training programme, and together they diligently removed the rats from St Agnes and Pugh by a system of poison traps and constant monitoring. Part way through the mammoth task of making the isles rat-free, the Manx shearwaters were bouncing back. With their triumphant recovery, Manxies, as they are affectionately known, have become symbols of conservation success, the islanders rightfully proud of their intervention. They are there, existing still, because of a small handful of committed people willing to defend the birds. As I stood on

St Agnes, the world shrank to a single sound, a single territory, a single ribbon of hope: not only were they back, they were thriving.

The UK supports 8 million seabirds made up of twenty-five species including shrewd chip-thieving species of gulls and the well-loved puffin. While 8 million seabirds sounds like a lot, this group of birds is one of the most threatened, declining by 30 per cent in the last twenty years with a loss of 2 million birds. Seabirds face many challenges, from climate change to plastic pollution, habitat loss, non-native predators, oil spills and becoming accidentally caught up in fishing lines, which is the gruesome, unnecessary, heartbreaking fate of 300,000 seabirds globally each year. For many, extinction looms. With increasing exploitation of the marine environment, combined with bigger ocean storms and sea temperature changes, they face an uncertain future. Seabirds are a key indicator of the health of the seas and coastal environment, acting as a lens through which we can look at our island nation as a whole. One of the worst hindrances for seabirds is overfishing, and in particular sandeel fishing.

A 2021 report by the RSPB, 'Revive our Seas', outlined the case for stronger regulation of sandeel fisheries in UK waters. The report found that several declining seabirds dependent on sandeels were faring the worst, including kittiwakes, whose UK population has halved since the 1960s, as well as puffins, with both birds declared at risk of global extinction. Making clear the link between seabird decline and reduced sandeel availability, the report also uncovered major flaws in the way the North Sea sandeel fishery was being managed. Although warming seas, as a result of climate change, are held primarily responsible for the decline of sandeel availability, commercial fishing was making the problem much worse. Every year, industrial fishing fleets catch hundreds of thousands of tonnes of sandeels in the North Sea, crippling the ability of seabirds to find enough food to feed their chicks. This is the equivalent of farm crops being poisoned with chemicals that decimate the insect population for swifts and all insect-eating birds. No food, no future. So the RSPB had started a campaign, led by Principal Marine Advisor Euan Dunn . . . twenty-four years ago. A seabird guru, Euan has been sounding the alarm for over two decades, knowing that closing industrial sandeel fisheries would help build seabird resilience at a critical time for the natural world. In other words, threatened seabirds *might* survive when they almost certainly wouldn't if the unsustainable sandeel fishing continued. Trying to ban the annual quota of over 17,000 tonnes of sandeel, worth £3.8 million, was always going to be extremely difficult, especially as it is an industry that supports another industry: poultry farming. With over 23 billion chickens alive at any one time on Earth, a huge part of their diet is fishmeal, largely made up of sandeels. The irony of the world's most common bird eating the food that should be going to the world's most threatened group of birds mirrors the mess we have carved out for ourselves as a species. It was almost enough to make anyone become fatalistic and stop even trying, but Euan Dunn had refused to give up on the seabirds and I could see why. Every time I heard the patter of razorbill feet on the flat boulders where they nested, followed by their warning growl as their eyes caught mine, I fell in love.

The same was true for the people who worked throughout the breeding season on the rat eradication projects, keeping guard of the fluffy grey Manx shearwater chicks with remote camera traps and constant monitoring. For all the midnights I stood as the sole person among the Manx shearwaters, I was fuelled by this love, pocketing it for the swifts for when I returned home. All around me the Manxies flew in low from the sea, calling as they returned to their burrows. I couldn't see them but their wingbeats and calls placed me right in the middle of their colony. When the wind died down, the distant calls on the uninhabited island of Annet carried over the water, giving me goosebumps. Their calls have perplexed and frightened pirates, islanders and explorers, deterring people from settling, sparking haunting stories and provoking names of places like 'Trollval' on the Isle of Rum, the Viking word for 'Troll Mountain'. But to hear it, knowing who was calling, was to grin into the night. This signature sound doesn't just belong to the birds now but to those who have come to their aid, actively safeguarding them, because without conservation I would be standing alone in the dark in a silence that would wail; a ghost of sorrow in the wind.

Just as this landscape is only whole with the sound of Manx shearwaters and heathlands are only whole with the churring nightjars, our urban environments – our villages and towns and cities – our homes – are only whole in the summers when swifts are screaming above. This was what we were all fighting to protect but absence is difficult to illustrate. It is also a double threat. Researchers have concluded that extinction of experience doesn't just mean the loss of opportunity to experience nature but also the loss of emotional affinity with nature.

*

I returned home with the news that the date of the parliamentary debate was finally set for 10 July.

'Oh God, you know the whole reaching the almost impossible 100,000-signatory target?' I said to Robin, a feeling of sickness rushing through my body in panic.

'Yes,' he replied apprehensively.

'Well, it's going to be pointless unless I can secure MPs to speak in the debate.'

Robin shared the same sinking expression, putting his arm

round me. 'Let's watch *The Lord of the Rings* tonight. I reckon the
hobbits will help you,' he said.

Tolkien's hobbits did help give me a morale boost, but I had no
idea how to engage with MPs, politicians existing only on my periph-
ery. My friend Jemma who worked in Parliament became a lifeline,
along with Wild Justice's Mark Avery and the RSPB's Jeff Knott.
Without any fuss they quietly advised me on protocol as I navigated
the political web I had found myself in. Until I created the campaign,
shamefully, politics was an alien subject. Rewind a couple of years
and I couldn't think of a single conversation I had ever had about it.
I hadn't even known my own MP's name. I had never aspired to be a
campaigner, never been to a protest, nor had it ever occurred to me
that I should use my voice for nature. In fact, the terms 'protester',
'activist' and 'campaigner' made me feel uncomfortable. My vote was
flippant, fickle, inconsiderate, felt irrelevant and mildly inconvenient,
like a chore without consequences of punishment or reward. I rolled
my eyes when a gobby person inflicted their political views on me
during a dinner party, regurgitating some extreme blanket statement
one way or the other that they'd heard on the news. Most concern-
ingly, I never ever made the link between the natural world – or my
love for it – and politics. I had been blind to how interwoven these
two things are – how the people in our government have nature in
the palm of their hands and that we have put these people in power.

I booked my first-ever 'surgery appointment' with my MP.
With the classic polished, friendly look about him, Tory MP Robert
Courts shook my hand heartily, but as we sat down I felt myself
instinctively distrusting him, until he said, 'I used to have swifts
nesting in my roof as a child. I love them.'

This gave me a glimmer of hope.

'Will you speak in the debate?' I asked, pinning my judgement
of him on his answer.

'Absolutely.'

My shoulders relaxed and for a short fifteen minutes we chatted over the key points and he said he would put the date in the diary. As I was leaving, he said, 'Get as many MPs to speak – the more the better.'

So lobbying MPs became the new game. I sent emails, rang numbers, wrote letters. I engaged the public, utilising the support, making it easy for everyone by sending them bespoke letters tailored for their specific MP that they could amend and send on. A keyboard warrior, I sat on my computer for twelve hours a day until my eyes were crossed and my neck ached. Several MPs got over fifty emails. I know because I steered them all. Most MPs didn't reply to a single request and, with the public effort being ignored, outrage built across social media and the SLN.

Some MPs replied but were flaky, giving a lot of chat that came across as insincere, proven by their lack of commitment or action. A few said yes immediately. The hit rate was slow. I calculated that for every fifty emails, we got the commitment of one MP. But the joint effort of hundreds of people and the weight of the local groups from the SLN amounted to twelve cross-party MPs committing to speak in support at the debate, a record for a petition debate about nature. Crucially, Matt Vickers, a Conservative MP on the petition committee who was leading the debate, had decided to champion it. Then a housing developer, Thakeham, stepped in with active support, their sustainability director, Josie Cadwallader-Hughes, trailblazing for swifts in her industry.

'We'd like to pledge what you're asking. We've been installing small numbers of swift bricks already but we'd like to install one swift brick per house we plan to build from now on and I fully support your recommendation to government,' Josie said on a video call.

'Really?' I asked.

'Yes!' Josie said.

'How many houses do you build every year?' I asked, wanting to know how many swift bricks she had just committed to.

'We've got nearly 700 in the plans for next year,' she said. 'I know it's not enough for the swifts on a national scale but I will do as much as I can to drive a change in the industry.'

She meant it. I could tell. There was something obviously genuine in her manner, proven by her suggestion that I set up a community interest company so I could formally consult Thakeham, and other companies, in the space. Channel 4 News invited us to do a joint feature to be released just before the debate and so Thakeham officially went on record.

10 July was a hot classic summer day with blue skies and sunshine and screaming parties of swifts. On my way to the train station, they wheeled down the high streets, head height, mirroring the children rushing through their summer holidays below.

In London, I went to stand outside 10 Downing Street to pretend to deliver the petition, a tradition for generating news coverage, flanked by Rewriting Extinction's founder Paul Goodenough and Jeff Knott from the RSPB, who had become a crutch of support in the run-up to the debate. Happily fully clothed, I was interviewed by ITN and the BBC for the six o'clock news.

'How do you feel?' a reporter asked.

'Like I am made up of 100,000 people who care,' I said, feeling proud and optimistic.

At 4 p.m. I entered the Houses of Parliament, walking into the vast Westminster Hall. Robin and key supporters greeted me, excitement in the air. We were all led to a side room up some stairs and settled down in the small public gallery which was full of members of the SLN. The MPs filed in, including my role model, former Green Party leader Caroline Lucas.

The stage was set. Within a stuffy, strip-lit room that was verging on vomit-coloured, Matt Vickers began, his opening speech surprisingly emotional.

'Many of us watch out for swifts, believing they herald the beginning of British summer. Their status as an established British icon is clear from the support the petition rallied, capturing the imaginations and support of the public from a wide cross-section of society and from across the entire United Kingdom. The number of signatures alone clearly demonstrates the public's concern about losing these iconic birds completely, which would be a huge loss to our country's biodiversity and culture.'

As I listened, the words took on a new meaning in this context. They were being said formally, and by someone who was part of the government. With his words came tangible hope.

Once Matt Vickers had finished his opening speech, one MP after the next, representing the Labour, Conservative, Green and Liberal Democrat parties, stood up to give their speeches. It was like watching a live courtroom drama except there were no negative words, no arguments. It wasn't a debate, but a declaration of unity. Politician after politician unanimously supported the petition's aim. They even heckled each other to agree. While they structured their speeches with facts and statistics, every single MP was humanised by their own personal love for swifts. Caroline Lucas quoted a Ted Hughes poem, the words hanging in the air like an aria. She extended her thanks to me, calling me an inspiration, while Robert Courts credited my passion, the formal recognition making me feel like a kid at school winning an award from my favourite teacher. I had hatched this plan in the street during a heatwave. Now the birds we all cared so much about were being passionately fought for in Parliament. For two hours, I felt heard, each MP doing the birds proud. I allowed myself to dream that we might have a home run: that the government minister would get up and love the swifts too – and declare action.

Because the petition's ask regarded buildings, the relevant department was the Department for Levelling Up, Housing and Communities (DLUHC). Dehenna Davison, the minister delegated the task of attending the debate, got up to give the government's decision.

She opened her speech by acknowledging the decline of swifts, but her tone was jovial, as if she had failed to engage in what she was saying. Her air jarred. After a lengthy spiel about the government's concern, she made the department's concluding statement.

'This is a rare moment of cross-party unity, but the government also believe that we need to be cautious when it comes to mandating national planning conditions. We should not impose conditions and ensure that planning permissions are subject to additional and unreasonable requirements to accommodate species that are not present in an area, while creating financial burdens to comply with and to discharge the condition.' She said it all with a manner that implied the words meant nothing to her.

The reasoning contradicted the facts. What she was saying was no, and it was absolute bollocks.

I screwed my eyes shut, my hands turning to fists, my fingernails digging into my skin. I felt robbed. I had played by the challenging rules set by the government to warrant their time and consideration. Now both the minister's manner and her words felt like the department was condescendingly flicking me away like an annoying fly. As if to add salt into the wound, she had the audacity to brag about all the nature schemes the government was doing that had nothing to do with the nesting habitat of these birds nor the petition's ask of mandating swift bricks. Not allowed to speak, or even make expressions, I kept my head lowered, my eyes closed. One after the other, the MPs stood up, fighting back.

Robert Courts MP politely but firmly confronted her. 'The government are doing a lot, but the point that we are seeking to make is that they are not doing anything to help swifts.'

Caroline Lucas MP stood up, visibly exasperated, and said what everyone in the room probably felt. 'I cannot believe what I am hearing! This brick costs about twenty-five quid, right – that is a tiny amount for new developments. I cannot believe that she is refusing to do it!'

It was a statement that ended up being viewed almost a million times on social media in the coming days.

Caroline Nokes MP reiterated the sentiment in a gloriously sarcastic tone, 'Mandating a standard brick per dwelling does not seem very complicated to me.'

But it was no good. The decision, to do absolutely nothing, had been made. The debate finished. A steward led me out. I walked down the stone staircase into Westminster Hall. Happy tourists filed past. I felt as hollow as the vast room, a cave of emptiness. Suddenly the minister was approaching me, inappropriately light-hearted to start with, her expression changing to sympathy in reaction to my face.

'It wasn't my brief. I was handed it at the last minute,' she said, as though she was apologising for something small, like a spelling mistake or a wrong drinks order.

I looked at her, speechless.

'Can I give you a hug?' she said, launching at me before I could process what she had asked, and decline. Suddenly I was being clasped within the grip of a woman who I wanted to push away, too surprised to stand back and reject what felt like guilt, not sincerity.

Robert Courts shook my hand firmly and turned to the minister, asking her to meet us in the autumn to discuss it. She smiled, with her sympathetic expression still in place, agreeing. I was almost certain she would do nothing of the sort. I was right. By the autumn she had resigned as minister. For her, this afternoon was an awkward encounter where she hugged a campaigner whose name she didn't know. While it wasn't her fault, wasn't personal to her, while she was 'just doing her job', it was personal to me. It was personal to the birds whose homes and future we were destroying. She represented the government, and the government had just completely fobbed me, and the British public, off. Much, much worse, they had just fobbed the birds off. While spouting decline statistics that represented not only the death of hundreds of thousands of individual swifts but the threat of national extinction of a species that had existed for over 50 million years, the government had decided it was right to do nothing, even though the ask centred on a simple, and urgently essential, brick.

Matt Vickers hugged me, a firm, real hug, which was welcome but the kindness provoked unwanted tears. I stood outside, Parliament looming behind me, and just started swearing. 'Fuck's sake! The bastards! The absolute fucking bastards!' I yelled at the Houses of Parliament, which felt appropriate given that the authoritative politicians seemed to be made of stone.

Jeff Knott and my friend Will stood with me, swearing too, their anger a relief, knowing I wasn't alone in mine. The state of rage I felt I had never experienced before. It was anger with the absolute clarity of injustice, spattered with betrayal. This state of mind was an interesting one, considering I was about to go back into Parliament, this time for a reception hosted by Natural England, the government's environment advisor. It was a coincidence that the drinks reception fell on the same day and I had been invited in recognition of my campaign efforts. I said goodbye to everyone, going alone, and walked through security, clutching my swift brick.

'Oh, what have you got there?' the security woman asked.

'It's a swift brick,' I explained flatly, getting ready to justify why I had it.

'Oh my gosh! You're the swift campaigner!' she said, beaming. 'I signed your petition!'

At the back of Parliament where the reception was being held, several conservationists were waiting for me. In a group, they approached me, giving me hugs and congratulating me, looking at me in horror as I explained what had happened in the debate.

'You should go and speak to the secretary of state for the Department for Environment, Food and Rural Affairs. She's here. We'll come with you,' they said in supportive unison.

I nodded, words still evading me.

I did not trust the secretary of state. She was the minister I'd listened to at Christmas who had declared that Defra was 'the voice of the voiceless' the same week her government department reversed bans of the toxic agricultural chemicals, neonicotinoids. She had been elusive during every stage of the campaign. Her local swift group had lobbied her like mad. In their surgery with her, she had been positive and suggested they pose for a photo with a swift banner, smiling into the camera, and then she had done nothing. Hoping I had got her all wrong, I went to ask her to her face whether she was going to do anything to help swifts.

When she saw me coming, she gave the distinct impression of assessing whether she could avoid me. I introduced myself, explained what the government had said and asked her whether she was prepared to help.

For about three minutes she spoke about how it was a local government matter and about how she had no power over the decision despite being the secretary of state for Defra. I knew how little local government had done, how ineffective and lengthy the process was to get something like this implemented right down to the exact number of local planning authorities that hadn't acted, which was 441 out of 450.

Then, palpably irritated by me, she said, 'Now, I think I've given you quite enough of my time. I hope you are grateful for my advice.'

She looked at me as though expecting me to say thank you. There was such unhidden disdain in her face, and such absence of care, her invitation was like a red rag to a bull. I paused, holding her stare, calculating the risk of what I was about to say. And then I said it.

'What you've just told me is bullshit,' I replied, calmly.

The secretary of state went beetroot red, her manner transforming from clinical to pissed off, but with the anger came useful insight. She told me the government would never mandate swift bricks because it would open up the 'floodgates' for other accessories like bee bricks, hedgehog holes and solar panels.

Then she left.

The other conservationists came up to me, one clutching my arm and whispering, 'You're my hero. I've always wanted to call her out.' A few minutes later, I left, so angry I was shaking, tears falling down my cheeks in the most annoying way. On the train home, the tears didn't stop as I leaned my head against the window. But with the tears came defiance. Having assumed I would deeply regret confronting the secretary of state, feeling a surge of anxiety that reminded me of the fear of being awarded a detention at school, I realised I was glad. I was more than glad. I was proud. If I had said anything less, I would have done myself and the birds a disservice. I had just spoken truth to power, and it felt excellent.

Chapter 9

Lord Goldsmith's
Swift-Brick Amendment

A week after my petition debate I was invited back to Parliament, this time by Caroline Lucas MP. She was hosting the launch of Nature 2030, a campaign intended to ensure the government environment targets were met and added to. The launch was a chance to bring leaders in the conservation world together and for relevant politicians to engage with the topic. The campaign was created by Wildlife and Countryside Link, a coalition of over eighty conservation organisations including the National Trust, the RSPB, Friends of the Earth and The Wildlife Trusts. Its CEO, Richard Benwell, is a charismatic force for nature, and had become a mentor. An erudite man, he has an impish flare about him which is exaggerated by his resemblance to the actor Elijah Wood who played Frodo in *The Lord of the Rings*. We had first met when I joined the All-Party Parliamentary Group (APPG) for Nature as the only member of the public, halfway through my petition. Richard had congratulated me on the campaign and I had confessed I knew nothing about politics. We had met up for a coffee the following week and he had advised me to try to find a political champion, giving me a list of names that might be bird-friendly. Richard had promoted the petition on the Wildlife and Countryside Link blog, provided quotes for newspapers, sent supportive bulletins around Parliament and had continued to encourage me.

'Try every tactic and don't give up. Persistence is key. And if all else fails, follow in the footsteps of someone like Guy Shrubsole,' Richard had said, his advice ringing in my ears like an instructive bell.

Guy Shrubsole, the journalist and environmental activist best known for his campaign to restore Britain's rainforests, could also be described as impish – his twinkling intelligence spoken with unflinching conviction. That morning, I found I was face to face with him and he was inviting me to sit next to him. We sat in the front row listening to the political speeches while muttering to each other and picking apart the contradictory political statements, as though we had known each other for years.

When Caroline Lucas, someone we both heartily respected, took the stand, she wove me and my campaign into her speech. I couldn't believe it. The room was full of conservation leaders and politicians in environmental positions, and Caroline Lucas was namedropping *me*. 'This is your chance,' Guy whispered, offering to introduce me to a few key politicians after the speeches. I nodded, very grateful, my mind racing. If I was going to find my political champion like Richard Benwell had advised, today was my best hope. My mind raced through all the political names I could think of and stopped on one: Zac Goldsmith.

Two weeks before my petition debate, Zac Goldsmith had resigned as minister for overseas territories and the Commonwealth. In a letter to then prime minister Rishi Sunak that was published in the national newspapers, he stated his reasons. He began by explaining how he had become involved in politics because of his 'love and concern for the natural environment', declaring our dependence on nature for everything and that 'logically, there is nothing more important'.

He explained how, as minister, he was able to turn nature restoration agreements 'bit by bit into law'. Then he wrote, 'but I have been horrified as, bit by bit, we have abandoned these commitments – domestically and on the world stage.'

In a hard-hitting conclusion, he had outright confronted the prime minister by stating, 'The problem is not that the government is hostile to the environment, it is that you, our Prime Minister, are simply uninterested. That signal, or lack of it, has trickled down through Whitehall and caused a kind of paralysis . . . This government's apathy in the face of the greatest challenge we have faced makes continuing in my current role untenable.'

If I took his word to be true, the government didn't care, but Zac Goldsmith did. I didn't know him but he had been sharing my social media posts with words of huge encouragement and support. While he had resigned as minister, he was still a life peer, and as it happened, a particular bill was going through the Lords in its final stages: the Levelling-up Bill.

The process of politics is something that I had not understood until I had the support of Richard Benwell and others like Jeff Knott whose experience was rock solid, his advice laced with one of the best senses of humour I had ever come across. Jeff explained that the key was to keep up with what was going on – get the low-down, keep looking at options, understand the lay of the land. What I learned immediately after the petition debate was that if the campaign was to be any use at all, I had to find another route in to spark change, and quickly. My MP Robert Courts had explained that there were various ways I could potentially influence policy but the easiest would be to find a bill that was being created and add an amendment to it. Once a bill was passed it would become an Act and so any amendment that won a vote would become primary legislation. The first task was therefore to find a bill; the second a politician willing and able to table an amendment. The Levelling-up Bill was perfect because it was created by the right department, the DLUHC. It was also perfect because it had been through the Commons and now was going through the House of Lords, meaning an amendment could only be tabled by a peer, not an MP. Theoretically, Zac Goldsmith could table a swift-brick amendment but he was not at the launch of Nature 2030. I wasn't sure how to approach this intimidatingly senior, famous politician, but I guessed that he was not only the birds' best chance but possibly their only chance. So I emailed him with Guy sitting next to me, egging me on. To my amazement, he replied, suggesting we met later that day.

A few hours later, I lingered nervously outside the Peers' Entrance of the Houses of Parliament. Out Zac Goldsmith came. He had no air of authority, his impeccable politeness mixing with a touch of scruffiness making him instantly and irresistibly likeable. Sitting in one of the Lords' tearooms that resembled a set of a Jane Austen film, instead of talking about politics, we started by speaking about birds.

'Why did you decide to launch this campaign, which is brilliant by the way?' he asked.

I looked down, hesitating, wondering whether I should make up something that sounded appropriately serious, but instead I just told the truth. 'I love birds,' I said, as though it was a confession. 'I rescued, hand raised and released a finch who lived in my hair, and a swift, and then some crows, and these birds changed my life,' I explained, half muttering, feeling embarrassed.

Nodding, he started asking me questions about the birds no one had ever asked me. Questions that made me think he knew something of raising birds himself, a guess which turned out to be true.

'I know how it feels to have that sort of bond,' he explained. 'I've raised a couple of jackdaws, and that kind of love is so strong.'

He explained that he had recently rehabilitated fledgling jackdaws, one in particular who he had shared a special bond with, Johnny. Johnny had been delivered to him by a friend after the bird had fallen down a chimney. Quickly imprinting on Zac, Johnny became Zac's avian sidekick, demanding almost constant attention. While Zac conducted meetings with global leaders and worked on groundbreaking environmental legislation, Johnny would nudge his head into Zac's arm, hand, neck, asking to be stroked, particularly partial to tickles around his neck and face, lolling sideways, closing his eyes. When Zac didn't tend to this desire, Johnny would playfully bite Zac's earlobe. When that didn't work, Johnny would hop down onto the keyboard and pick off the letters, hiding them. He hid lots of items, the shinier the better, caching them. As Johnny got older Zac took him outside for long walks, where Johnny became increasingly curious, making short flights to perches before returning to Zac, who walked around with a pocket full of live, wriggling, mealworms.

Zac winced, expecting me to judge him, but I had done the same. I didn't have to convince him of anything and this shared experience felt like a natural, and instant, bond. It didn't feel like I was talking to a politician or someone who felt obliged to talk to me and very soon he moved on to asking how he could help.

'You could table an amendment to the Levelling-up Bill,' I said.

'OK,' he replied.

There was no resistance. I looked at him and laughed in surprise.

'The only issue is that the deadline for amendments is next week, the day before parliamentary recess,' I said anxiously, wondering whether this would screw it up.

Zac got up and said, 'Let's do it now then. We've just got to find the Billings Office in this place,' he said, smiling. 'Think it's somewhere on the third floor.'

A jolt of adrenaline raced through me as I got up in delighted disbelief, following him down the long red-carpeted corridor of the House of Lords. In a small office tucked away, we sat down with a clerk called George and began to draft an amendment. Just like my speech and the petition wording, this small collection of words had to explain, engage and convince. Words that, if supported, would become law for birds. Words that had the potential to save swifts.

Swift bricks and boxes

(1) It is a condition in any grant of planning permission for new-build developments greater than 5 metres in height, that there must be a minimum average of one swift brick or box per dwelling or unit.

(2) Where feasible, swift bricks integrated into walls must be installed in preference to external swift nest boxes, following best practice guidance.

(3) A planning authority may grant planning permission with exceptions or modifications to the condition specified in subsection (1) in exceptional circumstances, where possible following best practice guidance.

(4) Where a planning authority considers that there are exceptional circumstances under subsection (3), it must publish those exceptional circumstances.

(5) For the purpose of this section –
'Swift brick' means an integral nest box integrated into the wall of a building suitable for the nesting of the Common Swift.

'Swift nest box' means an external nest box suitable for the nesting of the Common Swift.

'Best practice guidance' means the British Standard (BS 42021:2022).

Members' Explanatory Statement

This amendment would make planning permission for new developments and certain home extensions conditional on the provision of a minimum number of swift bricks. These bricks provide the only permanent nesting habitat for Red-Listed cavity-nesting birds who are almost solely reliant on these sites to breed. Also known as universal nest bricks, they provide habitat for other small urban birds and invertebrates.

As we left Parliament, the precious amendment submitted, I realised it was one year to the day since I had made the promise to the swift babes who had led me here. A whole year had spun, and now I had one of the most famous politicians in the country agreeing to champion them.

The amendment would be tabled in early September, after parliamentary recess. Over the same six weeks, our swifts would leave their homes in our walls, making their epic migrations to the Congo Basin. Once more, the anxious mourning surrounded me in their wake, the swifts' departure like sand in an hourglass trickling fast. As the amendment sat patiently, my thoughts were with the swifts as they flew into Africa, over the Sahara Desert and on, crossing the endless landscape where tall grass, bleached flaxen by the sweltering heat, sways for hundreds of miles uninterrupted. They flew where round mud-hut villages pop up every now and then, hours away from anything else, built near huge old mango trees with gnarly trunks and canopies that splay outwards in a block of glorious dark shade. Water is scarce. Deep wells sit between the smaller villages, strings of women and children walking with buckets and pans on their heads to collect water. Small lakes shine silver, full of crocodiles, hemmed by palms and acacias full of weaver ants, making bridges out of their bodies, spitting acid at anything in their path. Little donkeys pull carts of firewood, driven by children who wave and scream in shock and delight when a car drives anywhere near them, and dusty clearings full of barefooted children play football with rags tied into balls. The swifts' view was one of huge skies and blocks of blonde grass, of snakes bathing on rocks and drongos sitting in trees. They flew over places so dry that trees catch fire when hit by lightning, far away from British high streets and fish and chip vans, from pubs and housing estates, cottages and farms.

At night I scanned the August sky for the Perseids, the highlight of the meteor calendar in Britain. Each meteor emphasised the depth of the sky, their light show originating from the constellation of Perseus, caused by Earth hurtling through the debris left behind by the Swift-Tuttle comet. I smiled up into the sky at the name. The swifts were all up there too. Some, like the two swifts in the hole above the garage, were experiencing their first-ever migrations, while others were making a familiar journey: commuters whose route was lit up not by street lamps but by meteors made by their namesake.

In early September, on the third day back after the parliamentary recess, Zac Goldsmith woke up to carry out the first-ever task he performed as a life peer. Greeting me at the Peers' Entrance, he no longer felt like a stranger. Over the recess we had lobbied, working on a briefing note together, sending it out to as many peers as possible. Other Conservative peers had stepped in to help, personally and privately raising support for Zac's amendment, two of them – Lord Randall of Uxbridge and Lord Blencathra – sponsoring it in formal support. I had met Lord Randall on the day Zac tabled the amendment, with the RSPB's CEO, Beccy Speight, in a tearoom in the Lords, and he had politely warned me that changing the law takes a long time, normally several years. I had hoped maybe this tiny tweak would be different.

'It is impossible to tell what time our amendment will come up,' Zac said as we walked through the House of Lords, noting he had described the amendment not as his, but 'ours'.

'The list is long, and while there will be a target of how many amendments go through today, they are often missed,' he explained, looking at his watch. 'It's 11 now, and I suspect the earliest we could hope for is 3 p.m. but that gives us time to lobby because, well, I've got good news and bad news.'

I looked at him anxiously. 'What's the bad news?'

'Well, you know how each peer will be told which way to vote depending on what their party whip says?' he said.

'Yes . . .' I replied, feeling sick.

'Well, the government has whipped against us,' he said. 'No idea why.'

'For God's sake!' I said, exasperated, not even trying to hide my reaction.

'I know. I'm sorry. It's awful. BUT, all the other parties are whipping in support, which means we need to round up Tory rebels and lobby them to either vote for us, or at least abstain from voting.'

'How do we do that?' I asked.

'We go and find Conservative peers and personally ask them to support.'

'OK,' I said, pretending I was far more confident than I felt, the bitter memory of approaching Conservative politicians at Christmastime resurfacing. But this was entirely different. I was flanked by the birds' ace card.

Our campaign field was the Royal Gallery, the largest room in the Palace of Westminster. A room of historical significance – the end of both world wars had been announced here by George V and George VI. Addresses had been made here by Kofi Annan, Ronald Reagan and Bill Clinton. I'd never seen so much gilt, almost every part of the room highly decorated. It felt like a vast, high golden vault in which the politicians, sitting at hexagonal tables, were miniatures. Two enormous paintings depicting the Napoleonic Wars dominated the walls, reminding me we were in a battle, just not a bloody one fought with cannon balls and bayonets. This one would be fought with small, quick conversations between the Westminster elite. *And me.* Somehow, I was in the mix, walking up to peers in a gilded political palace, armed with a swift brick.

Lord Randall was instrumental, quickly educating me on which peers to look out for, and which ones to avoid. He juggled between speaking to politicians as they passed by and sending messages on his phone. One after the other, Tory peers simply agreed to vote for the amendment, the consensus being that it was a 'no-brainer'. Zac would disappear and reappear, checking how I was doing.

'At this rate we should definitely hold a vote. There's a good chance we will *just* get the majority. If I don't think we will, we shouldn't vote because if we lose . . .' he paused, '. . . if we lose, the campaign sort of dies. It would be much harder to pick it up.'

Hours ticked by. I realised I was enjoying it. It was thrilling and we were building momentum. Jemma appeared and we moved from the Royal Gallery, down the long corridors, lobbying Tories as we went. In every room, live TVs showed the amendment listings in the different houses, like a departure lounge screen in airports. Zac and I went back to the tearoom, snacking on piles of peanuts, talking quickly but quietly about which peers had agreed to vote or abstain. Our eyes checking the screen every minute, we watched as the amendment number slid back and back in the schedule.

There was no sense of time other than the TV screens. The artificial light and the big rooms were all about what was going on inside them, as if the outside world didn't exist. Cocooned in politics, those who worked here would rarely see even one bird during their day. Only at the terrace bar was the real world let back in. By now it was evening, and in warm sunshine we sat waiting, our eyes half on the screens. With the Thames swirling next to us all along the side of Parliament, a single herring gull perched on the wall. Everyone else seemed to ignore it, but we both looked at the bird, and I hoped the gull was a good omen.

'Problem is, by 7 p.m. everyone will start to drift home. By 9 p.m. the whip will lift except for the government whip, which means if our amendment is later than 7 p.m. our support will likely have gone and it will be too risky to hold a vote,' Zac said.

7 p.m. came and went. The amendment was still nowhere near, our hopes fading with the light. By 8 p.m. Zac had to tell the government whip whether he intended to hold a vote or not.

'I think it would be too risky, but it's your call,' Zac said.

'Say no,' I replied, reluctantly.

'I'm sorry,' Zac said as he sent the message that would stop the amendment from becoming law, our hopes and hard work dashed.

Just after 8.30 p.m. as the hustle and bustle had diminished as people went home, the grouping the amendment was in flashed on the screen. It was time. While there would be no vote, Zac and the other peers still had the opportunity to speak as strongly as possible in the chamber. We rushed to the Lords Chamber, up the stairs from the terrace bar and through the lobby. Leaving me to watch from the members' gallery, Zac took his place. As he sat down on the famous red-leather bench, he gave me a quick glance that spelled out an alliance forged for swifts.

On the order of business, in among amendments for multiple tiny tweaks to planning provisions, Amendment 221A, in the name of Lord Goldsmith of Richmond Park, was there to try to stop one of the most ancient species of bird from becoming nationally extinct. And the government had whipped against it. I stared at the single line of text on the parliament-headed booklet. Despite the crushing reality of this amendment being unable to succeed without the vote, the very fact it existed was something to hold on to. Lord Goldsmith's amendment was the first attempt to safeguard these birds through national legislation in British history.

Zac stood up, opening his speech by acknowledging me. 'I first want to heap praise and thanks on a campaigner who is simply formidable. I am pleased that she is in the gallery today, probably holding a swift brick. Hannah Bourne-Taylor has single-handedly made what for many people appears to be a niche concern into a national campaign – not least by walking naked through London painted as a swift and causing quite a stir, as noble Lords can imagine.'

The other peers murmured in surprise.

'She has turned this into a national cause. It is because of her that this amendment exists.'

Blushing, I went as red as the leather bench I sat on.

After he had outlined the amendment and the reasons, one after the other, both Conservative and cross-party peers got up to speak. It was almost identical to the petition debate, except there was even more passion and exasperation. Baroness Pinnock described seeing her first swift of the year as 'a joy'. Baroness Hoey asked the question 'Why have we not done it before?' and then explained her concern for future generations growing up without the joy of urban birds. Lord Lucas described mandating swift bricks as a 'symbolic act that would show this government will make room for nature' while Baroness Bennett of Manor Castle reminded Parliament of the significance: 'If you are a swift then a swift brick is not a small thing. The fact that you need somewhere to make your home and raise your young is a matter of life and death.'

And then Lord Blencathra got up and expressed what I and so many people across the country felt. With palpable exasperation, he said, very loudly in his soft but crisp Scottish accent, 'Installing these bricks is an absolute no-brainer! They cost between £25 and £35. Last year, the big four housebuilders – just four of them, Barratt, Berkeley, Persimmon and Bellway – made profits of £2.749 billion. I am sure they can afford a £25 brick for the 300,000 homes they might or might not manage to build next year, my lords.'

He did not stop there. As if he was just warming up, he launched into a second attack, 'I learned today – I hope, wrongly – that the government may be opposed to this measure. That, too, would be a no-brainer if they are! I wonder where the opposition has come from!'

I liked this man. Very much indeed.

'I understand that in the Commons, the government said they could not mandate this nationally and it must be left to local voluntary discretion.' His voice got louder in exasperation, reaching a much higher pitch that was laced with sarcasm. 'Housebuilding left to local voluntary discretion? You cannot build a house anywhere in the country without the government almost dictating the colour of the curtains!'

Having thought he had reached his peak, his conclusive statement was one spoken with such vehement conviction, he deserved a standing ovation.

'If it is the case that the government are opposed to this, I would really like to know what idiot has decided to oppose this. Why in the name of God should a Conservative government oppose this?' he said, verging on shouting.

Just like in the petition debate, I had to stay mute when all I wanted to do was jump up and down, cheering him on. I found myself grinning, catching Zac's eye as he smiled back at me. Lord Blencathra's words, which would be archived forever in the official record, Hansard, were proving him to be a legend for swifts.

The government had been urged to change its mind and passionately accused of idiocy but to no avail, because with no vote, the Levelling-up Bill was a ship that had sailed without the amendment, a ride that had left the birds behind. For the eleven hours swifts had been spoken about informally in the galleries and tearooms of Parliament, and through messages and emails, and then formally in the Lords Chamber, the birds were far away. Four thousand miles they had flown from us, arriving at their wintering grounds in the Congo Basin, still in non-stop flight. Just like the politicians existing within the Palace of Westminster, they, too, were in a world of their own, only theirs was a world of green. A laby-rinth of trees and vines where nothing belonged to itself, nothing was separate, intersecting, overlapping in the barge of insistence, of ravenous existence. In a similar way to the warped time of the day here, time would be skewed there, the measure abstracted or concentrated, expanded or diluted into simply growth, the sounds muffled and echoed, dulled and sharpened by the living wooden treasure box below them.

Standing in the central hall of the House of Lords, I looked up at the ornately painted ceiling dotted with stars, thinking of that *other* world we were a part of that felt so distant under this roof. I clutched my swift brick, now a comfort blanket. They had all tried so hard, a team of twinklingly passionate politicians collectively fighting for birds in the halls of power, but it had not been enough.

As I left, Zac rushed out to say goodbye. 'I'm sorry,' he said, 'but . . .'

He was smiling. 'It's not over. We've been promised a meeting with Michael Gove.'

Chapter 10

The Rt Honourable Michael Gove, Secretary of State for the DLUHC

One year and three days after I launched The Feather Speech campaign and petition, I stood outside a Pret a Manger, on the corner of Westminster's Marsham Street, waiting for Zac. I was nervous. At 3 p.m. we had a meeting in the Home Office with Secretary of State Michael Gove.

Out of all 67 million of us in this country, besides the prime minister, Michael Gove was the person who had the authority to mandate swift bricks. He and the DLUHC had said no twice. Thank goodness he had agreed to meet, but why had the government chosen not to act when they had been told what was at stake? Why had they turned a blind eye when they knew they were the only people who had the power to act? Why had they ignored when the public, scientific and political support was so strong? Did they care at all? Did caring have anything to do with it?

This thread of care is what had brought me to the pavement outside the Home Office and it was also what linked Zac Goldsmith to the campaign. For all the vast differences separating me and Zac, one thread bound us together in a bond that felt, on principle, unbreakable: we were incorruptibly loyal to nature.

For him, this stemmed from an innate connection to nature that he had always known. As a child Zac had kept mice under his bed and hated the idea of caged animals so much so that he would let friends' pets out of cages, liberating them from their entrapment, rescuing caged birds, taking them to his house where his family made the most enormous aviary for them. A dove was first, trapped in such a small cage it had been unable to stretch its wings at all. For several weeks, the dove's flight muscles were too weak and it sat forlorn. Zac persisted, gently helping to condition the bird's wings by encouraging it to move, resulting in it being able to fly, its existence expanding to something resembling what it should have always been. He had grown up spellbound by the natural world through Gerald Durrell books, the work of Dr Jane Goodall DBE, and watching Attenborough documentaries. Spurred on by his father, the tycoon and politician Sir James Goldsmith, Zac became the editor of his uncle's magazine, *The Ecologist*, transforming its format to broaden its appeal. It was through his love of the natural world and learning how much trouble it was in that Zac became a politician. Campaigners come in many forms and while the image of an activist is one outside Parliament, holding a placard, Zac entered politics in order to campaign from within.

I thought back to my father and the toads at Hilbre and all the birds I had raised, Zac's childhood actions so similar. The brilliant truth is that anyone can protect the little lives that surround us. Not just the celebrated ones but the humble, overlooked creatures. Forgotten and unknown wildlife that would otherwise be in peril, helped and conserved by many individuals who care as much as my dad and Zac. People who work all day in offices without a background in science, without an expert status, older people, schoolchildren and everyone in between, including at least one senior politician. Anyone can help the underdogs of the wild, but the question was, would the secretary of state?

If you google Michael Gove, the first image that comes up is an official portrait of him. His expression is, at best, playful, at worst, somewhat absurd, portraying the opposite of what a secretary of state is, because surely, above all, a secretary of state is a real, proper, unmistakable, grown-up. Yet this was a man who had also fronted a 1990s flop TV show on Channel 4 called *A Stab in the Dark* in which he was filmed delivering supposedly funny satirical monologues and riffling through the contents of Sir David Attenborough's rubbish bin to judge how environmentally friendly he was. One episode featured Michael Gove likening Prince Charles to Hitler through their 'Green credentials', ending with Gove saying, 'There is one difference, however. When Adolf's wife tried to commit suicide, she succeeded.'

Michael Gove had gone on to establish himself as a career politician described as a 'king maker' with a reputation of being highly intelligent. Coincidentally, my first insight about Michael Gove was an anecdote about him and Zac Goldsmith, told by the Duke of Beaufort, whose book I had edited. As we had walked around Badminton House, the duke had told me a story about regularly playing poker years ago with them both. At the time these politicians were not on my radar but I had listened, intrigued. Zac was an infamous poker player with impressive wins against pros, and against Michael Gove he had never lost. As I paced outside Pret, I wondered whether it was going to play out like a poker game – requiring luck but also genuine skill; each player the master of his own fate. While to both politicians this was just another meeting, I had never entered into one with such high stakes. In the political arena, I had so far been silent, my campaign taken on by the professionals. Yes, I had briefed them, steered them, thanked them, but so far it had been their performance, not mine. What if I bottled it? What if the fate of swifts rested on whether or not Michael Gove liked *me*?

I had tried to work out who Michael Gove was, if there was any common ground between us. I had read his Wikipedia page, tracked his life from Scotland to Oxford University, from a Sunday school teacher to journalist working on the Leveson Inquiry, from Labour to Conservative. His roles within government had been extensive: education secretary, chief whip, justice secretary, environment minister. The first thing he had done as environment minister was to ban microbeads, stopping manufacturers producing them and shops from selling products containing them. He was the minister behind the 25 Year Environment Plan and biodiversity net gains, but he was also the minister who, a couple of months before, had tried very hard to throw out 'nutrients neutrality', the protective rule to prevent developers from being able to pollute in particular nature areas already under threat. The attempt to reverse this legislation had turned into a saga during the summer when the amendment was added to the Levelling-up Bill. Highly publicised, many Tories rebelled, going against the amendment.

As I waited for Zac, I tried to see the positives, reminding myself that the secretary of state had a broad brief and a very busy schedule: it was remarkable I even had the chance to meet him. He had agreed to make time to talk to me about birds, which was a feat in itself, thanks, entirely, to Zac. When Zac arrived, his advice was clear. 'I will be right next to you, ready to step in but this meeting is all about what you want to say, you'll have the floor,' he explained.

'Oh God!' I said, my palms sweating, my heart beating so fast I could feel my top moving.

'Hannah. You are formidable. You have become basically the world expert on this niche topic,' he said, giving me a quick, firm stare of confidence.

What he was deliberately not saying was that what I chose to say, and how I delivered it, would make or break the campaign. As we were escorted through the Home Office to the DLUHC, I was about to go up against one of the most significant Conservative politicians of the day who could run rings around me if he chose to, so my goal was to make him not want to.

We were led through the enormous glass-fronted, open-plan building to a huge corner office with a long oval table. In front of the table stood a line of civil servants and special advisors. At the end of the table, near the windows, waited Michael Gove: markedly smart, slick, neatly pressed. I shook his hand, thanked him for his time, and once again, a battle fought with words began. After Zac had said a few pleasantries with his signature politeness, the floor was mine. I could say anything I liked.

'Look, not only could mandating swift bricks be great PR for the government whose reputation with nature lovers is rock bottom, but without swift bricks there is no safe, guaranteed nesting habitat for swifts anywhere in Britain and there never will be,' I said, putting the swift brick down on the table. I had adorned it with playing cards, each one depicting the eight birds known to nest in swift bricks. I had worried it would come across as childish, but Michael Gove looked at it with interest. It felt like an effective engagement tool – through the playing cards, the birds were in the room, helping to sing for their supper. I examined his expression, looking for a flicker of emotion, of reaction, but he had a poker face.

He nodded, blinking his eyes slowly. His hands were clasped and he made a small but distinct noise. A sort of grunt of acknowledgement, the same tone as those antique bears that have a mechanical roar when you turn them slowly upside down, slightly Bagpuss-like. He shuffled some notes and began asking me questions. I liked the questions because whoever had written them had engaged with the topic. I was acutely aware that he could be completely playing me, but he did not come across as insincere. Then again, surely, he was an expert bluffer.

The adrenaline, combined with his specific, reasonable questions that I knew the answers to without even having to think, made my responses articulate. I answered each one-line question with a one-line answer. Each time I answered, he nodded and emitted the mini Bagpuss noise, which somehow humanised him. He was, after all, simply one fifty-six-year-old man. His questions became a bit more in-depth. He raised concerns echoing the secretary of state for Defra's statement about swift bricks opening the floodgates to other measures, and I politely hit back.

'Imagine swift bricks and the other biodiversity measures like hedgehog holes and bee bricks are in the Odd One Out round in the TV show *Have I Got News for You*. Swift bricks are the odd one out. Yes, they are bunched with the others, because they're marketed and made by the same manufacturers, but they are unique in their necessity. All the others are supportive measures and clearly wildlife needs all the help it can get, but swift bricks are the odd one out because they are urgently critical nesting habitat and therefore the only one that is essential for the existence of species. Therefore, you could easily justify mandating swift bricks and keep the others in guidance,' I explained.

I felt instantly guilty about hedgehogs, knowing hedgehog holes would be such a help for them, but also knowing that if I tried to champion absolutely anything else, or even raised concerns about anything else, it would not work. Michael Gove looked at me differently this time, as though beginning to assess me as a person. I had shot down his concern firmly without hesitation. Maybe he was reassessing me as a different sort of campaigner, more ruthless. He sat up, stroked down his tie.

When he asked the important question, 'Have any other countries—?'

I interrupted him before he could finish. 'Gibraltar and The Netherlands,' I said, feeling like it was a quick-fire round of *Question Time* – which, effectively, it was. This wasn't a thirty-minute meeting he had scheduled to discuss swift bricks, but a thirty-minute assessment of whether he should take me and my proposal seriously. I was there to convince him that I knew this topic like the back of my hand so he would see a woman who had managed to get a meeting with him because she was right.

Perhaps he thought I was, because the meeting ended with his invitation for us to come back, this time to meet with the minister of housing and the members of the Home Builders Federation, which was the only way government action would be able to happen.

'You nailed it,' Zac said as soon as we got out of the Home Office.

'Why are you so sure?' I asked, fretting, shaking slightly with the rush of adrenaline.

'He would never have invited us to a second meeting if he didn't respect what you'd said.'

Chapter 11

Amateurs

The second meeting wasn't until February, but in the meantime, my network grew. A shift had taken place since the summer, and I was being invited to environmental events in Parliament and considered part of the campaigner club. Dominic Dyer, best known for being an animal rights campaigner, had set up the first-ever environmental awards for politicians and invited me. At the drinks reception, I spied one of the peers who had spoken with such conviction in the House of Lords supporting Zac's amendment, and made a beeline for him. 'You're an absolute legend!' I said, knowing he would recognise me because I was holding my swift brick. When I explained Michael Gove had invited me and Zac to a meeting, he replied, 'Michael Gove is famous for his logic and arguably the best secretary of state for Defra Britain has ever had.'

He paused, looking down before saying in an exasperated tone, 'Now we could lose that good reputation because of opposing a thirty-five-quid brick in a house wall to save swifts. So, let's hope Michael Gove sees that and acts. I have no idea why he wouldn't. It would defy logic.'

I was buzzing; the feeling of being able to walk up to politicians and talk to them instead of begging for their attention was a relief, but the best thing was that my identity had become firmly and officially bound to swifts: to be the 'swift campaigner' filled me with pride.

The reception was emotionally charged with both hope and frustration; campaigners and politicians drawn together by common goals that got rid of the barriers normally separating what, effectively, were two almost identical sets of people. Most of the politicians in the room had climbed their way up to the top with minds full of determined intentions to change things for the better, one way or the other, for nature. There could be stigmas attached to both labels – 'politician' and 'campaigner' – but tonight there was a smidgen of equality in the air. Caroline Lucas said to me, 'We rely on campaigners like you. It's so much easier – and I'm not saying it's easy by any means – when there is a cause we can show is being raised by the public. It gives it so much more weight. We can't drive change without campaigners to galvanise public support to show it's a public concern.'

Her view felt revolutionary. It had never occurred to me that there were politicians waiting to find a figurehead among the public so that a change could be demanded. The problem was that public voices had to get heard, first by the public, then by the media, then by a political champion and then by enough of government to make progress. Protests seemed to be the preferred communication method for many campaigners but with mixed results. Some were boycotted by the media, like the XR 'Big One' in 2023, which was the organisation's first-ever non-disruptive action, and only got one piece of coverage despite 60,000 people turning up. I remembered the day when Zac had tabled his amendment. As we sat in the Lords Billing Office, squirrelled away in a compact room in the House of Lords, there was a distant rhythmic boom coming from the front of Parliament. It reverberated around the walls as march after march had gone past. Amplified voices rang out from tannoys, drums beat, people yelled, thousands of footsteps thudded. But it was all muffled, a perpetual background noise. I heard one of the civil servants mutter to a colleague, 'It's such a racket, whatever they're banging on about *this* week.'

'It's not like anyone listens!' came the reply. The remark was said in a flippant way that implied she, and perhaps many others in the building, were simply inconvenienced by – and most tellingly, numb to – protests.

'Seen it all before,' said the first civil servant, confirming the tone.

I had sat there, processing their point of view. They had not even considered the logistical difficulty, planning and cost of getting crowds of people together, let alone considered the reasons. Perhaps from their point of view, passion was just a sign of unprofessional weakness, not unfaltering conviction. Whistleblowing was just an inconvenience to roll eyes at, not an alarm to be taken seriously, or perhaps the sheer number of issues reduced engagement. I tried to picture what it was like to be them: of a working life within the Houses of Parliament. Every day they came in to take instructions from, and offer advice to, peers. At the start of each Parliament, they dealt with an ever-growing mass of new amendments crammed into a tight, rigorous schedule that covered every range of issue going: cost-of-living crisis; immigration; conflict; healthcare; education. And then there was everything else, from ongoing Covid inquiries to legislation about people murdered by a single punch. Somewhere among the rubble of human issues, among the noise and the business and the budgets and the party politics and the in-fighting, and the inter-office fallouts and love affairs, hangovers, maternity-leaves and promotions, there were the mounting environmental issues. Zac's amendment, 221A, requesting a tiny change to legislation to save a species, was grouped with hundreds of small amendments about things that were irrelevant to birds. In the same way, the entire joint issue of biodiversity loss and climate crisis was buried somewhere under the rising costs of living and the agenda of each politician.

Even the reception was a maquette of this reality. While everyone in the room was talking about nature, everyone had their own concern, their own aim, each one fighting for a slither of attention and a crack of light. How could anyone hope to achieve anything in this disco inferno of noise? But that wasn't the question I focused on. The question I focused on was who else was like me, because the answer gave me a fuel far more powerful than petroleum or caffeine. The answer gave me the ability to have enough faith to keep going, to persist, the only thing left when all other routes are pending. And that answer – that faith – came that night in the form of Mary Tester.

Dominic Dyer introduced us as he walked past. 'You two. You two will get on. Mary, Hannah. Hannah, Mary,' he said without stopping, busy in energetic conversation with someone else.

I said hi to Mary, an American woman about my age with blonde hair and a beautiful smile.

'I'm just trying to get the government to mandate swift bricks to save swifts which is proving much harder than it sounds like it should be.'

Mary laughed. 'No wonder Dominic thought we should meet. All I'm trying to do is get the government to agree to give seals basic protection.'

Mary explained that she had set up Thames Seal Watch, partnered with Seal Alliance and British Divers Marine Life Rescue (BDMLR) to work alongside Defra and local councils to stop seal disturbance, protecting seals from interaction with the public and from dog attacks. When she said the last words, 'dog attacks', her voice faltered.

'What made you set up Thames Seal Watch?' I asked, intrigued.

She explained that five years before, she had moved to London from California, where she had been a whale observer for the American Cetacean Society and had rehabilitated seals.

'We only moved here because it was a better decision for our family, but I felt like I left a huge piece of myself behind. I wasn't sure how I was going to fit in here, I still don't.'

'I get you,' I said. 'I know that feeling of being out of place and without purpose.'

'Yes, exactly,' Mary replied. 'It's the lack of purpose that eats you up. I became a volunteer diver and medic for the Thames but I knew that while there were seals here, I would probably never be needed.' She paused as a waiter offered us canapés.

Mary continued, 'I felt the lowest I'd ever been because I felt like I had messed up everything . . . and then there he was, Freddie.'

Mary explained that Freddie was a grey harbour seal pup who had decided to make a stretch of the Thames his home in early 2021. The ten-month-old pup had been named Freddie Mercury after he was found abandoned on a Dutch beach. Underweight, he was taken into intensive care and the staff at the Pieterburen Seal Sanctuary had named him after the Queen frontman because 'no one's gonna stop him now!' After his release, Freddie swam to England, finding himself on the Thames. The community loved him, as did the media. He became a local celebrity when he was rescued from Teddington Lock after a fishing lure got caught in his mouth. After being released at the Isle of Sheppey, he soon returned to the Teddington and Twickenham stretch of the Thames. For him, the stretch of river and beach along Teddington, Barnes and Putney was home.

'It's a tough thing to talk about Freddie,' Mary paused. Her voice choked, her eyes glistened with tears.

'I went to go see him for the first time and there were already crowds of people because he had been featured on *This Morning* and other TV shows and his photo was all over the press. It made me really nervous seeing so many people around him, but he didn't seem to care. To start with, I didn't understand why he wasn't bothered, but I know now that he didn't care because he'd been rescued so many times before he was used to people. That wasn't great either.'

The waiter came back, this time with glasses of fizz. We both grabbed one and took a swig.

'I was with him for a long time that first day, and when I came home, I drank a bottle of wine and then sat in the bathtub and cried,' she said. 'I never really fully understood why I cried like that. I've had these moments in my life where I knew I was in a place where something big was going to happen, so I've always had these moments that mark change, but this one came out of sadness. I had an extreme emotional reaction because I felt immediately protective of him.'

Every day, she went to see Freddie, to check he was OK. Normally he spent hours lying on a boat ramp that was in use, so Mary would put back up the barrier that had been made with rope and cones that had often fallen down. Each time she visited, she noted that people didn't know how to act around him. They'd walk down to try to take selfies, and one time, Mary witnessed a woman trying to get her dog to go and play fetch in the water next to him. Another time, she saw a woman trying to feed him fish.

'I felt so guilty I couldn't be there all the time, but I didn't have help,' she said, gesticulating in exasperation.

She put posters up to explain what to do and what not to do around him and then one day in March, Mary went to see Freddie and there was a man who was putting up signs on the trees saying

'Put your dog on a lead'. Mary explained how the man, Paul Brown, told her he had seen a dog almost attack Freddie. Nervous of the threat, Mary gave him her number, asking him to call her if he saw or heard anything else. She went home and made more signs, putting them on more trees.

'Less than forty-eight hours later, Paul texted me telling me Freddie had been attacked,' Mary said.

Mary had got on her bike and within ten minutes had arrived where Freddie lived. She didn't even take off her bike helmet, rushing through the crowd of people to get to him. By luck, there was a vet and someone who worked for swan rehab and they both knew how to restrain Freddie, because if he got in the water to escape, he would never get help. There were two school pupils who had been bitten by Freddie while trying to get the dog off him. Telling the boys to go to hospital, Mary took over and started coordinating with the British Divers Association to get help and forge a plan.

'And I was hopeful,' she said.

Triggered by the memory of that hope, Mary started crying, her tears flowing, and in that moment, I could see her heart break all over again.

'I was hopeful that he was going to make it,' she said, looking at me.

She explained that although there was significant damage, she knew the founder of Hanger Clinic, who make prosthetics for marine animals and had made a prosthetic flipper for a turtle and a tail for a dolphin. She rang the founder, asking whether he could make a flipper for Freddie.

'He said yes,' Mary said. 'But Freddie's infection was too serious, and he wasn't eating and the next day they put him down.'

Tears started rolling down my cheeks and together we stood in Parliament, crying because of a seal.

'My heart broke. I felt so guilty. I felt he had saved my life. He had given me hope and purpose and I couldn't save his,' she said.

She explained how what happened to Freddie spotlighted what needed to be done. Nothing happened to the woman who owned the dog. The community was so angry. Mary knew there needed to be more education and awareness around the code of conduct about how to act around seals. She realised the community, by and large, was ignorant about the wildlife in the area, many assuming the river was biologically dead. Mary wanted people to know that what happened to Freddie happens all around the country.

'All the other Freddies out there don't get the press that Freddie did,' Mary explained, going on to fill me in about the reality seals face.

The grey and common seals of Britain face an extensive list of threats, including climate change, toxic pollution, entanglement, collisions with vessels, kayakers, paddleboarders, surfers, plastics and other marine debris. Of these threats, disturbance from human interaction is a significant and growing problem. Seals are vulnerable to any kind of human interactions, either deliberate or unintentional. People don't necessarily know to keep themselves, their children and their dogs away from seals, not to feed them and to take rubbish home. Young seals like Freddie are most affected by disturbance and only 25 per cent are likely to survive to the age of eighteen months in a bad year. According to the Seal Research Trust's 'People Protecting Precious Places' (PPPP), an annual average of 1,106 seals in Cornwall are seriously disturbed, compromising their survival chances. If people are being noisy or startle the vulnerable animals by getting too close, this wastes their energy, meaning young pups struggle to haul out of the water to rest and digest their food. Female seals are heavily pregnant or pupping during the summer and getting too close or disturbing them can lead to seals stampeding on rocks, which proves fatal to both mother and pup. The impact on seals can also be invisible, but results in mothers not being able to build sufficient fat reserves so they cannot feed newborn pups adequately.

'The laws weren't there to protect him. So that's why I started Seal Watch and the campaign. I started it because I had to do everything I could to make sure what happened to Freddie never happened again. I didn't want him to die in vain,' Mary explained.

Wanting something good to come from it all, Mary intended to try to make Thames seals protected like the deer are in Richmond Park, but after talking to the Seal Alliance Chair, Sue Sayer, Mary decided to join the organisation, as they were trying to make seal protection national. Together with the Seal Alliance, Mary worked on the government-backed and government-funded campaign Give Seals Space. The campaign distributed 68,000 leaflets and one hundred information signs nationwide, with Mary responsible for all the signs for the Thames area. Alongside the Give Seals Space campaign, Mary launched a petition, organised a debate against the fisheries minister and brought the Seals (Protection) Bill to Parliament, which, if adopted, would make seal disturbance illegal. The law would comprise an official code of conduct and the implementation of licensing for commercial tourist-boat activity. Disturbance measures would be added to marine protected areas, along with continued public information, the encouragement of engagement at a local marine stakeholder group level and no-fly zones over sensitive seal sites. An open, group letter, backed by Chris Packham, was written and signed by over thirty conservation organisations, including the Marine Conservation Society and the RSPCA. It was so blindingly obvious. So simple. And clearly so necessary.

'Sadly, we still haven't crossed the finish line. We had a date booked in at Defra where we thought it was going to be agreed but then they cancelled it. It's like pulling teeth trying to get anything done. But I will keep trying until I tick off every box, until I fulfil every promise I made him,' she said, her voice breaking again.

I knew this promise. It was identical to the one I had made.

Chapter 12

Alliance

Every time I walked past the new development of thirty houses on the outskirts of the village I paused, my eyes fixed on the nine measly swift bricks that I had fought tooth and nail to have installed. Originally there were zero. To get these nine swift bricks, I had sent emails to the developer without receiving any replies; had phoned the developer only to be told no one was available and that I should send an email; contacted a leading local swift conservationist who contacted a local ecologist who had worked on the original plans (without including swift bricks) who put me in touch with her replacement who said she would look into it. Finally, after several months, the developer confirmed they would include some. All that for nine swift bricks.

It was so inefficient, when government action was not only justified but far from radical. Other countries had already stepped up, seeing the combined problem of nesting habitat loss and modern design as a way to embrace futureproofing our buildings for birds as well as ourselves. Many EU countries had granted year-round protection of swift nesting sites too, and the stable population trends were perhaps a testament to this.

I knew swift bricks worked on a national scale because Gibraltar had already done it thanks to one man who became, albeit remotely, a mentor: Professor John Cortes, Gibraltar's environment minister. Lord Randall had been the first politician to mention John Cortes, referencing Gibraltar's measures during the House of Lords amendment speeches in support of Zac's swift-brick amendment. Following up, I had made contact with the minister, hoping to get the specific information about what had been put in place, but I got a lot more than that: I made a new ally.

'I've loved birds all my life,' John said over the phone. 'They're really why I went into politics.'

Just like Zac, John was a nature campaigner who had gone into politics to try to lead change, and he had been successful. Considering there is only one local planning authority in Gibraltar, he hadn't needed to push for legislation and used a planning policy instead, which ensures swift bricks are included both in renovation and in every new build. He did this in response to the decline of Gibraltar's three species of swifts in the 1990s. Thirty years on, the swifts are not only still there but thriving.

'It works, which is fantastic because we as a government and the public were simply not prepared to lose them. Swifts are part of life in Gibraltar and so there was no resistance. Why there would even be a hesitation is extremely depressing.'

We chatted through the ins and outs of the campaign, me asking him devil's advocate questions, using the opportunity to pick apart the mind of a senior politician. Because of John, every single species of bird in Gibraltar has a full protected status, no mean feat considering the headland's location in the middle of the Mediterranean, a place infamous for catching, killing and eating hundreds of thousands of migratory songbirds every year.

Soon after our first call, I got a letter in the post, formally printed on Gibraltar government paper, pledging support for the proposal, stating all the reasons why it was an urgent and necessary measure to adopt via legislation in the UK's case, complete with the robust reassurances of the measure working. John wrote a similar letter to Michael Gove and the minister of housing too. Through this letter, foreign powers were wading into the campaign in a bid to help birds. In a separate note, John had written, 'Hannah. You will win because you are right. Do not give up.' My heart swelled at this politician's support. Here I was, reading my post in my pyjamas with my hair fuzzy and my eyes puffy, living in an almost constant, mute despair, and I had been given ammunition *and* a dose of belief from a foreign environment minister who had protected *all* birds.

The Netherlands had embraced swift bricks too, adding requirements for them into their building regulations in 2024. Although not yet enacted by the new 2024 Dutch government, this legislation included all new builds but also any renovations in which 25 per cent or more of external walls were being changed. This was a legislative dream and something Zac and I decided to propose to the government at our next meeting.

Over the course of the campaign, we had gathered endorsements from people across the conservation space and within politics, and we checked in with them again, creating a coalition of experts who sense-checked and moulded the ask. Michael Oxford was a key player in the proposal, as he had chaired the British Standards Institution's Technical Committee on Biodiversity and had created the British Standard that would act as guidance to enable legislation. Mike Priaulx from SLN, Richard Benwell and the RSPB contributed. Urban ornithologists, including Dr Thais Martins, added their stamp of approval, along with other experts in their fields that together represented each sector that needed to support the idea. When I shared the draft with Sustainability Director of Thakeham Josie Cadwallader-Hughes, not only did she agree that it would be efficient and practical to deliver but she agreed to come to the government meeting.

Zac and I sent our proposal to Natural England, the government's environmental advisor, explaining the overall reasoning of why it was felt necessary for the government to mandate swift bricks. Natural England Chair Tony Juniper and his team considered the proposal. I met Tony and we discussed it in detail. Dr Tony Juniper CBE is a big fish who has led major organisations, run global campaigns and advised at the highest levels. Out of everything Tony could have led with when we met, he launched into his love for, and understanding of, birds. We spoke about the Spix's macaw that Tim Flach's studio had been full of photos of, the campaign coming full circle because Tony had worked as an ornithologist with BirdLife International, spearheading the programme to prevent the extinction of this critically endangered parrot. Most of all, we spoke of swifts. Once again, I witnessed a political figure light up at the mention of these birds, and the clear alliance Tony has with the natural world.

Zac and I joined a video call to speak with Natural England scientists and then we were sent a statement:

> The inclusion of nesting bricks wherever possible in new housebuilding (as well as retro fitting wherever appropriate) would represent another great step on behalf of the industry and its partners towards supporting the essential recovery of iconic national species such as the swift for future generations.

I read it over and over, my face eclipsed by the grin that formed. This was another little paragraph that held so much significance. But where some people dedicated their lives to nature, there were others who had the extraordinary ability to ignore, dismiss and not care. Some of these people lurked within the government. While Michael Gove had appeared to be willing to consider government action, and we waited for the second meeting, I found out that the DLUHC was playing hardball.

The discovery had come on Christmas Eve, moments after I had cooked a feast and laid it on the table to share with merry mouths. I got a message from a politician telling me that the deputy director of planning policy had invited housebuilders to the second meeting as planned. However, in the email, the civil servant had told the lobby group that the government was generally resistant and that they thought it would burden the housebuilders.

I reread the words, feeling my blood pressure rise and a physical rage seep up through my body. I wanted to swear at the top of my voice; instead, I slipped off in silence to message Zac from the hallway, wondering exactly how much of a line I was crossing by contacting him on Christmas Eve. He rang me immediately and talked strategy, both of us suggesting options while sense-checking the other. Then I said something I had been thinking about for a while, keeping up my sleeve in case it felt necessary.

'I don't know whether this will even work, but I'm willing to pull another naked stunt to get the campaign back in the headlines, if you think it will add useful pressure to the government,' I asked, knowing that Zac would never humiliate me but might find a kind way of dissuading me.

He agreed at once. 'That's an excellent idea. How about walking to the government meeting? I'll walk next to you, though I'd prefer to keep my clothes on otherwise I think I would guarantee the death of your campaign!'

I double-checked with him via message but his reply was unflinching: 'I'm in.'

In my hallway, as everyone started scoffing the feast and drinking until their faces reddened and their voices slurred and their eyes drooped, I abandoned my plan of joining them. 'Well, that's

Christmas cancelled then,' I muttered to myself, knowing that for me to go naked again, I would not be eating my body weight in Christmas food. As I glanced at my reflection in the hallway mirror, my scowl turned into a grin at the new, secret scheme. Telling Robin the plan, checking he was OK with it, he nodded. 'Clever idea,' he said. 'They won't see that coming,' he added, putting his arm around me in solid support. I messaged Jemma, who replied instantly, saying, 'Now that's one way to outgun the government. Brilliant. I'll be there to help with your clothes.'

I submitted a Freedom of Information request and was sent the email with the relevant information that showed the DLUHC was not supportive blacked out. I stayed angry, the resentment channelling my focus on getting my body toned again to ensure I looked the same as I had sixteen months before. It wasn't just a physical aim. I knew the exercise and the disciplined routine would help my mindset. Instead of feasting and boozing, I was on the rowing machine for an hour every day, wearing Robin's old Olympic rowing Lycra all-in-one, which was enormous. As I rowed, I swore at the civil servant who had actively tried to derail the campaign, having full-blown arguments out loud, shouting over the top of Eminem's 'Lose Yourself' on repeat. His words became my mantra, and I changed from the sweating woman in the street who began the campaign into a sweaty woman in a shed, sixteen months angrier. When I finished, I'd lie on the floor, listening to Edward Elgar's 'Nimrod'. It was epic, and epic is what I needed. The exercise and the music put me in a competitive and disciplined mindset, making me obsessively focused on the goal. Robin kept encouraging me, and his friend, three times Olympic champion Pete Reed, reassured me that I wasn't overreacting. Pete was like family, having rowed with Robin in the GB team and in the University Boat Race for Oxford. When he asked how I was, I let my guard down:

'I need a pep talk. I think most people would worry I'm not coping very well.'

'But, Hannah, you're in a fight, right?' he said.

'Yes,' I replied.

'So, when you're in a fight, this is what it feels like.'

'The way I see it, if I am not exactly like this, what is the point of the last sixteen months of my life, and by extension, the point of the 60-million-year existence of swifts? But I'm not sure if I'm losing my mind,' I said, pausing, realising that to row in three Olympics means ultimately obsessing about perfecting rowing every single day for twelve years, just for three sets of races. I knew this – Robin had rowed in two Olympics, his friends spanning every Olympic games for decades, but it was almost too close to see and not directly relatable.

'I used to be so familiar with constantly fighting to achieve what I had set out to, which is what I think you're feeling now. This feeling in itself is a testament that you are achieving something, because if you weren't so close to your goal, you wouldn't feel like this. You've got something to fight for and you know you *can* achieve it. I know it might be hard to believe, but I miss that feeling and one day you will too. You're in the thick of it, Hannah. You're in a fight. It isn't supposed to be easy, so keep scrapping,' Pete said, giving me a huge hug, his arms like the wingspan of an albatross.

Robin and Pete's other rowing friends reiterated their own version of the advice, not batting an eyelid at my intensity but instead telling me to cherish it. With this personal coaching team of former international athletes, I tuned into an odd little world where I woke up every day pretending I was Rocky, and watched Arnold Schwarzenegger's documentary about taking no bullshit, on repeat.

A few days before the meeting at the start of February, I was in a good headspace but my mind was still fickle. Clad top to bottom in waterproofs, I was drawn to the song thrushes one rainy Saturday afternoon, their pale dotted chests like beacons of soft light. Their song trickled, a musical crown on the top of the bare trees. On the muddy ground there were tractor tracks through the soil, the rain collecting in little puddles where the tyre grooves had shaped the earth into neat chevrons. The bare ground was about the size of a double bed. It looked inviting. Spontaneously, I felt an irresistible urge, and hoping my clothes were fully waterproof, I lay down. My back sunk into the mud, and with my head cradled by the hood of my anorak and my feet upright in my wellies, I was comfortable.

I stared up into the sky at the nimbus cloud, an indigo ink spill running across the grey, listening to the song of the thrushes. Out of the corner of my eye, hunkered down between the new barley, low to the ground, I saw a baby hare: a leveret. I turned slowly onto my side to look at it. With damp fur in little flattened patches, it was darker, stained by the rain. Its long ears were pinned to its back. Its big amber eyes looked at me, but it didn't move. This was its spot. Stillness and camouflage were the leveret's defence, its mother leaving her babies in different safe places during the day where they would stay put, unmoving. At sunset, she would be back, visiting each one in turn to suckle them with her rich milk, the only feed they would need each day. The hare sunk its body lower to the ground, nuzzling its soft round chest, twitching one ear and closing its eyes. An unexpected wave of tiredness washed over me and, like the leveret, I closed my eyes, cradled in the shallow muddy puddle, sinking into invisibility. I exhaled slowly, encouraging my body to flop heavily into the ground, listening to the tap, tap, tapping of the rain as I felt my eyes rolling slightly back. I needed these elements: the vast sky that built clouds that blew fresh air down on the trees and fields below, reddening my face, softly blowing the leveret's fur. I needed the wildlife, the natural world. Without it, I felt unbalanced. With it, instinctively safer. This is what I was fighting for.

*

I kept the 'naked stunt' plan quiet, half worrying Zac would get talked out of it or change his mind over Christmas, but he didn't, and neither did I. Monday 5 February was just a normal day at the office for the vast majority of Brits but not for me. Staying at a friend's house in London, leaving Robin and the dogs at home, I woke up to blackbirds singing in the garden square as I dialled the number for the Press Association.

'Hello, PA media. Make it quick,' said the man who answered.

'Hi, I've rung to pitch you something that I hope you'll cover,' I said.

Just like the last time I had rung, the response was intimidatingly curt. 'You've got fifteen seconds.'

'I'm a bird campaigner and today I will be walking to a government meeting at the Home Office naked, and Tory peer Lord Zac Goldsmith will be right next to me,' I replied.

'Bloody hell. What time? We'll be there,' he said, taking my details.

Just after one o'clock I met Zac outside the Peers' Entrance of the Houses of Parliament, just like I had done the first time we met, except this time underneath my black jumper dress I wore no bra and a G-string that had no sides, stuck on with glue. Covering the small patches of knicker and my boobs were black-velvet swift shapes stuck on to my skin. We looked at each other with expressions of mischief, then walked through the Lords' cloakroom, which looks just like a school cloakroom with golden name tags complete with full titles, arriving at a small red room to one side. Thankfully, it was empty.

'You OK?' Zac asked, smiling.

'Yeah. Bit quiet. Are you OK?' I asked, still worrying he was going to back out of it.

'Yes, but I'm not the one about to be brave!' he replied.

We talked through the plan and found ourselves walking up and down the little room next to each other, checking our pace, practising for when we walked to the meeting a few hours later.

'Did you manage to get any press?' he asked.

'Yes. The whole press pack is coming,' I replied.

He gulped.

While he was more nervous about the walk, I was fretting about the meeting. Three days beforehand, the DLUHC had capped our attendees, telling us it was a small round table. Zac had challenged this, but it had made me feel on edge. We went through my briefing note, and Zac went through the choreography. In contrast to the meeting with Michael Gove, this meeting, with the minister of housing and members of the Home Builders Federation, would be much more political, so Zac would be leading it accompanied by the former housing minister, Kit Malthouse MP, who had spoken so brilliantly in the petition debate.

Zac walked me out to the front of Parliament and I began the first stage of the plan that didn't involve him or the press. While Zac went to get a cab for us, I met Jemma, Ben Cook and Ubdhav Maik, who had kindly agreed to film and photograph the stunt. I whipped my dress off, chucking it to Jemma, and stood in front of Big Ben. It was cold and as I took my dress off, the crowds of people filing past did double takes. Groups of tourists aimed their phone cameras not at Big Ben but at me. For fifteen minutes I posed on the road when the pedestrian light went green and then rushed out of the oncoming traffic as the lights changed. It was oddly fun, the high energy of the small crew rubbing off on me. This was a domain I felt comfortable in. After all, I had done this before, walking unclothed right past this spot. With the press pack due to be on the street corner of Marsham Street, where the Home Office is, at 2.30 p.m., I put my dress back on and we all walked to the Peers' Entrance where Zac was waiting with a cab.

'This is Lord Zac Goldsmith,' I said, introducing him to everyone. It was a surreal moment. Every now and then I would realise that the person who had become as much a part of the campaign as I was – the person who I had begun to completely rely on, trust and feel deeply fond of – was a senior politician. This label, this status, was invisible almost the entire time because Zac himself did not wear it at all. Not once did he remind me of how important he was. Never had he patronised me or told me I was out of my depth. His generosity of spirit had become the wings of the campaign.

The short cab ride down Westminster roads was a blur. Ben got out his camera and started filming me and Zac. The others spoke, the cabbie getting excited, asking where he would be able to see whatever we were about to do. I half heard Jemma reply but my mind had checked out. I had planned to go through everything for the millionth time. It wasn't really a big deal. All that was about to happen was that Zac and I would walk down a road next to each other on our way to the most important meeting of my life and be photographed. I just so happened to be naked. Not only would I be taking *all* of my clothes off in front of Zac, and the others, but my naked body would be seen on the national news. What if my stuck-on knickers fell off? What if my bikini wax wasn't as thorough as I thought? What story would the images tell? In my mute panic, I felt dramatically body conscious, my mind flashing back to the thousands of mean comments about my small breasts, worrying about the thickness of my thighs, my wonky eyebrows, my bum that used to be so pert but now was beginning to sag. Then, just like the first time, I remembered the swifts, and every issue I had with my body was eclipsed.

The cab stopped a few minutes from the Home Office, round the corner from the press so they couldn't see us. I took off my dress again and handed it to Jemma. 'Just a normal Monday meeting,' I joked as I got out of the cab, stung by the cold, the breeze twisting my hair across my face. Zac lingered, for a moment not entirely sure what to do, while the others walked off in front, getting into their filming positions, and Jemma checked round the corner.

'The press are here!' she said, smiling back at us. 'All of them!'

Zac and I glanced at each other. 'You OK?' he asked, his voice ever so slightly nervous, his stance instinctively protective.

I rubbed my hands together, looked at him, and nodded. 'I cannot believe we're doing this,' I said, and off we went.

With Zac beside me, we walked down the pavement. Other people, smart and suited, likely to be working for the government, walked past. With their expressions, our nervous, quiet mood turned. There was a feeling shared between us of a childhood sense of mischief – an innocent daring only made fun and possible because of us being in it together.

'Did you see that double take? God, I'm never going to forget that!' Zac said. 'Oh, and another!' he added, laughing.

As we got closer to the Home Office, the press pack descended on us, journalists darting all around for the shot, so it felt as though we were walking through a flock of pigeons. We didn't react, walking steadily as if all these people with video cameras and tripods running around us weren't there. At the entrance, the kerfuffle had alerted two security guards, who walked quickly up to the scene. Zac strode in between me and them, and Jemma flung me my dress.

While the press pack started asking questions, Zac fielded the security guards. 'We're just going to a government meeting,' I could hear
him saying. They didn't believe him, didn't know who he was, and I
giggled into my dress, feeling a little thrill of the contrast of it all.

Just after I had put the dress on, Kit Malthouse arrived. While
Zac had suggested I told him we were doing a small stunt that
wouldn't be taken into the Home Office or the meeting, I had
decided against it, worrying he might not turn up to the meeting.
He was far too important to our cause for me to scare him off. Kit,
wearing an owl tie, greeted us, having no idea what we had just
done. 'Impressive amount of press here, well done you,' he said.

Zac glanced at me, smiling as we went in, the doors of the
Home Office separating one strategic line from the other. Inside,
we were playing a different game.

We went into a very small room with windows looking out
on to the street. Below, the pavement was filled with press, the
video recorders set up on tripods waiting for us to come out. The
people we were meeting had no idea. On one side of the table I
sat with Kit, Zac and Josie, who represented the only housebuilder
that actively supported the campaign, while on the other side were
members of the Home Builders Federation. It was awkward. These
people had been invited by the government, encouraged to object
to our proposal by one of the civil servants who was attending via
a Zoom call, her face projected on an enormous television that
loomed over us from one side of the table. This was the woman
who I had thought about every time I had got on the rowing
machine while I was channelling Arnold Schwarzenegger.

In came the minister of housing, who was new to the position after his predecessor had been reshuffled. He didn't look me
in the eyes when he said hello and opened the meeting by telling
us he would leave promptly at 3.30 p.m. despite being six minutes

late. His manner made it abundantly clear this meeting was a twenty-four-minute inconvenience. There was not even a flicker of acknowledgement of the sixteen months it had taken for me, a member of the public, to get the meeting.

Sitting at the head of the table, the layout of the guests echoed why this meeting was happening: Michael Gove had set me and Zac the task of discussing swift bricks with the Home Builders Federation to allow the industry to raise concerns, giving them an opportunity to object. The logistical challenge of the meeting was that there were nine of us round the table, three on video call and we only had twenty-four minutes to lay our case. It was absurd. The minister took up another four minutes by inviting everyone to introduce themselves.

'I'm Hannah, I've worked every day, unpaid, solidly, for sixteen months to be in this meeting,' I said.

'I'm Kit Malthouse and five years ago this was my office,' Kit said.

It was Zac who outlined the context of why Michael Gove had set up this meeting as a way to remind everyone that the secretary of state was not opposed to our proposal. 'To be honest, I can't quite believe we are here, still discussing this when it is not only urgently necessary, but so easy. It's a win for everyone and a burden on no one,' he said, his tone somehow positive, not exasperated.

Then it was my turn. I outlined the need, moving quickly on the wealth of testimonials, theatrically handing each formal letter to the minister who tried to resist taking each one.

'This one is from the RSPB and its 1.2 million members.

'This one is from Wildlife and Countryside Link, the coalition made up of eighty conservation organisations.

'This is from your own – the Conservative Environment Network.

'This is from the environment minister of Gibraltar, who wanted to come to this meeting.

'This statement is the official decline statistic from the British Trust of Ornithology, which estimates there are 45,000 UK pairs of swifts remaining and by next year there will be fewer than 40,000 pairs.

'This is the official statement from Natural England in case it's useful to be reminded what your own environmental advisors say.'

'What do they say?' he asked.

'That you should add swift bricks to building regulations,' I replied.

With a slightly vexed expression, the minister asked, 'If these birds are reliant on our buildings, where did they nest before humans?'

'In cavities in trees in primal forests, but in the seventeenth century we cut them all down, and astonishingly the birds adapted,' I replied.

Kit was next, explaining the guidance he had added to the National Planning Policy had been widely ignored by housebuilders, who were, of course, represented in the room.

Then it was the turn of the housebuilders. One of them explained the industry's wish to carry on doing it voluntarily with their own commitments, while another added that guidance really needed to be fully considered.

Josie, from Thakeham, replied. 'It already has. There is a specific British Standard on swift bricks, created so industry-wide action can be taken. Since building regulations are basically framed on British Standards, it's all perfectly set up.'

'Yes, and unlike policy, which will be ineffective for a whole host of reasons, building regulations will ensure that existing nesting sites are directly mitigated when there are renovations,' Kit said.

The civil servant spoke from the huge television in response to Kit's comment.

'Oh, I hadn't realised about that. You make a good point.'

I quivered with anger. This was the woman who had made a concerted effort to ensure our proposal failed, yet had not even considered one of the most obvious points. Having minimally engaged, this person in a position of authority was ignorant of the issue she was influencing the outcome of.

There was a bristling of tension as members of the Home Builders Federation had their say. One commented that a bit more research was needed.

'No, it isn't,' I said. 'Not only is time running out, but there is plenty of research. This step isn't even radical. Gibraltar did it thirty years ago and stabilised their populations of swifts. The Netherlands is implementing exactly what we propose this summer. We've even drafted the wording for the requirement in building regulations,' I said, audibly exasperated.

The civil servant made a condescending comment about how good it was to know how passionate I was about the subject. I sat in polite, silent rage.

The conversation moved back to the housebuilders, whose overriding verdict was one of willingness, declaring their huge commitments that had been recently made, scheduled to be implemented in the autumn. Members of the Future Homes Hub (FHH), which comprised about 70 per cent of the industry, including all the big developers, were committing to install one swift brick per dwelling. Steadily, the industry, helped by Josie's advocacy, had begun to recognise that swift bricks were necessary. This commitment was huge – if implemented. It was theoretically the aim of the campaign. It sounded like a dream but as soon as I had seen the collection of people who had turned up as we were in the lobby,

I had whispered to Zac and to Kit what the battle was about. The housebuilders' stance was going to be that their commitments and progress and leadership were enough and government action was unnecessary. While the FHH had managed to successfully get commitments from all of their members, a coup in itself, this commitment was voluntary, unchecked and temporary, promised only until 2030. It was significant progress but it wasn't enough. It wasn't permanent, enforceable and legally binding, and unchecked, it was only as good as the housebuilders' word: either a problem solver or a paper tiger. I was sceptical: surveys of developments instructed to include swift bricks by local planning authorities in Hertfordshire had resulted in 64 per cent non-compliance.

Zac confronted this issue positively as ever: 'The reason why the Environment Act, which I helped lead through Parliament, even got to the point of legislation, was because the industries affected stepped up. Instead of lobbying against or saying legislation wasn't necessary, they actively supported it, leaving the way clear for government action. A swift-brick policy is so utterly insignificant, yet it would have a huge impact, so I ask you all to actively support this proposal going forwards. It's so easy, and so important.'

None of them said yes or no. They probably couldn't, since none of them were CEOs. The minister, who had been looking at his watch throughout the meeting, and had stifled a yawn, got up. Having been hardly in the conversation, he was now ending the meeting. Kit and Zac both tried to get him to commit but he said no.

'Well, will you at least commit to letting us know your decision?' I asked.

'Yes,' he replied.

'Just before you go, can I just ask the main question while you are here. Is there any objection to this proposal from housebuilders?' Zac asked them.

'No,' they replied.

We left the meeting. Zac and I walked back to the Lords. I swore as usual but Zac corrected me. 'It doesn't matter. The challenge Michael Gove set was for us to meet the housebuilders to flush out any killer reasons for not agreeing the proposal. And we did. We were accompanied by some of the world's greatest authorities and testimonials, and not one of the housebuilders raised arguments against mandating swift bricks. We answered and met the challenge. Hannah, we passed the test. Michael Gove has no barriers to stop him from doing it.'

Chapter 13

Safe Passage

I processed the day's events and Zac's optimism as I stood in a dark alleyway in Westminster, nipping out of a bar where I'd been having a drink with Jemma so I could be interviewed live on Radio 4 for the *PM* programme. My phone kept buzzing with editors from newspapers telling me the story was lighting up the news desks of all the nationals, and by that afternoon the coverage had begun. '"Naked" Campaigner Urges Government to Take Action to Help Swifts'; 'Ruffling More Feathers Zac? Scantily clad former model Hannah Bourne-Taylor is joined by former minister Lord Goldsmith as she arrives to lobby the government to help nesting swifts – while wearing a nude body suit'. Swifts were news until 6 p.m. that evening, when a shock announcement about the king having cancer eclipsed everything else.

As I lay awake, wired, processing the surreal afternoon, what stuck out more than anything was how Zac's presence, conviction and support felt tangibly like a protective force field. I trusted him to have my back, to listen to me, to react fairly, to act in our common interest. Surely, this was the sort of feeling that the government should aim to give the electorate in a democracy. Instead, the label of 'the government' depicts a faceless, vague, inhuman entity where there is almost zero accountability. It felt more and more like a formal smokescreen used by some politicians – both elected and officials behind the scenes – to duck and dive, point fingers and run away from any engagement, responsibility or action.

I sent the formal proposal with the drafted wording and placement of the swift-brick requirement in building regulations to Michael Gove, and Zac fed back to me updates about other Conservatives who were personally lobbying him. Hundreds of people who had supported the campaign sent handwritten letters and postcards to Michael Gove, asking him to mandate swift bricks. The recurring dreams about Michael Gove, of his face with his classic, playful impression floating in front of mine, became the norm. Journalists sporadically asked me whether I was secretly dating Zac, paparazzi photographing us together meeting for a coffee, alluding to a romantic relationship, but when asked in magazine interviews, I explained that we were not having an affair and, in fact, the politician I was dreaming about was Michael Gove. One morning I woke up thinking I had just walked into the Home Office to be greeted by Michael Gove naked, standing with a quilt wrapped around his body, surrounded by swift bricks. I wondered whether this man, whom I had inadvertently become obsessed with, thought about the campaign at all. It was the year of the General Election; he had a big, stressful role but he was also getting personal texts and WhatsApp messages from many Conservatives about my campaign. At some point during some of the days, surely, maybe, just for a few seconds, swifts must have been entering his mind while I lost mine.

By the third week of February, the season had shifted but the government stance was stagnant. Aconites and snowdrops were being joined by violets. The year's first bumblebees and butterflies were adding colour to the air and the first major migration was taking place: on drizzling, clear nights, the amphibians of Britain were making their way back to their ancestral ponds to mate.

It was the toads who gave me a break from thinking about Michael Gove. Thanks to Froglife's 'Toads on the Roads', a part conservation action scheme, part citizen science, I was a toad patroller, along with thousands of other volunteers. Between February and April, the toads appear, hell-bent on returning to their ancestral ponds, migrating using the same routes, many of which have roads running through them. On dark, drizzling nights, all over Britain, people descend on toad villages to help. They come with torches and buckets, wearing high-vis jackets, and walk along the roads that the toads use, sometimes all evening until the traffic stops or until there are no more toads to help. When they see a toad, they pick it up, put it in their bucket and decant the passenger on the other side of the road, in the direction the toad was heading.

I walked along a road on the outskirts of a particularly busy toad village in Oxfordshire, wearing a head torch and carrying a bucket, looking for toads. Filling the track, like a scene from a bizarre film, were dozens of pairs of eyes, lit up in the dazzle of my head torch. Sat in puddles, hunched along the side of the road, taking great, slow slides as they crossed, they immediately transformed the road into a spectacle. Crouching down, I peered at the nearest one, who was sat in a puddle as though part way through bath time. I picked it up, expecting it to leap away from me, but it sat still and squeaked, revealing it was male by the sound. Mottled golden, his eyes were metallic bronze like a pair of tiny pools of liquid metal. He was heavy in my hand and sat upright, his front feet like the hands of an old gentleman, almost clasped, ready to tell a story. At my feet, a female was striding past, being followed by three males who bundled on top of her, trying to mate. Other little gangs of males filtered past. It was uncannily similar to a pub on a rowdy Friday night an hour before closing, just playing out in silence except for the odd squeak.

There were no cars coming but the danger to the toads was obvious. Sprawled across the road, they were oblivious to the risk. I counted twelve in one puddle in the middle of the road, so I started picking them up, carefully placing them in my bucket. Further up the road there was a splatter of casualties, a smear of toad bodies with strings of intestines splayed out, mixing with the tarmac grit and the rain. I moved quicker, collecting all of them off the road before another car came. With the contents of the bucket reaching forty-two, the road temporarily empty, I walked over to the track where they would be safe and placed them down one by one, delighting in each one in my hands. I lay down next to them, surrounded by small piles of toads. One walked over my arm, another sat next to my face. In no hurry, I felt part of their quiet gang. If there was no risk of others being run over, I would have stayed with these toads all night, making my way with them to the ponds, watching them splash in.

Normally, about 5,000 toads are chaperoned across the road I was walking down, over the course of a season. On either side, there are steep banks that turn into stone walls – a pretty wood cut in half, so each year the toads slip and fall down one steep side of it only to have to climb up the other. Many of them struggle, ending up in the leaf litter, trying to find a way up the walls. But these were lucky toads, thanks to a woman called Amy who had grown up in the village, her childhood memories full of seeing squashed toads in the mornings outside her house. She lived in a long cottage between a house with a neat front garden and a pretty row of cottages on either side of the road. There was a phone box and a car park. It all looked so prim and proper, except for the trail of toads making their way silently past pansies that lined the garden wall opposite. For Amy and this village, this amphibian odyssey was the norm for three months of every year. During the season,

Amy would come home from work, eat quickly and go out. Other members of the patrol came from neighbouring villages, checking in with each other on a WhatsApp group to make sure that someone was always out and all routes were covered.

'If we didn't do it, the roads would be full of squashed toads. One car can wipe out hundreds of them,' Amy said.

One volunteer, Richard, walked with me and explained the connection he felt. 'There is just something different about toads,' he said. 'While frogs do these amazing gymnastics and leap across the roads, the toads sit there unhurried. There's something important about that. About slowing down.'

He talked about the purpose that he felt from helping the toads, about the wider link they gave him to his surroundings. In return, he checked every single drain down a two-mile stretch of road in case the toads fell in, stuck.

Further along, we bumped into another volunteer, Enid, who was beaming.

'The darlings are out tonight in force,' she said. 'They're toppling every which way, laughing at us nutters.'

'Enid talks to the toads,' Richard explained. 'I often hear her chatting away in the dark going from one side to the other.'

'Well, there's something charming about them. They've got so much character. And you know, if you manage to save one female full of spawn, you've actually saved hundreds,' Enid replied.

Because of these people and the many loyal volunteers, collectively, across Britain, between 70,000 and 120,000 toads are given a helping hand every year. These efforts stem from the scheme championed by the co-founder of Froglife, Tom Langton, and his childhood love for toads. Growing up in North London, Tom often visited three old toads living in the neighbouring basement well. Clambering down to their green damp dell, among the moss and ferns, he'd pick them up. Marvelling at their bellies in his cupped hands, their eyes golden, their chins lightly pulsating, a passion grew. During the summer of 1966, as others were engrossed in the World Cup, Tom helped thousands of toadlets marching across the narrow lane outside his house. Using flowerpots, filling them with soil for cushioning, he scooped the toadlets up and moved them into the adjoining gardens.

For ten years, every summer, Tom rushed out to stop them getting run over, noticing the numbers dropping significantly. He went on to study ecology, his career in conservation allowing him to share toad stories with like-minded peers which led to 'toads on roads' leaflets and car stickers to get more people interested. Formal toad patrols had been underway in the Netherlands, Germany and Switzerland since the 1950s. Spurred on by these initiatives, signs were made to temporarily divert traffic on certain roads, eventually leading to a national road warning sign authorised by the Department of Transport in 1985. Tom persisted, supported by many herpetologists, and toad patrols across Britain began more formally, building steadily.

Even with this nationwide effort, the common toad, although not endangered yet, is diminishing, the population declining by two-thirds in the last thirty years. Twenty tonnes' worth of toads are run over annually, while others migrate only to find their ancestral ponds have been filled in and built on. While these statistics are both sad and concerning, the idea of toad patrollers filled me with hope, tinted with a sense of childlike fun that made me grin. Thousands and thousands of toads *had* been helped. Toads had been spotted, scooped up and carefully laid on the other side of the roads, by all sorts of people. Bakers, electricians, bus drivers, engineers, schoolchildren, retired couples. Through entire evenings, instead of watching television or going to the pub, meeting friends or going to the gym, hundreds of people, scattered across the country, choose to walk along in the dark looking for toads: our jewelled-eyed neighbours, some rambunctious, some chilled out, all of whom are just trying to get back to their home ponds. This narrative, of individual people going out of their way to help individual wild lives, played out across the country with all sorts of species. For every toad patroller, there was a hedgehog, swift, bat, hare, badger or fox rehabber, dedicating whole seasons to individual animals in need of help.

In return, the nature on our doorstep provides a sense of home, and in the nights I couldn't sleep, worrying about Michael Gove's silence, I stood in my garden next to the shrub where I knew the house sparrows were fluffed up and asleep inches away from me. I marvelled in the knowledge that they live alongside us just as they lived alongside Edwardians and Tudors and Anglo-Saxons and cave men. Written references about these gregarious neighbours of ours date back to Greek mythology. Over the centuries, they've been described as being prolific in their ability to reproduce, but ironically, since 2002 their population has declined. One of our oldest symbols of love, dating back to Aphrodite's sacred sparrows, they now face national extinction. They're the birds who *are* recognised and familiar because, luckily, their population baseline is still in the millions yet, since the 1980s, the UK and Europe have a staggering 247 MILLION fewer house sparrows. A study of UK and EU birds by scientists from the RSPB, BirdLife International and the Czech Society for Ornithology found that one in every six birds, totalling 600 million breeding birds, have disappeared in the past forty years, with another swift-brick beneficiary, the starling, having 75 million fewer individuals.

Others are being wiped out of our collective national consciousness, outlaws of memory, almost entirely forgotten. The cost of this amnesia is also grave. The endangered yellowhammers I feed to keep alive were once so keenly observed they were known as scribbling larks, or scribbies, because of the irregular lines on their eggs. There used to be so many skylarks, people described seeing 'clouds' of birds. So abundant, they were hunted with nets for our dinner tables, a single nightly haul of a hundred or two common. Amazingly, their 63 per cent decline to the tune of 68 million fewer across the UK and EU is not from Victorian lark hunters but from the last forty years of modern farming practices. With this loss comes a silence in the sky, only heard by people who know the difference between then and now.

This silence should be filling us all with horror because it directly affects us. The birds' decline is wrapped up in lack of habitat and food, and their food – seeds and insects – is what we also rely on. We have bumblebees to thank for our pizza nights, chips dunked in ketchup and Bloody Marys, because bumblebees are the sole pollinators of tomato crops. Ancient Egyptians worshipped bees and believed they stemmed from tears shed by the sun god Ra, yet the activists and scientists who raise awareness about the need to protect our pollinators – and the birds who rely on them – are dubbed by the media and some politicians as 'eco-zealots'. *Zealot: a person who is fanatical and uncompromising in pursuit of their religious, political or other ideals.* It is a worrying label, implying we have collectively reassigned our understanding of scientific fact to be an ideal.

The separation between us and nature has grown steeply over the past century. Only one hundred years ago, rural people knew the nature on their doorsteps because their daily lives were intertwined with the countryside, to the point of depending on it. Entire lives were lived locally. As my neighbour Wendy once told me, 'I was born in 1935. We all grew up getting our food from the daily market, only eating what was grown locally and in season.

I had a poster of a banana on my wall and still vividly remember the treat of first tasting one.' Hers and previous generations impressed a date by giving flowers like scabious, the pretty purple round-headed wildflower that grows in road verges and meadows, nicknaming them bachelor's buttons, while the hollow stems of the smaller common hogweed were once used as water pistols and as straws to drink cider. Hedge woundwort was, for centuries, made into a poultice for cuts. Herb robert was once commonly known as a 'cure-all', meadow-clary, meaning 'clear-eyed', now one of the rarest plants in Britain, was used as a remedy for sore eyes. The tall straight stem of great mullein, which grows like spires with clusters of yellow flowers, was also known as Our Lady's candle. Stems were cut, dried and dipped in tallow to make torches and lamp wicks. They are links to the past, layered in ghosts of every age before us.

Knowledge of flora has become the domain of experts, not commonplace. There is a sadness in letting go of centuries' worth of carefully built-up knowledge, and a danger in our ignorance because we still rely on plants. Accounts of plants being used for medical purposes go all the way back to the first records made. An ancient Egyptian scroll, the Ebers Papyrus, written in about 1500 BC, is a 110-page, 20-metre-long list of medicinal herbal knowledge. Today, many of the plants on the list remain in medicinal use. The bark of the willow tree was chewed to alleviate aches and pain. Today, the active ingredient in willow bark – salicylic acid – has been synthetically replicated and makes up the over-the-counter medicine aspirin. More famous are the opium poppies that are the base of codeine and morphine as well as the class-A drug heroin. A natural alkaloid called galantamine, extracted from snowdrop bulbs, is now used to slow the progression of Alzheimer's disease and mitigate its symptoms, such as memory loss, working by slowing the decline in the transmission of chemical messages in the brain. Proteins from snowdrops are also being investigated as a possible treatment for HIV. Plants are used for fighting cancer, including Taxol, a compound in the chemotherapy drug Paclitaxel, which is from the Pacific yew tree and is on the World Health Organisation's Model List of Essential Medicines. Wildflowers found in Britain proven to have cancer-fighting properties include a member of the carrot family commonly named bishop's weed or false Queen Anne's lace; milk vetch; camellia; pennyroyal; common myrtle; milk thistle; garden thyme; wild pansy; and nettle.

We have dislocated ourselves from what we once knew, so even when there is a connection, it often goes unseen. This collective blindness, this forgotten truth, was something everyone I knew who loves nature was trying so hard to reverse, and swift bricks had become my clarion call for reconnection.

Time ticked on, the season change emphasising the time passing with no word from Michael Gove, who wasn't just holding the swifts' future hostage by floundering on making a decision, but inadvertently also my own. The limbo caught me out in moments where I would suddenly feel physically depressed, weighted down with gloom. My mood slowed into a strange, paralytic state. I wondered whether I was entering into a mental breakdown, finally realising that the so-called democratic process I had been governed by, that had subsequently derailed my whole life for almost eighteen months, felt like a complete farce. Robin kept finding me in tears and was beginning to worry, trying to help me manage my emotions and compartmentalise the campaign. I was snappy and riddled with self-doubt, then suddenly I started walking into walls like I was drunk, my head spinning, losing balance, unable to stand.

'You've got labyrinthitis,' the GP said when Robin had half carried me into an emergency appointment. 'It's an inner-ear infection that causes severe vertigo. There's no cure or prevention but many people get it when they become stressed. Are you stressed?'

I stared at the doctor, trying not to fall off my chair.

'Is there a reason why you'd be stressed?' the doctor said.

'Michael Gove,' Robin muttered.

'What?' the doctor replied. 'Look, the only way you will get better is if you do absolutely nothing and you must alleviate the stress.'

After the appointment, Robin set me up in bed, sitting on the side.

'What's sending you over the edge, do you think?' Robin asked.

'I feel like I'm holding my breath,' I replied. 'I cannot comprehend why a person with the authority to help an endangered species so simply . . . hasn't. Is it because Michael Gove and the team around him don't believe it's necessary, or because they do, but they don't care? The thought is just a loop in my head. Why wouldn't they care?'

For ten days, I lay in bed feeling as though I was spinning, as though I had misplaced my own spirit level, unsure of what way up I was. All the while it was the garden birds' voices – the chirping sparrows and the wren's trill – who were my constant companions. Different countries have different names for wrens, each one showing a connection made through close vicinity and observation. In Hebrew the wren is called 'fence master', in Bulgarian, 'little walnut', Fins call it 'thumbling', while the Faroes call it 'mouse-brother'. 'Little king of winter' is its name in Dutch, while in Serbian the wren is known as 'red-tail'. The name 'wren' originates from the Middle English word *wrenne* meaning 'little tail', and as I lay, I pictured the wren's tail flitting in the dappled light of the garden, grateful for his company.

A 2022 study from the Institute of Psychiatry, Psychology & Neuroscience at King's College London found that seeing or hearing birds is associated with an improvement in mental well-being. I know this is true even on ordinary non-spinning days. Every morning, I play a game in my head where I note the first bird I see. It feels like a treat each time I wake up as I spy out of my window, step into my garden or walk into the fields. Noticing the birds allows me to feel like I am part of a community, all of us getting up to start a new day together: wood pigeons shuffle along rooftops, cooing to each other, heads nuzzled; dunnocks appear like crouching tigers, striped and alert as they spy on me; in the highest branches of garden trees, robins sing, starlings adding their chortling from the wires. For the past three years every morning I've posted my first bird on X with the hashtag #FirstBirdOfMyDay #WhatsYours, and across Britain and around the world, people play it with me, commenting with their first bird. Through this daily interaction, not only is there an informal survey of first birds, but people tell me how important the birds are to them, how much they love and value the ones they see. For some, the birds shed light in the darkness of illness, disability, divorce and mental anguish and the daily stresses of life. For all, the birds have created a community of strangers who come together in a positive morning ritual.

After a fortnight, the dizziness went away. Robin urged me to take a break from my ordinary routine, so for a few days I went to the wildest part of north Devon to try to escape my mind. Hartland is a place full of movement and sound, of roaring waves from the Atlantic swell that ride upwards, clashing with the wind that whips up and smacks you right between the eyes. Great blocks of rock, created millions of years ago by submarine avalanches, fold upwards in angular shards from the beach, chevron-shaped cliffs that jut along the bottom of the shore and out to sea like granite ribs. Nestled between wind and water, just off from the edge of the cliff, is a single white-washed cottage with red windows and doors.

Listening to the waves filled me with a mixture of excitement and relief that I was warm and cosy in a little single bed as the waves stayed up on their night shift, keeping guard. Virgo hung over the cove, its bright star of Spica like a spotlight on the earth that was blooming. Virgo is associated with the spring goddess Persephone. In Greek mythology, her abduction by Hades to the underworld is what leads her to becoming the personification of vegetation which surfaces in spring and withdraws into the earth after harvest. She summoned the snowdrops, celandines, violets and primroses and anemones, covering the wooded areas around the cottage. Underneath February's full moon, aptly called storm moon, the wind wrapped the cottage up in a howling sea fret, engulfed by the sound of the swell. Here the sky and the sea are obviously connected, working as one, bound together by the moon, which glowed like a giant sea pearl. George Darwin, the son of naturalist Charles Darwin, calculated that the moon is slowly spiralling outward, away from Earth, by a few centimetres a year and eventually, once it has moved much further away, billions of years from now, Earth could become tidally locked, and some parts of it will never see the moon again, just like Pluto and its moon Charon. There is nothing any of us mere mortals can do about the moon strolling away through the sky, taking the pendulum of night and day, light and dark. This acceptance of change, because it was out of my hands, granted me a relief because my irrelevance was absolute.

In the cold blue light of dusk, I watched a peregrine falcon from the window. Just outside, directly above the cliff edge, the falcon suspended herself in the sky, hunting her kingdom of gorse and heather. Steady in the air, she rode the wind, pausing in a flutter of movement replaced by stillness, the wind reined in by her in avian magic. Sweeping suddenly, she hurled herself ground-ward, pouncing at whoever was there. Out of sight for a moment, among the bright stars of gorse flowers, I wondered whether the smaller heart beating below had been stopped by her or propelled an escape?

This feathered goddess has been interlinked with humanity for millennia. In ancient Egypt they were deified in the form of Horus, the sky and sun god, the ancestor of the pharaohs; now they have taken up homes in many cathedrals in England. This bird also had a truth attached to her that made me feel conflicted because, as a peregrine falcon, she posed one of the biggest natural threats to swifts. Her kind had been hunting swifts for millions of years. These two birds were well matched, evolving to compete for their own survival, the peregrine dependent on the swift's downfall in the same way as this bird was reliant on the death of whoever was in the undergrowth. Yet for all her kind's killing, the swifts and the mice and the sparrows and the lizards who the peregrines had preyed upon for millions of years had managed to live alongside their hunters. An agreement had been kept, a balance and rhythm remaining.

The delicateness of the balance of the natural world spoke of bigger warnings that, as I had campaigned, had sunk in. Because the campaign had dragged on, and the strategies employed were a joint and active effort, by the time I was waiting for Michael Gove to make a decision, I had spent hours with Zac. We never made small talk, or asked questions about each other's lives, so in some ways we hardly knew each other. We only ever spoke non-stop, intensely, about either the campaign or nature restoration on a broader scale. For hours we talked in his office surrounded by beautiful sculptures he had made. A life-size bronze of his jackdaw, an intricate collection of hummingbirds, a huge bust of a gorilla. As environment and overseas territories minister, he had led policy change all over the world. Zac is a lifelong environmentalist camouflaged by the untrusted status of being a politician, but to spend five minutes with him was to see him for what he is: head over heels in love with nature. He'd talk of scratching the tummy of a manatee in Guyana, his eyes brightening, his whole face lighting up. Every anecdote had a wild creature: a gorilla he'd watched who had taken his breath away; macaws who had landed on him as he'd been awarded a prestigious conservation award by the president of Colombia, the parrots proceeding to remove all his shirt buttons during the ceremony, to Zac's delight. Zac's unhidden love for nature reminded me of something Sir David Attenborough had said to President Barack Obama during an interview at the White House in 2015. When asked by Obama why he loved nature so much, Attenborough replied, 'I've never met a child who is not interested in natural history – from the simplest thing of a five-year-old turning over a stone and seeing a slug and saying, "What a treasure!" Kids love it. Kids understand the natural world and they're fascinated by it. So the question is: how did anyone lose the interest in nature?'

Zac, nearing fifty, had never lost it either, his love of nature seeming to be his heartbeat. Despite the setbacks that had led him to resign as minister, Zac's manner remained both focused and optimistic. He was a dogged problem solver, jackdaw-like. During one meeting, he said, 'I think many people believe nature restoration is either unrealistically expensive or somewhat irrelevant but neither is true. Solutions that restore nature and, by doing so, help combat climate change *and* create sustainable economies for communities exist. They are just the exception, not the rule.'

He had handed me a government policy called the '10 Point Plan for financing biodiversity', launched as part of the UN General Assembly. Zac and the rest of Defra had created the policy in the run-up to COP15, the biodiversity conference that had coincided with the launch of The Feather Speech. When I had walked through

London naked the first time, Zac had been busy at the United Nations Conference. He had worked for days upon days without sleep, meeting endless world leaders, negotiating both informally and formally on behalf of nature, disguised as a politician. I read the first paragraph. It had Zac's fingerprints all over it:

> Nature is our source of life. It provides the foundation for nearly everything we value. Yet nature itself is not being properly valued – or protected – by our economic and political systems. It is being destroyed at an unprecedented rate, throwing our planet into one of the most dramatic extinction crises in history.

I looked at these facts I knew so well, printed with the government crest. These words had been agreed on not just by the UK government but by forty-one countries led by Ecuador, Gabon, the Maldives and the UK. But this landmark policy came before Zac's resignation.

'So, what happened? I see it says it is a "non-legally binding political narrative", so did the UK keep this commitment?' I asked, already guessing the answer.

'No,' Zac said.

'Yet it states it is a document that "defines a clear pathway for bridging the global nature finance gap and to manage the significant risks of biodiversity loss to the global economy and public health",' I said, reading it out before adding, 'Sorry, maybe I'm being stupid, but do you mean to say that the problem of biodiversity loss has been effectively solved and therefore, so has climate change, and the government is just ignoring it?' I asked.

'Yes,' he replied, his eyes burning with exasperation. 'This plan, that got as far as government policy, along with The

Leaders Pledge for Nature, which I believe is the most radical and thoughtful manifesto for nature that has ever been created, demonstrates how we can restore the natural world and by doing so, our own future.'

Only Zac's energy and care stopped the conversation from being the bleakest I had ever had. 'I think some people see green issues as meaning we have to all cut everything out, that it's some big virtue-signalling party for do-gooders, but it's not true. We just need to find a balance that comes with investing properly to make changes and plans that go beyond short-sighted elections,' he explained. 'If it wasn't absolutely necessary and doable, some of the poorest nations wouldn't be the biggest advocates for nature restoration, but they are, because they are on the frontline and they can see for themselves it is the answer.'

Zac lingered next to his exquisite sculpture of bronze hummingbirds. 'Net zero is a tiny part of the story. It doesn't matter how many solar panels we stick up, if we lose the Congo or Amazon or the great forests of Indonesia, it is game over. It really is as simple as that. There is no technological substitute for the extraordinarily complex ecosystems we all depend on. The Congo produces more than half of Africa's rainfall. If we lose it, we will see a humanitarian disaster of biblical levels and a refugee crisis we couldn't even begin to solve. A climate plan that doesn't have nature at its heart is not a credible plan.'

Zac's words had stung like the wind on my face now as I walked outside, watching the peregrine who had resumed her position in the sky, the heart in the bushes still beating, escaped. What was agonising was the realisation that Zac and many other politicians across the world do care and the government was still floundering on the vital progress he and others had made. It was a horrible truth.

Suddenly I let out a wail. I filled my lungs, arched my back and wailed a low-pitched scream of despair. My ears rang with the effort but my voice was swallowed up by the crashing waves, the remnants collected by the gale, flung out across the peregrine's territory.

Chapter 14

The Campaign Club

Spring equinox came. Still no word from Michael Gove. The birds woke the dawn quicker, carolling the day by singing. The ivy glistened in the rain-soaked hedgerow where I fed the farmland birds, and above me the fluttering specks of skylarks poured their notes onto the landscape, their voices carrying twenty times clearer at nighttime. I watched the flock feeding, the chaffinches mingling with the reed buntings who always stood taller, as though their reed habitat had improved their posture. Intermixed were the yellowhammers, like threads of gold.

The first blackcaps and chiffchaffs arrived, 8-gram birds who had flown all the way back from North Africa to sing with gusto in these hedgerows. I bathed in song, cocooned in their avian world. But this ecstasy was forever tainted. This was the first dawn chorus I had heard with a knowledge of politics, a topic that I had never understood to be directly related. As I listened, the part of me that was afraid and overwhelmed half wished I didn't know what I had found out. Naively, before I started my campaign, I thought that the problems facing nature came about because politicians didn't have the budget or simply didn't know about certain issues. Along with Zac's insight, that left me with the burning question of 'Why is it all like this?'; what Dominic Dyer told me left my rose-tinted glasses stomped on and shattered into a million pieces.

Dominic Dyer, alongside Chris Packham, is Britain's best-known animal rights campaigner, perhaps most famously associated with badgers. Dominic is energetic, switched on and frank, and comes with a background that gives him a useful contextual insight: during the late 1980s and 1990s he worked as a civil servant on environmental issues ranging from animal welfare to marine pollution, food manufacturing and agricultural commodity issues within the EU. He helped deliver New Labour's animal rights campaign to stop fur farms and animal testing. In 2002 he was coaxed away from the government, poached by a food and drink lobby group that would pay through the nose for his inside knowledge and wealth of connections before being poached for more money into an agricultural lobby group.

As we drank beers in a pub in Oxford, I asked him what working in a lobby group was like, hoping to glean some insight that might help me navigate my campaign.

'It was all about assessing opportunity versus threat, always from a monetary point of view,' he said, summing up the system. 'Everything I did was about how to create more – more yield and therefore more profit. This often conflicts with environmental issues to the point where politicians and civil servants are programmed to dismiss them for fear of risking a price increase of something, normally food. The lobby groups play this card to their advantage all the time. I know this because I did it.'

To my horror, I listened to Dominic explain how he had successfully lobbied the government not to ban neonicotinoids in 2008. At the time, the EU was decreasing pesticide use because scientific studies had shown that neonicotinoids were decimating insects. Neonicotinoids make pollinators unable to navigate, suppress their immune response, lower their sperm viability and shorten their lifespans before eventually killing them. From the farmer's point of view, neonicotinoids work well because they kill a wide variety of insects and they're not contact-based but systematic. Water soluble, they are absorbed into seeds as they grow, making the plant itself toxic to the insects: all of it from flowers and leaves to nectar and pollen. Toxic pollen then disperses, landing on new ground, poisoning it too. They also make soil toxic, leaving the target area free of insects. From a crop point of view, whole swathes of farmland can be insect-free. The cost of insect-free crops is that the neonicotinoids transfer poison into us too. Scientific studies prove we are extensively exposed to neonicotinoids, which in turn are linked to renal, insulin, glucose, testosterone and semen issues, and cancer. Neonicotinoids have been registered in more than 120 countries. According to the GMI, the neonicotinoid pesticide market was valued at around $5.1 billion in 2023 and is expected to witness over 5.4 per cent compound annual growth rate between 2024 and 2032. In Britain, two-thirds of the country is a death trap for insects in order for farmers to create the biggest yields for the best prices . . . for us.

Dominic explained how during the 2000s, pesticides were being tirelessly campaigned against by a solo campaigner, Georgina Downs, a singer-songwriter in her twenties. Having become chronically ill due to pesticides being sprayed near her rural home in Sussex, Georgina had founded the UK Pesticides Campaign in 2001, which successfully influenced the EU legislation through the inclusion of residents as a 'vulnerable group'. After seven years of campaigning, in November 2008 Georgina took the government to court and won. It was a landmark victory, the high court ruling that she had produced 'solid evidence' that residents exposed to chemicals used to spray crops had suffered harm. In his ruling, Mr Justice Collins highlighted that the 1986 Control of Pesticides Regulations states that beekeepers must be given forty-eight hours' notice if pesticides harmful to bees are to be used. The judge said, 'It is difficult to see why residents should be in a worse position.'

However, in July 2009, Defra appealed and won, the court overturning the previous ruling. In reaction, the CEO of a big lobby group said the judgement was a victory for common sense, stating, 'Without pesticides to keep weed, pest and disease pressures in check, crop yields would fall by around a third, something we can ill afford at a time of heightened concern about food security and population growth.'

'The CEO was me,' Dominic said.

I stared at him, gobsmacked. This was a man I knew because he had acted on *behalf* of wildlife.

'It was my job,' he said, nodding in acknowledgement of my appalled reaction.

He explained that following issues raised by Georgina Downs, the UK's environment minister at the time, Hilary Benn, was very much intending to follow the EU's decisions to decrease or ban the chemical entirely.

'Just like it had been my job to stop formidable campaigners such as Georgina Downs, it was my job to stop Hilary Benn from banning the very lucrative pesticides. I had to find an angle that would persuade the government not to follow the EU. It was easy. It was the age-old food security/cost-of-living threat: the price of potatoes would go through the roof and the public would start hating the government.'

'And it worked,' I sighed.

'Yes,' he said. 'Within days, I received a letter from the prime minister himself, Gordon Brown, personally assuring me that the government acknowledged the food security risk and would not go ahead with the ban.'

Dominic explained how the prime minister had also responded to the All-Party Parliamentary Group on Science and Technology in Agriculture saying he shared the industry's concerns communicated through the *Farmers Weekly* campaign Save Our Sprays.

I shook my head in disbelief.

'It's how it works. The trade lobby groups dictate the prices and want to keep their profit margins, and they will use any tactic necessary to maintain their growth, including threatening press releases that will scaremonger the public. These companies make billions, so they have enough money to protect us all, but it's not in their interest, nor, clearly, is it in the government's interest,' Dominic said.

'Even when the government is presented with scientific evidence?' I replied, finding this new truth almost impossible to accept.

'This is what you're up against, Hannah,' he said. 'You've got to think about two things: the lobby groups which the housebuilding industry are famous for, and the government itself. You've got to work out *where* the problem lies or, more usefully, *who* has a problem with your ask. If it's not directly related to money, it will be indirectly related. Or it might just be that the civil servants and advisors have been programmed to flick away anything environmental so as not to burden the industry, which comes back round to money one way or the other.'

I tried to process what Dominic was telling me.

'You've just got to keep at it. Stay energetic. Push your argument. Find the barriers. Work the angles. Look ahead – think about a strategy for a year's time as well as now because Labour will be in power. Labour will have one main filter in their head: the price of a chicken. They will be governed by this, ensuring that all decisions made will never increase the price of a chicken. Keep your bum to the fire. Be unpredictable. You are making a colossal impact.' Dominic was energetic, focused, fox-like.

I sighed, inadvertently slumping my head on the table for a second, half hearing his solid advice about lobbying Labour, feeling exhausted by the thought.

'I know it's hard. I've spent many a night finding myself crying as I try to get to sleep,' he said.

'What made you switch sides?' I asked.

'When I was working alongside the National Farmers' Union on pesticide policy, my employers made it very clear to me that I should not raise concerns about the NFU lobbying the government to increase the cull of badgers, even though I was chair of a wildlife protection charity that had campaigned for decades against the killing of badgers over bovine TB in cattle. The plan I was supposed to leave unchallenged eventually cost £100 million of taxpayers' money and killed 500,000 badgers despite no peer-reviewed evidence that culling badgers reduces bovine TB in cattle, and despite culls being ineffective.'

He paused, taking another sip of his drink. 'I couldn't do it. I was walking back from the pub late one night in London and a badger crossed my path. Beautiful, and managing to exist even in our capital city, ironically less at risk there than in farmland. This badger, and all badgers, were being persecuted because they didn't have a monetary value. They had no value in their own right. I know I had been incentivised by money and the status of being a CEO "in bed with the enemy" but the badger made me stop and think. The badger confronted me with my own accountability.'

'So a single badger turned you into a wildlife advocate?' I asked.

'Something like that,' Dominic said, smiling.

Giving me a hug as we said goodbye, he said, 'Never give up, Hannah, you are winning.'

My head spun. I had never thought my little swift-brick campaign would end up in me discovering information like this. My mind returned to the phrase 'food security' as I thought about its complex meaning. Through Farmland Bird Aid Network I had got to know Ian Wilkinson, a leading regenerative farming advocate. He had transformed a local farm into a demo farm – FarmED – that has a learning hub. Here the team engage farmers, policymakers and anyone interested, with the agroecological farming techniques that help make soils more productive, minimise the use of agrochemicals and pollution, and enhance crop diversity. When it came to the diversity of farmland birds alone, surveys conducted on FarmED land showed a rise from forty-four to eighty-four species between 2014 (when the farm had been bought) and 2020, a clear display of solutions that did not involve chemicals. I had seen with my own eyes how wildlife could prosper at the same time as crops, resulting in poison-free produce.

On the bus back home, I searched online for more information about pesticides and herbicides, thinking about the farmland flock and the swifts and how so much of nature recovery depended on living without these chemicals. There was little point managing to secure nesting habitat for birds who then risked starving to extinction. Insect restoration had been put on my to-do list by so many supporters, but I wondered whether they had any idea what they were requesting I went up against. As other passengers played Candy Crush and scrolled through social media, I researched glyphosate, the world's most widely used weedkiller. It's a product that many farmers use in order to reliably provide us food at an affordable price, but the discoveries I made about the cost of this product to our health rocked me to my core.

The European Food Safety Authority (EFSA) assures consumers glyphosate is safe. So does Defra, stating its approval process of the chemical is to 'protect the health of people, creatures and plants and to safeguard the environment', reassuring us all that glyphosate 'has been approved as safe and efficacious for a number of years now'.

If it is safe, then I suppose it doesn't matter that a Soil Association study conducted by Defra in 2015 showed that 1 million hectares of UK cereals were being sprayed with glyphosate, resulting in nearly a third of bread tested containing traces of the chemical. Friends of the Earth tested the urine of volunteers from European countries in the same year. Out of the ten volunteers in the UK, seven of them had traces of glyphosate, and it had been found in the breast milk of German women.

However, a paper published in the *Entropy* journal explained how the safety assurances about glyphosate by the EFSA didn't give the whole picture because it is a chemical rarely used on its own. Many of the tests were done on just glyphosate – not on the cocktail of formulations – conducted by the product-maker and corporate giant Bayer. Toxic formulations – petroleum-based compounds such as arsenic, nickel, chromium and lead – above the admissible levels in water showed up in toxicology reports but when glyphosate was looked at in isolation, these poisons were omitted, even though the chemical cocktails were part of the product. The paper went on to state the diseases linked to the toxins found in pesticides, including (but not limited to) liver disease, cancer, cachexia, developmental and fertility problems, Parkinson's disease, multiple sclerosis, autism, Alzheimer's disease, zinc deficiency, bowel disease, obesity, cardiovascular disease, heart failure, permanent developmental immunotoxicity leading to later development of allergies, asthma, autoimmune diseases and mood disorders including depression. The report's conclusion stated, 'Glyphosate is likely to be pervasive in our food supply, and, contrary to being essentially nontoxic, it may in fact be the most biologically disruptive chemical in our environment.'

I looked around the bus. So much of biodiversity loss was linked to chemicals but the connection to our poor health was news to me. Did anyone else have any idea about any of this? If they didn't, would they be appalled if they found out? Did farmers know? Did the policymakers know? Did any of them check or read the incredibly long leaflets stuck onto the back of chemical products, printed in tiny font? Did any farmers think that the government had it in hand? Did our government challenge the product makers? Had I been alone in thinking that the politicians would do everything they could to keep us all fundamentally safe and healthy because they too lived in the same society, bringing their own children up in it? When I got home, I saw another warning waiting for me like a Trojan horse in the form of the mundane shape of a Fairy Liquid bottle. It told anyone who cared out of the 13 million British households who bought 150 million bottles of it a year, in plain sight, to stop using it through its own label that states, 'Harmful to aquatic life with long-lasting effects.'

I felt like I had been sleepwalking through my whole life. Not only had I been naive to the existence of lobby groups but I had no idea the food we ate could be poisoning us. I sought Georgina Downs out, wanting to learn from her experience.

'I knew nothing about politics when I began,' she said via email. 'I genuinely thought at the beginning that if I provided the evidence to politicians, the government and its advisors and regulators would immediately take action, knowing that millions of rural residents' health was at risk from the continual spraying of poisons near homes, schools, children's playgrounds. How wrong I was. Successive governments have only protected the multi-billion-pound pesticides industry and big farming unions whose primary concern is ensuring the continued sales and use of pesticides and will fight tooth and nail against anyone who threatens that.'

When I asked her how she kept going, she explained, 'Not only are these toxic chemicals in our air, our water and our wider environment, they are being used on our food. If people really knew what is being sprayed on food in the process of growing it, I think more people would be demanding food free of such poison which would then free residents from it too.'

The risk of being poisoned was her bottom line. Mine was the swifts' existence, which was fundamentally linked to pesticide use.

When I explained to Margaret what I had learned over a cup of tea, she almost spilled hers, horrified too.

'And there was I thinking that eating meat and food imported from countries thousands of miles away was bad for the environment. I never thought to consider British grub being such a cause for concern, not just for wildlife but also for us,' she said numbly.

'I had no idea the fight for a brick would unveil all this mess. How can we trust the government? How do we make sure nature restoration is actually taken seriously? How do we begin?' I asked, bewildered.

'Do you ever wish you hadn't started this campaign?' Margaret asked, uncharacteristically quietly.

It was a question that I had asked myself so many times that it had become my personal, secret elephant in the room.

'All the time, in a way,' I replied. 'I've put all my effort into this for eighteen months and for what? I haven't achieved the law change and instead I've discovered how complex so much of nature recovery is. But the thing is, I made the promise to the birds because I meant it. I said I would do everything I can to save them and I will. I just didn't think it would be this hard.'

Margaret didn't reply to start with. She just stared at me, contemplating. Then she said, 'I think we all need to find a way to begin. We have to start somewhere and you have done that, with bells on.'

Conservationists were steadily making progress to shift government priorities to help nature recover. It was Richard Benwell who had first cooked up the idea of what had become the groundbreaking Environment Act. He, together with his team, Rose Dickinson and Paul McNamee, had sat together in a pub in Westminster and come up with a draft bill. Working with the RSPB and The Wildlife Trusts, they produced a policy paper to bring the mapping idea to the table. The Nature Bill was tabled by none other than Lord Randall as a private members' bill in 2015. Years passed in which negotiation and evolution led to Lord Krebs tabling an amendment, which Richard wrote with Matt Shardlow from Buglife, working with lots of the Greener UK partners at the time. The result was the government's draft Environment Bill, which gradually got closer to the original vision for the Nature Bill. Six years after Lord Randall's PMB, with the help of Zac Goldsmith as a Defra minister, it became law in 2021. It may never have happened without Brexit. The secretary of state for Defra embraced it with open arms when faced with the political imperative after Brexit to replace the important environmental functions that had been carried out by the EU Commission and courts. Almost all the people who had hatched this brilliant plan, I knew; some of them key to me and the birds, including the secretary of state at that time, who, ironically, was Michael Gove.

Richard Benwell had continued to be critical to the ongoing nature restoration in the UK, with Wildlife and Countryside Link's Nature 2030 campaign at the forefront of this aim. It proposed to help the government reach its goals to halt the loss of wildlife and manage 30 per cent of the land and sea for nature by 2030 with five policies: a pay rise for farmers, doubling their support to make sure that they can deliver nature-friendly farming and nature restoration; making polluters pay, ensuring that businesses have nature and climate plans in place and setting new duties to drive private investment in species and habitat recovery; making more space for nature by restoring more protected sites and landscapes by 2030, and creating a Public Nature Estate across England with the support of local and national partners; creating more green jobs in urban, rural and coastal habitats, and in species recovery through a National Nature Service delivering wide-scale habitat restoration; and a right to a healthy environment – establishing a human right to clean air and water and access to nature.

Each one was robustly thought through by teams within teams of nature advocates. At the heart of this enormous task, Richard remained brimming with energy for change: an atomic bomb for good with genteel manners, dressed in a suit. I met Richard for a catch-up in a pub in Oxford, and asked him why he had committed to nature restoration.

'Because of a magpie's jumble of bright moments which turned into my identity as a nature campaigner,' he explained. 'There was never a blueprint. There was the day my grandfather passed on his ancient, battered binoculars; the brilliant teacher who showed me hawfinches and water rails near the centre of Birmingham; noticing the contrast of the diesel-belching bus home or the debris along the canal sides, where cheese-and-onion crisp packets tried to outshine a kingfisher.'

He talked about how the hope-filled news of the Kyoto Protocol had been an eye-opening time for him – a boy of fourteen then; he had thought it amazing that the whole world could agree on a treaty that would reshape human behaviour to avoid catastrophic climate change. 'What hope for humanity that people could agree to change their lifestyles now to avert a danger decades away!' he said. 'Realising political change could take decades came more slowly, but with it came conviction to be part of the solution,' he added, his voice moving up and down in pitch as he focused on the hope, then back to the reality of how hard political change is.

'Winning the world's first legally binding target for nature recovery with the Environment Act was just 5 per cent of the battle – the next six years will be the campaign to make sure it happens, because the government are currently not adhering to it which means the government is on track to break their own law.'

This grapple for a healthy environment was at the heart of another campaigner's aim too: James Wallace, who had become another mentor. Like a relay, James picked up much of what Richard and Dominic had told me about the battle to change governance. He gave me more insight into the Pandora's box I had opened for myself, naively thinking in the same way as Georgina had, that if the government knew, they would act.

James, a co-founder of Beaver Trust, is now the CEO of River Action. He was calling out Thames Water for the excessive amounts of E. coli found in the River Thames, and confronting the pollution in the River Wye thanks to chicken shit run-off. The Wye valley is the chicken factory farm capital of Europe, with hundreds of intensive poultry units (IPUs), often with hundreds of thousands of birds in each, comprising 23 million chickens at any one time – about 25 per cent of UK poultry production. That means 20-million-plus chickens' worth of chicken shit. It has to go somewhere, so the farmers spread it all over the fields because it is a precious fertiliser. The problem is chickens poo all year round, so the farmers spread the poo all year round, even during the winter when there are no crops (and far fewer hedgerows) and this causes run-off. The chicken poo run-off, full of phosphorus, ends up in the river, changes the chemical balance in the water and makes it toxic.

The government regulator, the Environment Agency (EA), should have been enforcing the law to stop this but they weren't.

What's more, the government *could* have been incentivising farmers by giving generous grants for sustainable slurry storage. The government *could* have been scaling up buffer zones such as the Woodlands for Water scheme, a coalition of conservation organisations, including Beaver Trust supported by Defra, aiming to create 3,150 hectares of trees in six river-catchment areas from Cornwall to Cumbria. But they hadn't. So James Wallace and River Action had acted. Their campaigns to save Britain's rivers had been headline news for months, leading with humour with slogans such as 'If you give a sh*t do something about it!' and 'This is Sh*t!!' But behind the engaging poo-themed videos, there was a deadly serious issue, culminating in legal action where River Action took the EA and the government to court. During the judicial review in February 2024, the KC speaking on behalf of River Action said that there was indisputable evidence that the Wye was in an 'ecological crisis', with the single biggest contributor being agricultural run-off, highlighting that the EA had failed to enforce the law, quantified by 31 per cent of farm inspections between January 2020 and October 2023, found to breach regulations yet suffered zero consequences.

'Anything to do with the agricultural lobby groups?' I asked, as we sat down, neither of us fond of small talk.

'Quite possibly. They have been pushing for deregulation to help maximise productivity and increase profit and market share of the large food and agriculture corporations,' James said, adding, 'Problem is, these lobby groups call themselves the voice of farmers, when actually they are the mouthpiece of multi-billion-pound agrichemical and intensive agriculture interests. It's similar to the water industry – or sewage pollution industry – where powerful internationally owned corporations profit from pollution, rather than invest in their leaky infrastructure.'

'By the way, is there a name for this corruption?' I asked.

James nodded. 'Regulatory Capture,' he replied.

'Regulatory Capture,' he continued, 'is a much-denied strategy of corporations to "capture" and influence – stifle and silence – the regulatory powers of a government, like ours, which results in further enriching of the rich and powerful at the cost of the public, customers and nature. These corporate giants and lobby groups, whether it be the big agribusinesses or water companies, have invisible back channels with a government and negotiate the split between what we as taxpayers and customers pay and what their shareholders pay – usually nothing. In the case of the water industry, they have taken more out in profits and executive pay than invested in cleaning up their shit since privatisation over thirty years ago. It's the same for all industries, including the notorious housebuilding lobbyists that you're up against.'

Housebuilding lobby groups like the Home Builders Federation have been accused of creating the 'housing crisis' by sitting on land without building – 'landbanking' – in order to sell it on for more profit. Most of the time, the housebuilders, some of whom were prominent governing party donors, got what they claimed the industry needed, incentivised by their own bonuses that were awarded in their multi-millions.

But as well as telling me the outrageous realities, James's energy focused on the solutions. James had created systems to restore nature that, if implemented and enforced, would work not just for the rest of nature but for us too. His attention had been focused on wildlife – including beavers – and rivers because they were so systemically important. From food production and industry to schools and hospitals, everyone needs abundant, clean and healthy water.

'What is more important than the lifeblood of our land? Both beavers and rivers are just that, and protecting things that keep us safe makes the most sense to me.'

He spoke so enthusiastically he almost sounded as if he were singing. His reasoning flowed out of him and, eyes bright, he explained how Britain and Europe were once covered by beaver wetlands made by these ultimate ecosystem engineers.

'They are a totem for life. Who else creates whole wetland habitats full of food, water and habitats? No other species does that,' he said, a hint of pride in his voice at the official allegiance with the wild he had carved out.

He co-founded Beaver Trust in 2019 with a group of friends. Beaver Trust brought together big stakeholders, ranging from the big NGOs to regulators like Natural England and Defra, landowners and anglers, to discuss and agree on a future for beavers. That led to the creation of the English Beaver Strategy written by James and colleagues, supported by dozens of collaborating organisations, and finally amended and adopted by the government as the national strategy for beavers. By working with the cross-sectoral stakeholders and diverse groups and communities, Beaver Trust managed to get a landmark achievement, making beavers recognised as a native species and protected in England. Then James turned his attention to the habitats themselves – rivers – because they haven't had enough systemic protection and restoration. Quite the opposite: our rivers in Britain are in just about the worst state of anywhere in Europe, thanks to a chemical cocktail of sewage, manure, microplastics, pharmaceuticals and recreational drugs. Since rivers need every element of a community to collaborate in restoring them, the silver lining is that rivers can and are bringing communities together. River Action was doing just that.

My understanding of the nature crisis expanded far beyond my own campaign, the breadth of insight creating a political context that felt impossible to win against. Yet here was James, still scrapping and simultaneously trying to heal and unite, encouraging me to do the same.

'How did you get here? Why is it *you* doing this weird dance of fighting *and* helping the government and not someone else?' I asked, curious.

James explained how he had been the odd one out and had been bullied at school, instead finding a natural affinity with nature: the sanctuary of the wild. But his nascent connection with nature hadn't been enough to save him from dark times that led him to substance addiction and a stint on the streets.

'You wouldn't know it by looking at me now, but I was a punk. I had piercings, a Mohican and I was falling apart,' he said.

Fast forward a few years and James was enrolling in a Holistic Science degree, studying systems theory and ecology, giving him direction and purpose. 'It left me with the question of "how I can bring about change?" Change in everything – all of our systems from food, farming, energy, everything,' he explained. 'I'm still a punk rocker but now I live by the rules, poking the government, calling them out for breaking their own laws.'

By focusing on systems, James looked at problems holistically, able to see the complex overview as well as the detail.

'And how do you cope?' I asked, admitting I was struggling, wondering how someone who was engaged in multiple legal battles with the government, who was subject to repeated online abuse, who was in the middle of fighting this reality, was not brimming with despair.

His answer left me in tears.

'My wife, Becca, died a year ago from cancer. She was ill for ten years and it was unbearable. I am now a single parent with two girls to protect and nurture.'

He paused and got out his phone to read me a poem he had written. 'I think you will understand. I want you to hear it.'

The six-verse poem was beautiful despite bursting with violent, graphic, all-encompassing grief. James's words put me in a trance but instead of feeling awkward or full of sorrow, there was a release, a liberation of sorts, summed up by the poem's final sentence, 'Scatter my life in all that lives.'

I looked at him. Here was a man who had endured his love being ripped away from him and his daughters in slow motion.

'Compared to losing Becca, the stress and despair of fighting the government and corrupt corporations is nothing, right?' I said.

'Yes,' he replied.

'And are you committed to nature restoration because we are a part of nature and because if you don't, we will all lose it too?' I asked, tentatively, worrying I was overstepping the mark.

He nodded. 'Between us, we can and *will* make them change. We have to.'

James's achievements were something to stop and examine and take hope from. Despite having to go up against the richest lobby groups, Beaver Trust had successfully reintroduced beavers and got the government to make them a European Protected Species. River Action had raised public awareness of river pollution to an all-time high. James and his colleagues and many collaborators had proved that rivers and beavers were the perfect conduit to mobilise people and give hope and purpose to whole communities to demand change to secure our future. James was living proof, in the flesh, looking me in the eye, that hard work and perpetual effort paid off. He showed how anyone who wanted it badly enough and could channel their hopes and dreams into strategic, viable, proposed solutions could save nature. Britain needed more beavers, and it also needed more James Wallaces.

A man with grit and love and sense, as a fellow campaigner, albeit far ahead of me, James understood why I was trying so hard for birds. We sat there a moment, quiet, intense.

'I really love swifts,' I replied, tears brimming.

'I know you do. It's the first thing anyone notices about you,' James said, smiling.

Later that afternoon, on my way home, I got off the bus and went straight to the fields, on a sudden pilgrimage to seek out the farmland flock. Across the fields, in the rain, I tramped, processing what James had told me. On the Salt Way I sat in a dip in the ground, halfway into the hedge, watching the farmland flock congregate, foraging for the seed I had put down that morning. Two hundred souls, feasting. The lone male yellowhammer was still there. Bright in his spring plumage, he stood tall when the others dashed for cover as a small flock of starlings dispersed, like a scattering of sequins lit up by the intermittent sunshine. A year ago he had reminded me to stand steadfast. He had managed to survive talons of kestrels and hawks others had not. He had survived storms and drought, heatwaves and snowdrifts, small and mighty. He was the splendid, singing sun.

Overhead, there were other feathered talismans. I walked on for miles, following not a route but a single sound: skylarks. In the organic farmland they were everywhere; in the neighbouring farm, the sky was an empty block of silence: a harsh line of life and death, of prosperity and doom. I watched the closest one soar upwards before stopping in the air, hovering. Opening his wings out, he positioned himself for a second before bursting into song. Others joined him in their own spaces of sky, suspended in light that cast no shadow like stars. Without warning, the nearest one dropped to the ground, a quiet dot in the vast field. I kept hold of his position, knowing that if I blinked, he would become invisible like a needle in a haystack, yet his presence dominated the landscape. Here was another heartbeat intent on thrumming loud enough to hear, able to snap attention away from even the biggest space. There was sunshine and the first blue sky of the year. I tilted my head back and closed my eyes as I walked, the sun warm on my face. I basked. All around me the skylarks sang. James's love for his beloved wife and our mutual love for the wild merged into the sound of the skylarks, who sang back to me as if reciting Shelley's poem 'To a Skylark':

> Teach me half the gladness
> That thy brain must know,
> Such harmonious madness
> From my lips would flow,
> The world should listen then, as I am listening now.

Above, hope reigned the skies in song. A song that would soon coax the sun to shine and the grass to grow and the house martins, swallows and swifts back into the fold of home. The little feathered dot climbed higher, fuelled by the future and the promise of spring, despite the hardship and obstacles of a bleak winter. Despite everything that skylarks had lost, his little oh-so-resilient frame persevered energetically, embracing the moment while preparing for the future. The Latin name for skylark is *alauda*, from the Gaulish word *alawda* meaning 'tuft', linked to the tiny Mohican skylarks have. I smiled: James was the skylark. Just like James, these birds were punk rockers surveying the whole landscape holistically, calling for a future, lobbying *me* with prose and song to keep going.

Chapter 15

Underdogs

By March, there had still been no word from Michael Gove, or any acknowledgement or decision from the government since that early-February meeting. I had collected crumbs of knowledge indicating Michael Gove's decision-making process. Zac had ensured that he had seen all the news coverage of the campaign, but Michael Gove hinted at 'complications', which no one understood to what he was referring, and he had not responded formally. I had gone into Parliament several times to meet politicians, seeking their advice and hatching plans, and a core group of seven Conservative politicians that included a former housing minister and former secretary of state for Defra had sent a collective letter to Michael Gove. He hadn't replied. The SLN and the local swift group remained unfalteringly supportive but were left perplexed. Everyone was out of ideas. When I went round to Sylvia's for lunch, she was pensive, looking out of the window at the wren flitting over the drystone wall.

'Doesn't he get it?' she said. 'For some people, urban birds are precious, precious companions; to many they are all that is left of life. They are first and last memories. They are both casual and vital doses of joy who remind the old and the young, the weak and the strong, that we all share this planet and we are all still here, embracing another day, together.'

I was glad of Sylvia's anger because within it lay the truth at the core of my campaign, and a few days later, this truth was presented to me in the form of a nestling dunnock who had been kidnapped by a neighbour's cat. Although the bird was uninjured, it was displaced so, unaware of where it had come from and knowing it was too young to fend for itself, suddenly I was agreeing to adopt it. Collecting it in a small basket, I returned to my house, now a surrogate bird mother. Again. The likelihood was that the bird would die within twenty-four hours, but there was a chance I would be taking care of it for several weeks. I sighed at the thought of 12 million cats in the UK, many without the colourful collars with bells proven to give birds a much better chance of escape.

Auburn and speckled, the dunnock looked at me with its wide eyes and baby beak, crouched on its long spindly legs, unmoving. There's a particular 'look' baby birds have – one of being resigned to wait for their parents to come back and usher them somewhere, to feed them, to reclaim them in some way. The bird was cold and I didn't have a heat mat, so I put it under my shirt on my collar bone, a place the finch I had raised liked. Accepting of its new circumstances, the dunnock nuzzled down.

The dunnock didn't die. I used the table as a makeshift pen, wrapping the sides in mesh so the dunnock had a creche, complete with branches and logs, so under the table simulated being under a bush. Robin, not surprised to have another bird in our life, stepped around the garden kitchen. I dug up worms from the garden, apologising as I cut them up, and used tweezers to feed the bird, who ate them greedily, opening its mouth just as soon as it had swallowed the last mouthful.

Working on editing books at home meant I could easily feed the dunnock throughout the day, mostly leaving it alone, not wanting it to become too dependent on me, which it didn't. Its wild streak was strong, only coming to me for food, hopping towards me in a rush of legs and brown feathers, bright-eyed, open-mouthed, closing its eyes as it swallowed. Dashing back into the little kitchen bush, its legs scurried to a low perch. Then its eyes rolled closed, overwhelmingly tired after its feed. Head lolled, legs crouched, it snoozed, its little brown body so soft, so camouflaged within the branches I had brought inside.

When it was awake, most of its time was spent shimmying along the branches, pecking at thrips and aphids, only partially interested in the seeds I had scattered. This, too, was a bird who needed insects to survive – not exclusively, but still necessary, especially for the early-development stages, the need for a healthy insect population so clear through its amber eyes. I picked some off a garden rose, thankful for the aphids that I hadn't killed with chemicals, and the dunnock tucked in, its hunting instincts improving daily.

I made a pen outside so it was surrounded by other birds and could begin the rewilding process. A fortnight later, the dunnock was restless, eager to exit the pen and try its luck in the wild. We devised a luxury set-up: the bird was wild, with all the freedom and the risks that came with it, but when I opened the door and chirped, it appeared within the vine or the wall outside the kitchen door. Keeping a pot of wax worms with their pollen feed, I tossed a few out for the dunnock and every time the same thing happened: it caught my eye to tell me it was ready for me to throw its food. Gobbling the caterpillars up, it would then scamper back into the undergrowth of its garden territory, never going too far. Despite our differences, we could communicate successfully. We could form a trusted bond. We could learn from each other. We could prove that small actions have a big impact. We could live in harmony.

In mid-March, I met up with Jemma in Parliament, heads together, trying to think about ways I could get to Michael Gove myself, finding out the members' clubs he frequented, and the friends he kept. I fantasised about getting stuck in a lift with him so I would be granted a private inescapable audience with the person who could put me and the birds out of our misery. When I found out that Lord Ed Vaizey, his friend from Oxford and best man at his wedding, had gone on to become a Tory MP and was now a peer with his own radio show, I emailed him. His radio producer emailed back, inviting me onto the Friday-night show for a ten-minute live interview at 9.30 p.m. I said yes, hoping that if I could persuade him to lobby his good mate, then maybe Michael Gove would finally concede.

In the foyer of The News Building, the enormous lobby wall has lots of words written across it, including the line 'sticking up for the little guy'. I had noticed the phrase when I had gone there for a live interview just before the petition debate. It felt even more prominent now. Clutching my swift brick, I entered the radio floor – open plan with a series of booths, the producers welcoming me with a glass of prosecco, ushering me into the studio. On-air, I launched into my now practised spiel. I had lost count how many times I had said it, but I was grateful to reach a new audience – not the listeners, but the peer himself. This time, I knew I needed to convince *him*. I hadn't paid £50 for a train ticket to London, knowing I would get back home at one in the morning, for a ten-minute slot on the radio. I had gratefully accepted the invitation in order to lobby Michael Gove's best man. In a three-minute break, I explained that Michael Gove had yet to decide.

'Look, he's ghosting me and Zac Goldsmith, despite a whole load of Tories urging him to do it,' I said. 'He is well aware of the proposal,' I added. 'All he has to do is greenlight it.'

'I'll message him now,' he replied kindly, his air casual in contrast to my fun façade that was laced with growing desperation.

This is what I had wanted, immediately grateful. The adverts stopped and the segment moved onto another guest. I waited. Another light-hearted chat ran and then there was another advert break.

Lord Vaizey checked his phone. 'Michael's just replied. He says, "Why should I mandate swift bricks?"'

'Why should he mandate swift bricks?' I said in disbelief.

As the radio jingles were broadcast, I thought about the answer to that question and how much time, effort and money I had spent on the democratic process of earning the right to explain exactly why Michael Gove, as the secretary of state for the DLUHC, should mandate swift bricks. The public-facing campaign was the tip of the iceberg. Yes, I had bared my naked body, twice, and managed the consequences, but I had also sent over 4,000 emails, been to over twenty-five in-person meetings and countless video calls. I had passed the test that the government as a whole, and then Michael Gove specifically, had set. I had got public support, NGOs' support, government advisors' support, political support, foreign political and scientific support. Even some housebuilders had supported, but for reasons unknown, not Michael Gove.

Lord Vaizey made some funny quip on-air about Easter, reminding me it had been almost a year since the petition had successfully reached the 100,000-signature mark. As I sat there, I wondered why the government invited members of the public to embark on a journey to engage with them. It seemed so ironic since Michael Gove was a man *we* had elected. I felt like I had become the embodiment of the swifts and that we were the archetypal underdog, except this wasn't a sports match we were pitched to lose; this was our life, my existence trapped within the swifts like a blood oath.

In an odd twist of fate, I found myself in a lift with Lord Vaizey, so I said what I would have said to Michael Gove had he been in the lift.

'Without mandating swift bricks, swifts have no future in this country. I just want to look you in the eye to make sure you accept that as a fact,' I said.

He looked me in the eye, nodded and said, 'Yes, I understand.'

I sounded half like a ranty environmentalist and half like a strict mother. I regretted it. No one reacts well to this sort of intensity. It was awkward and his polite lack of engagement made me feel like I was irking him. For him, I was a random, energetic, swift-obsessed woman who had pounced on him at the end of his late work shift. For me, this was an exchange I had hoped would help secure the swifts' existence. We were unmatched, the imbalance making me feel uncomfortable. I said goodbye under the huge lobby wall and its words 'sticking up for the little guy', watching him walk off into the night, my campaign hopes sinking into the darkness, a lost cause. It was a peculiar exchange to have late on a Friday evening, drunken groups of revellers milling about the underground as I made my way home.

At the station, among the people, were the ultimate urban birds: feral pigeons. I crouched down in a quiet corner and chirped, the birds looking round instantly. I got out my bag of oats that I carry everywhere just for them and tipped some out on the floor. Every time I had gone to Parliament, dressed in my smart clothes, I would crouch, sprinkling oats when I came across the pigeons. A small group of four came quickly, their necks pearlescent, impossibly beautiful in the strip-lit station. Edging towards me, they winced as someone walked past but they persisted, their movements of simultaneous tenacity and doubt reminding me of how I had navigated the last eighteen months of my life. My campaigning status had made me feel like a pest that night and in the weeks before it as time had dragged on. Even supporters were remarking how good it was that I was continuing to 'pester' the government, the line between tenacious and pest-like thinning. It was a horribly vulnerable and degrading label to feel, the silver lining being that I was in the same club as these birds.

The pigeons were so gentle, despite being ravaged by us: one had a gammy foot from something being caught around it, leaving just a yellow stub where pink toes should have been. It hobbled gratefully towards me as someone passed, unnecessarily shooing the pigeons away, while another person muttered, 'Disgusting birds.' Classed as vermin, all over the country their nesting habitat is blocked by netting or sharp metal spikes. We take no accountability for having tamed these birds. They are descendants of wild rock doves that we bred, turning them into domestic homing pigeons. Feral pigeons are the bird versions of the dogs and cats of our world that at some point we discarded to the street, and because their ancestors' homes were rocks and cliff edges, these birds have adapted to buildings. I looked at the handsome male, his neck bigger and puffed up so it looked like a technicolour Tudor ruff, his eyes dark and cautiously friendly. Quickly at ease with me, he stood between my feet, his shoulders relaxing in the shelter of someone he trusted not to kick him. I looked around at everyone, most there because of leisure, in friendship groups and couples waiting to go home. In this country we are, fundamentally, safe and I wondered whether anyone saw the link between this status and the birds surrounding us. Less than a hundred years ago, at the outbreak of the Second World War, thousands of pigeon fanciers gave their pigeons to the war effort to act as message carriers, seconded into the National Pigeon Service. Pigeons carried their messages either in special containers on their legs or small pouches looped over their backs. Thousands of servicemen's lives were saved by these birds, who flew often in extreme circumstances, nearly a quarter of a million pigeons serving this country. An elite squad of couriers, their work contributing to winning the war. (Swifts had inadvertently contributed too, their remarkable manoeuvrability in flight inspiring the design of fighter jets.) From saviours to vermin, we kicked them, shooed them, maimed them and blocked them from their homes while other countries celebrated their birds: in France, the summer migrations of swifts, swallows and martins are tracked on the evening news as part of the weather segment and for years cathedral bells in New Zealand were rung to celebrate the homecoming of godwits arriving after their non-stop 10,000-kilometre flight from the Arctic.

The value of the natural world has, historically, been considered far more by the Conservatives than any other political party but, ironically, it was among Labour politicians that the birds had found an unexpected advocate. In tandem with my obsessive focus on Michael Gove, I had also begun to lobby Labour. First I met Matthew Pennycook, the shadow minister of housing, together with the RSPB's CEO, Beccy Speight. Steadily, we presented the birds' case, shifting the minister's relatively but not completely open mind in a more promising direction. A particularly detail-orientated and practical politician, the shadow minister had taken on board what we had said and kept in touch. Labour had whipped for Zac's swift-brick amendment, the spokesperson for the shadow DLUHC, Baroness Taylor of Stevenage, becoming an unexpected champion – unexpected because she had admitted her first reaction to the amendment had been resistant.

I met her in the House of Lords. Sitting in the same tearoom I had first met Zac, we had a frank conversation about my campaign.

'I deal with housing, doing everything to ensure people without means have shelter and when I first saw Zac's amendment, I resented that people cared so passionately about birds when there are so many human issues that so urgently need to be addressed,' she said. 'But then I thought about how actually these things needn't compete. We can look out for people and nature, and our urban planning, if it is to be sustainable, needs to include nature.'

I looked at the baroness in recognition of what she represents. As the shadow spokesperson for the DLUHC and the opposition whip, and with a career founded in local government, she deals with an array of fundamentally pressing issues. These include social-housing reform to address the 1.2 million households on local authority waiting lists and the 11,000-plus women living in refuges every year, reminding me how broad and completely unrelated to nature the DLUHC is.

Ultimately, as a member of the DLUHC, the baroness was at the heart of one of the most important parts of our lives – shelter – yet she had the grace and foresight to have room in her political breath to include swifts too. In support of Zac's amendment, she had stood in the House of Lords representing Labour and the DLUHC and said, 'We believe that specifically including swift bricks as a measure to be incorporated in planning law is justified because of the unique nature of these precious birds' nesting habits. They add to the biodiversity of urban areas, and I am particularly keen that we support that. I grew up as a townie and the swifts and house martins were a real feature of my childhood. Their decline has been very visible and sad to see. If there is anything we can do to either halt that decline or hopefully turn it around, we should certainly do so. There is definitely a clear and present threat to these species. We hope the government will accept this relatively small step, which could make a world of difference to protecting our swift population, and that it will not be necessary for the noble lord, Lord Goldsmith, to divide the House – but I hope he knows he has our full support in this amendment.'

When she reiterated this support in person six months later, I felt like there might be a far-off chance for swifts thanks to this politician who had the vision to include nature alongside people in her authority. Maybe it would be Labour who would bring the sun for the swifts. Maybe the political party most associated with urban environments would end up championing urban birds. Maybe Labour's tagline 'Let's Get Britain's Future Back' included swifts. The problem was that it was March and there would be no more votable orders of business until after the general election, which would be several months later.

Baroness Taylor gave me a spring in my step, the tangible hope shared with Jemma, whom I met immediately after in the Strangers' Dining Room in the House of Commons, excitedly debriefing her. With intelligence as bright as an iridescent beetle, Jemma always had an idea about how I could progress politically, but on this occasion, her first move was insisting we ordered a bottle of champagne that came with its own special 'House of Commons' label on it. We sat at a little table with a crisp white tablecloth in the wood-panelled and red-damask wallpapered room, framed by huge windows with a view of the Thames. Surrounded by politicians and advisors talking about when they thought the general election would be called, we got tipsy and, incapable of small talk, we plotted.

'Baroness Taylor's emphasis on fundamental shelter for people has given me another idea to spark a second legislative change to run in parallel to mandating swift bricks. I want to seek further protection of cavity-nesting habitat to ensure year-round nesting-site protection,' I explained, sounding like everyone else in the room hatching their own strategies.

'At the very least, it could potentially act as leverage,' Jemma replied.

'It's something the Swifts Local Network has always felt extremely strongly about but I dismissed in favour of swift bricks because I felt swift bricks would be less of a burden on the industry and therefore, ironically, more likely to get government support,' I said. 'Also, most EU countries have already done it, so maybe they'll be motivated into action.'

'It's a change that could happen through statutory instrument, not needing a vote and therefore not needing to set up and rally support for a votable order of business,' Jemma said, calculating the idea. 'It's effectively a stroke of a pen by the secretary of state for Defra.'

'Exactly,' I replied.

'Do it,' Jemma said with a glint in her eye.

She raised her glass. 'A toast to saving nature despite most of the people in this place,' Jemma said.

'What's that phrase . . . don't hate the players, hate the game,' I replied, clinking her glass with such force I almost broke it, trying to repress the bitterness that had surfaced with the alcohol.

There was a relief, though, of letting my hair down in the very place that had begun to derail my life. It made me feel like I belonged, like I could claim a piece of Parliament as my territory, for birds.

Walking round Parliament tipsy on champagne was something I never expected to find myself doing, but after dinner, Jemma took me through the labyrinth of corridors. We walked through the ornate lobby, past the famous chambers and down staircases until we were under Parliament and at the door that linked directly into Westminster tube station. As we left the Palace of Westminster compound, I turned round to glance at the entrance

and jokingly impersonated Arnie Schwarzenegger. 'I'll be back,'
I said, grinning.

The next morning I composed a letter asking Defra and
Labour's shadow minister for a meeting to discuss the idea. I rang
up James Wallace since he had successfully campaigned to make
beavers a protected species. 'In reaction to the government currently ignoring my ask, I'm going to double it,' I said to James,
explaining the idea.

'Naturally,' James said, laughing, offering to help write the letters.

I sent the draft letters to James, who added the specific ask,
and then on to Richard Benwell, who immediately discussed it
with the team at the RSPB led by Kate Jennings, who specified
the amendment. Within a matter of hours, together a spontaneous
coalition had approved the ask for Defra (and the shadow minister for Defra) to amend the Wildlife and Countryside Act and in
the NERC Act to afford protection of cavity-nesting habitat all
year round. I shared it with Zac and his brother Ben Goldsmith,
a prominent advocate for beavers as well as a leading voice in
nature restoration and the chair of the Conservative Environment
Network (CEN), who were both instantly supportive. Within
twenty-four hours, the signatory list was full of the main conservation organisations in the country, from the RSPB and the
National Trust to the International Union for Conservation of
Nature (IUCN) who compile the Red List of Threatened Species.
Richard Benwell had also sent a group letter from Wildlife and
Countryside Link supported by the NGO heavyweights, including
the British Trust for Ornithology, to Michael Gove, urging him
to act. I looked at the letters created from a chain reaction of the
country's nature recovery leaders working together for swifts. In
the face of the secretary of state's apathy, the whole conservation
world had immediately reared up in defiance.

The next day I met with Lord Randall who had been so key in Zac's amendment. The security guards in the House of Lords greeted me and my swift brick, beaming. 'Never give up! You'll get there in the end!'

In another damask-wallpapered tearoom in the House of Lords, I shared the idea, asking him to co-sign with Zac and me, and come with us to the meeting should Defra, either in this government or the next, grant us an audience. He agreed immediately, smiling at me, saying, 'You're not giving up, are you?'

I smiled back. 'When I first met you, you looked at my eager, fresh campaign face and warned me changing the law takes time,' I said. 'Years.'

He nodded, remembering.

'Well, I'm buckled in,' I said.

'That's what you said at our first meeting,' Lord Randall replied, nodding in acknowledgement of how far we had come and I nodded back, acknowledging how far we still had to go.

By the time I got home, it was dusk. On the outskirts of the village, I was greeted by a whirl of the local rooks, all on their way home to roost in the ash trees on the village fringe. There were over one hundred, clearly divided into mainly pairs with a few in threes. Each pair were lovers separated by a halo of darkening sky, a wing stretch away from their kin, journeying towards bedtime. On the rooftops of the old terraced houses stood starlings, chortling loudly, their necks rotund with song. As I opened my door, a flurry of house sparrows chirped, their noises softened, slower now the time had eked into the dregs of the day. Through my house I went, unable to stay indoors, my feet walking me out into the garden, to listen. Along with the dunnock who rushed for a wax worm, it was the blackbird who kept me company that evening, just like he does every spring. Blackbirds are also in decline, losing

18 per cent of their population between 1967 and 2020, but with an estimated national population of 5.1 million pairs, they were on the Green List for least conservation concern – a bird who didn't need the same attention as so many others, but one day they might. To love and notice common birds, I realised, was just as important as loving and caring for rarer birds. All risked oblivion at our hands unless we embraced them as neighbours. When I had lived in Africa, the single element of home I craved most was the song of the blackbird.

In the blue light of the garden, he perched in the apple tree and sang to me. Head back, eyes alert, his trickling melody so beautiful it resonated over me in a feeling of still, calm happiness. Every evening he sings, I listen. There is a melancholy tone so exquisite it touches on that subconscious awareness of mortality that breathes a philosophical note into his song. But most of all, his presence bathes me in a peacefulness. In the way the screams of a party of swifts make me grin so my face aches, blackbird song turns my mouth into a slower, steadier smile as if preparing me for sleep. A winding down happens in my mind as my thoughts are replaced with his music. As he conducts the day into night, I thank him, very much, for being close to me. Although he does not know it, he is my crutch, the bird I can depend on because not only is he here, but I don't have to worry about him. There is no sense of guilt or urgency, no feeling of betrayal. Our partnership is working well enough, for now. And in return, we witness each other's lives. I watch him as he sticks his tail up to balance when he has landed in the garden, and he watches me as I toss him currants and fill the shallow dish of water up. I look at his orange-rimmed eyes and he looks back at my grey-blue stare. He hears me swearing to myself, and I hear him swearing at the other male blackbirds. We are in sync. He likes the currants I give him, and I am head over heels for him. If I am going to be thought of as a pest to save his fellow urban birds and preserve our future with all of them, so be it. The joy-bringing, singing, soaring underdogs of the wild are, and always will be, worth fighting for.

Chapter 16

Nature Needs You

While Michael Gove stayed silent, blackbird song conjured spring. It is a combination of living things that define the season. A concoction of interlinked lives, triggered by sunshine. The temperature must rise to 6 degrees for grass to grow and then the race is on. Wildflowers spring in swathes of white, and with them hatch the insects. As the air warms up and more wildflowers bloom, astonishing journeys are enabled. Within the six-mile depth of the sky and atmosphere, there are tiny insect and plant-seed travellers, unseen. Swept up by convection currents, they rise from the ground surface, some deliberately, some accidentally. Winged aphids walk to the tops of blades of grass to hitch lifts to new territories to claim and conquer. Money spiders unravel a single silk thread, offering it to the sky, waiting for it to catch a breeze, and off they go, tiny eight-legged Mary Poppins. Some venture further than intended, carried halfway around the world, found at the top of the atmosphere by scientists, frozen solid but revivable when they fall to lower altitudes. The world is covered in routes of travellers who make astonishing journeys thousands of miles long.

Every spring that has ever been witnessed by humans, through this airspace fly homecoming birds including swallows, house martins and swifts. Just like every May, after patches of sky fill with the chatter of swallows and martins, I waited for the swifts to arrive. Standing in the field near the precious wall, there they hurtled through the sky. My eyes locked on to a single swift who flew in my direction. Nine months of non-stop flight and here I was witnessing the end of its journey as it flew over the river and across the field before entering the hole in the wall above my head: home. I wondered how it felt to be still after months on the move. I wondered what it felt like to be in a small, dark place after flying over Africa and Europe and England, after being above the green, humming, hot rainforests of the Congo Basin and surging oceans. Most of all, I wondered what it felt like for the swift to touch the ground of home.

I didn't know how many near misses this one bird had survived but other swifts had had a gruelling passage, with freak storms greeting them after hundreds had crossed the Straits of Gibraltar. Exhausted, hundreds had ended up on a wall in central Malaga, clutching the brickwork. SOS Vencejos, a local association for the protection of swifts and other urban birds, had sprung into action. Carefully retrieving each swift, some still clutching, some fallen, they put them in cardboard boxes and set up an emergency swift intensive care unit. Hydrating the birds, they gave them food and shelter, before releasing them so they could carry on with their journey; some of them would be on their way home to England. I knew this because one of the members had written to me saying, 'We have been able to save almost all of them. Soon, you have them in your land.'

It was a bittersweet thought that made a tear roll down my cheek as I glanced back at the wall. Here was a species whose breeding territory spanned half the world, connecting countries and cultures, people from all nationalities finding joy in this little bird. Here was a bird who was the world's poster child for biodiversity, who relied on safe passage, insect abundance and, like every living soul, somewhere to rest its head. A bird who united everyone.

Yet without secure nesting habitat, the swifts' efforts, and so many people's, would be in vain. I stared at the hole in the wall like I had done for months when it was empty, but now I knew there was a piece of magic inside, safely home. Shutting out everything else, I bathed in the quiet moment of relief and awe.

The swift's return marked almost two years since I had created the campaign, meaning I had one more year left until those young swifts I had promised to keep safe were back looking for a home. During this time, the insight that had unravelled, like a form of torture, was that the government was yet to grasp that sustainable economies and societies rely on nature, despite acknowledging it in words, even in law. The government still hadn't fully applied action that shows nature recovery is not something to resent, resist and dismiss but is centric to all governing, especially in this decade that the UN has declared as nature-critical. When it came to my small campaign, for arguably the easiest urgently essential biodiversity measure, the government had ignored both the swift-brick proposal and the year-round protection, the meetings and the group letter gone unanswered.

By mid-May, with still no response from Michael Gove, Zac posted a statement online that got picked up by the national news:

> The government's behaviour in relation to swifts has been distressing on numerous levels. The tiniest measure, one supported across the board including by the industry itself, could make the difference between survival and the disappearance of this iconic bird species in the UK. Michael Gove began the conversation full of enthusiasm. He set Hannah Bourne-Taylor and me a challenge to get the industry on side. We (or in reality she) did. And then Michael went silent and has refused to engage in any way

since. I have cheerleaded for Michael for years as I felt he deserved much more praise as environment secretary than he received. But there isn't a generous interpretation for his behaviour on this issue. He is a friend and it pains me to say it but he has simply not been straight. So now the future of this iconic species rests in one man's hands. His hands. And I fear he is willing to let them go. It is unforgiveable. After all his work, will this sordid chapter be his legacy? I sincerely hope not but the signs are not good.

This is one of those things that shouldn't require a campaign, let alone the brilliant, persistent and civilised campaign that Hannah Bourne-Taylor has been waging for over a year now. It is a no-brainer, a win-win, backed by almost everyone. What does it say about this government that it won't even agree to the very tiniest measure to ensure us to keep this iconic species alive? Michael Gove, you were sympathetic to this, or wanted us to believe so. Now you've gone completely silent. What on earth is going on?

Within a matter of days, word got to both Zac and another peer that apparently it wasn't Michael Gove stopping the campaign but No. 10 that was blocking it, the campaign making the national news again with the *Independent* publishing the headline: 'Fury as Rishi Sunak "blocks efforts" to save swifts from extinction'. I went on GB News twice to be interviewed about the government's inaction, and my social media posts about Michael Gove and Rishi Sunak were viewed half a million times by a public who was soon to be invited to vote to either keep the Conservatives in power or get rid of them.

The same week, Caroline Lucas hosted a parliamentary debate on biodiversity loss as one of her last acts of advocacy before she stood down as an MP. She, along with several other MPs, mentioned the need for the government to mandate swift bricks, demanding an answer from the minister for nature. I watched it live on parliament TV as Rebecca Pow, the minister, responded, smiling broadly as she claimed swift bricks were part of biodiversity net gain. It was either a deliberate lie, or she – the nature minister – hadn't engaged enough in the topic to know it was a falsehood. She went on to tell the MPs they should all do what she had not, and get their own local planning authorities to implement planning conditions. I swore at the telly, enraged. 'One may smile and smile and be a villain,' I said between pursed lips, deciding to resend the proposal to Michael Gove, calling out the minister for nature's response.

Two days later, everything changed. Suddenly, Rishi Sunak was standing in the rain calling a shockingly early general election. Immediately I decided to stand as an Independent MP against Michael Gove but the next day he stepped down. After twenty years as a politician, and after months of my obsessing about every minuscule detail of his political decisions, Michael Gove was instantly obsolete. I would never know who blocked the proposal or whether it was ever properly considered, but a few days later, at the end of May, the government formally said no. The government decision came in the form of a joint letter to Zac and me from the DLUHC. The same sentiment was relayed via letter to the Wildlife and Countryside Link and to John Cortes, Gibraltar's environment minister.

While the government had claimed building regulations was not a viable option for swifts because it was a route exclusively for structural safety, earlier that month, Lee Rowley, the minister of housing, had contradicted this line with the announced changes to building regulations to ensure single-sex toilets are provided in public buildings in the future.

Department for Levelling Up, Housing & Communities

Hannah Bourne-Taylor
Via email: ███████████████████

Lord Goldsmith
Via email: ███████████████

Department for Levelling Up, Housing and Communities
2 Marsham Street
London
SW1P 4DF

Our reference: MC2024/04115

31 May 2024

Dear Hannah Bourne-Taylor and Lord Goldsmith,

Thank you for your joint email of 14 February to the Rt Hon Michael Gove regarding swift bricks, and for your further email to the Lee Rowley and Rebecca Pow of 22 May. I am responding on the Department's behalf.

I appreciate how important this matter is to you, and I am sorry for the delay in responding. I understand you and your colleagues met Lee Rowley in February; and I know he appreciated you taking the time to explain the extensive work you are leading to support swifts during the period they spend in the UK each year.

You asked if the Government could review your request to mandate the provision of swift boxes within new builds and renovations as part of an update to the Building Regulations. In broad terms, Building Regulations focus upon life safety, rather than on other public policy objectives (however valuable and important). As an example, in Approved Document A, which seeks to deal with the structural soundness of buildings, the focus is on issues such as loading, ground movement and avoiding potential collapse. In general, where wildlife is referenced, it is because there is a direct relevance to ensuring structural integrity, such as the house longhorn beetle (an infestation of which can weaken the timber structures of a building dangerously).

While the Government has not implemented a mandatory scheme, the Department understands that the Future Homes Hub representatives are considering a voluntary scheme that some in the industry are indicating they will support. This proposal from the Home Builders Federation could have a big impact in the shortest timeframe for our swift population.

As you will be aware, the Prime Minister has announced that a general election will be held on 4 July 2024. Following the general election, it will be for the next government to make future policy decisions on the important matters you raise.

Thank you again for taking the time to write and for meeting with Lee Rowley, and I wish you the very best.

Yours sincerely,

Alex Badrick

Alex Badrick
Deputy Principal Private Secretary

As for the commitments from the housebuilders – it was exactly the block I had feared from the last meeting. While on paper the commitments sounded promising, they were not the most viable option, nor the quickest, with the planning route taking several years before construction began on commitments that were not only unchecked but temporary.

'If the housebuilders really are going to do it themselves, then there would be no issue about swift bricks being mandated,' I said to Zac, wondering what he would think of the long-awaited decision. 'It's a paper tiger!'

'I am beyond angry,' Zac replied. 'The government's reasoning is irresponsible and disgraceful. I never thought for one second we wouldn't have managed to secure this before the election. We will jump on every opportunity that arises come next Parliament, and we won't give up until we've won.'

Robin handed me a vodka tonic which I drank quickly before sitting with Margaret, who swore until her cheeks went red. We stared at the letter, my name etched into a little piece of government history.

'Thank goodness I was blissfully ignorant about the resistance and apathy I would face on the birds' behalf,' I said numbly.

Margaret replied with more swearing, shaking her head so violently it looked like it might come off. I felt so grateful for her fierce loyalty.

At bedtime, unable to sleep, I walked round the village, lingering next to the walls I knew were now made of part stone, part swift. At every point I had been questioned, tested, mocked, criticised, dragged through the mute and detached hell of apathy, but many people shared my love for swifts, turning the campaign into an ongoing fight. If millions of houses and dozens of new towns are to be built in this country, we need to rise up and engage the government so that they fully understand how much we value the nature on our doorsteps. We all need to ask our MPs for swift bricks, not taking no for an answer. While we will soon forget that there was a secretary of state named Michael Gove, and while every few months politicians will continue to be reshuffled into new roles, and governments will change, we are the ones who will remain constant. We are the ones who elect MPs. There are 650 MPs and 67 million of us. We hold the power, and regardless of which political party runs the country, it will be up to us to save our swifts and the rest of nature.

After the government dissolved, like a nightmare dissolves when you wake, the swifts' wheels and dives welcomed summer. With the sun came the insects that had conjured the swifts. Round my village I walked once more, chaperoned by the swifts. The May evening was warm, the sky blue and windless. As my eyes traced a single swift diving down the sky towards the stream, I followed. Mayfly hatches are triggered by sunlight, sometimes synchronised by dawn or dusk, otherwise by warm, still afternoons that summon them into the last stages of their life. The River Glyme runs through Oxfordshire, one field away from my village. 'Glyme' comes from the Brittonic for 'bright stream' and the river lies in the valley like cut glass on sunny days in a narrow path of water and dappled light. Through a line of horse chestnut trees, dense with white blossom like chandeliers patterned with flecks of neon pink, I arrived by the water. Here the river widens from its narrow line in a glossy pool before rushing under a stone bridge. Quiet and slinking, it flowed between the trees while all around it, under and over it, the mayflies were hatching.

In flying shoals, they flew above the water and over the field between the horse chestnut and willows. Up and down they darted: yo-yos in perpendicular lines, bouncing in courtship. Their wings, like tiny pieces of stained glass divided by black lead lines, glinted in the shards of sunlight that spilled through the gaps in the trees. They were everywhere, dancing their species' dance, a tradition that had lasted at least 300 million years. Creatures that preceded the dinosaurs, mayflies were one of the first winged insects to live on Earth, with 3,000 species spread out across the world except for Antarctica. Taking off my shoes and socks, lining them on the bank, I paddled, encased in an aquatic spectacle. Like fairies made from light, these tiny pixies jigged, as though on invisible strings, flying up and down over the water in between my legs, glittering in the evening sun.

Most of their life is spent as larvae, existing underwater for up to two years. Despite Britain being so depleted of wildlife, despite so many of our rivers being polluted, they were *still* here. I sat on the bank, dangling my legs in the water, a mayfly landing on my knee. I looked at its three long tails like single black hairs, and its body that changed from cream to brown, the same hues as popcorn. This was a sub-imago or 'dun', the first out of two different winged adult forms in their life cycle. In a few hours, it would shed its skin for the last time, transforming into a darker-coloured imago for its final hours. A nymph emerged on the water upstream, pushed up to the surface to moult. Pulling its body, the old exoskeleton split and out came its wings. Floating, too light to dent the water at all, it was taken downstream by the current where it would wait, not for its wings to dry, but for them to fill with fluid before flying. All along the bank, others were clutching onto stems of grass, resting and shedding their skins. An adult flew into the water, wings out, stuck to the surface, glittering as it went. Likely to be a female, she would muster enough energy to lay her eggs in the water before dying. She lay like Shakespeare's character Ophelia, depicted in John Everett Millais' iconic painting, floating downstream, surrounded by little rounds of white horse chestnut flowers. The name for the order of aquatic insects they belong to is Ephemeroptera, deriving from the Greek meaning 'living a day'. One species, *Dolania americana*, stays in this world in flying form for only five minutes, the shortest adult lifespan of any insect. These creatures' final hours were spent dancing in shards of sunlight surrounded by trees thick with green leaves and air that was warm and still. The drama unfolded in silence, each one falling when it was ready for perpetual rest. One by one they dropped into the water to be pulled away from this life within reflections of the sky they had flown in. The final life stage is also known as 'spinners' because they mate in swirling swarms over the water, and that's what they were doing around me: spinning into the sky, into the light and down to the water, and soon into another world, leaving a legacy of larvae in the riverbed to emerge on a future summer's day. This perspective on time – on life – broke it down so that every minute was accounted for, every second was important, their existence highlighting mortality, showcasing the opportunity to embrace life.

As I witnessed this glittering existence, I knew I would spend my life spinning in the sunshine with wild lives while doing everything I could to save them. In Britain, according to the 2023 State of Nature report, one in six species faces national extinction, including 43 per cent of birds. So I will fight apathy and resistance by finding the sunshine and the creatures who dance in it. For a moment, I was liberated from the stress of the campaign, of the burden of trying to protect the birds I love the most. The campaign and the constant multifaceted act of saving nature would always be about a team coming together that is greater than the sum of our parts. Nature needs me. Nature needs you. Nature needs every single one of us.

The next morning, as I cycled into Oxford to welcome the homecoming swifts in the tower, I realised that for all this time, some sort of devil has been whispering in our ears, telling us, 'You are not strong enough to withstand the storm.' As I pedalled in the direction of our beloved feathered neighbours, a smile formed, turning into a grin as I replied on our collective behalf, shouting skywards, 'WE ARE THE STORM!'

Epilogue
Feathered Neighbours

'Let me tell you the secret that has led me to my
goal. My strength lies solely in my tenacity.'

– LOUIS PASTEUR

In the two years since I launched my campaign, the estimated decline of the UK's breeding population of swifts has been a further ten thousand birds. House martins, starlings and house sparrows continue to decline with them. According to a Wild Justice survey published by the *Guardian* in late 2024, non-compliance of developers required to instal bird boxes in new builds by local planning authorities is 75 per cent. The Great British Insulation Scheme (GBIS), with its budget of £1 billion, will continue to insulate homes, the most popular measure being cavity-wall insulation, accounting for 61 per cent, ensuring the increasing national-scale loss of cavity-nesting habitat. A new planning law implemented by Michael Gove just before he stepped down, at the request of Jeremy Clarkson, allows farm buildings to be converted without planning permission. 'Clarkson's Clause' is another inadvertent nail in the coffin for birds reliant on buildings.

People all over Britain are not giving up on the birds who share our walls, with swift-brick petitions launched in Scotland and in Wales, where the swift is the most rapidly declining bird. But with an estimated breeding population of fewer than 40,000 swifts, there is a quiet agony I wake up with every day.

Throughout the summer of 2024 Robin and the dogs bounded through the days with me on walks, while Jemma and Jeff stayed in almost constant contact, engaging in everything from getting strategic plans ready for the incoming government to just swearing when I was feeling sorry for myself.

As July arrived and the new government began, a joint letter from Steve Reed and Angela Rayner, the new secretaries of state for Defra and the Ministry of Housing, Communities and Local Government (MHCLG), was sent to the conservation sector. The letter's sentiment was a commitment to acting with nature in mind while building 1.5 million homes by 2030, summed up by the statement, 'We are determined to transform the [planning] system to ensure a win-win for housebuilding and nature.'

In early September, after parliamentary summer recess, I sent my proposal to Matthew Pennycook, now Minister of State for Housing and Planning and scanned the news constantly for political decisions about housing and nature. Not expecting to get anywhere soon with a brand new government, I was surprised when my phone bleeped with a message from Zac.

'Steve Reed's said yes to a meeting. Are you free on 19 September?'

'Yes, anywhere, anytime. I will be there,' I replied, my heart racing.

I rushed home, ringing James Wallace: 'We've got a meeting with Defra.'

'Make sure you get the official I mentioned to the meeting. He's critical to decision making,' James replied. 'I'll ping you his contact details now.'

Five minutes later I had my phone in my hand, standing on a chair in the kitchen to get mobile signal, taking a deep breath. Then I cold-called one of the top civil servants in Defra.

'Hello, my name is Hannah Bourne-Taylor. So sorry to call you out of the blue but I'm the swift-brick campaigner and I wanted to introduce myself,' I explained.

'Ah yes, I know who you are. How can I help?' the official replied.

'Will you come to the meeting that Lord Zac Goldsmith and I have with Steve Reed?'

When he agreed, I emailed the chair of Natural England, Tony Juniper, asking him to relay the official stance of support and recommendation from Natural England.

'I'll be there,' Tony said.

Meeting Zac and Tony outside Defra's offices, I was relieved to be fully clothed. We sat in the autumn sunshine and I realised I was happy, not nervous; I was in the company of allies who had become friends. Tony quizzed Zac on his latest nature recovery achievement and the Sumatran tiger now named Goldsmith. Somewhere within the Gunung Leuser National Park – the only place on Earth where tigers, elephants, rhinos and orangutans coexist – Goldsmith roamed, the name a gesture of thanks after Zac had led efforts to secure an ambitious Memorandum of Understanding with the government of Indonesia to protect 15 million hectares of natural forest. Hearing Zac's positivity felt like a tangible antidote to the dire state of nature, although a little piece of me couldn't believe how this huge, complex and costly achievement could have been made within the timeframe of us *still* campaigning for a simple brick.

At two o'clock, we walked up to the reception.

'You're not on the list, I'm afraid. You can't come to the meeting unless someone vouches for you,' the receptionist said.

'I'll vouch for her. Obviously. She's the most important person in the meeting,' Zac said.

As we sat in the lobby, Zac turned to me: 'Apart from their not putting you on the list, I have a good feeling about this.'

'Me too. I woke up like it was Christmas morning today. I feel almost giddy with excitement.'

Walking up through the Home Office and into Defra, we were ushered into the secretary of state's office where a line of civil servants, Natural England officials, Steve Reed's special advisor and Steve Reed himself stood. Sitting down next to Zac, I put my swift brick on the desk and Zac broke the ice.

'Hannah's been to Parliament with this swift brick so many times, the security guards know what it is,' he laughed. 'Don't they call you the Swift Lady?'

I nodded, smiling, looking at Steve Reed, hopeful.

For a few minutes Zac and Tony talked about broader nature recovery targets, insect recovery in the UK and the fundamental importance of rainforest protection.

'Swifts are poster children for biodiversity,' Tony said.

'And since they migrate to the immeasurably precious rainforests in the Congo Basin, broader nature recovery targets both here and overseas are wrapped up in this iconic species,' Zac added.

Steve Reed smiled, turning to me.

'You're pushing an open door, Hannah,' he said. 'I've discussed this with colleagues in the Ministry of Housing, Communities and Local Government. We wanted to add it to the Labour manifesto, actually.'

'You wanted to add it to the manifesto?' I asked in disbelief.

'Yes,' Steve Reed replied.

In a millisecond my mind flashed through the two years of campaigning, the apathy of the Conservative government and the stand-off with the former secretary of state for Defra. I repressed the desire to cheer and asked whether I could give a brief overview, wanting to make absolutely sure that everyone in the room knew the key points. I concluded: 'I know this is such a small thing within the broader targets and you are in the hottest of hot seats, but we aren't exaggerating when we say this tiny measure is fundamental to the survival of these birds.'

'It's not a small thing to the birds,' Steve Reed replied, nodding, reassuring me he truly understood the stakes. 'We need legislative options. If you're able to work with my team, we can go back and discuss options with the MHCLG.'

'Could we include a swift-brick provision in the Planning and Infrastructure Bill?' I suggested, aiming for the holy grail of primary legislation.

Steve Reed nodded. 'I agree,' he said, standing up and shaking my hand. 'Well done and thank you for your impressive campaign,' he added as his team huddled round to give me their numbers.

As Tony stayed behind with his team, Zac and I walked through the building on our way out. We were grinning like children given the run of a chocolate shop.

'I'm trying to keep my cool until we get out of the building,' Zac said.

'Don't come anywhere near me then,' I replied.

As we went down in the lift, I was suddenly worried. 'Am I missing something here? He did suggest legislation. He has said yes, right?'

'Yes,' Zac replied. 'And importantly, he said that he had already had a positive discussion with MHCLG about it.'

'Will they listen to Defra though? I mean, Defra seems to be further down the pecking order?'

'True,' Zac replied. 'But you've got Defra on side and actively lobbying now, so there's no reason it can't happen. I can't believe it hasn't already happened.'

*

The train journey home went by in a surreal daze. Robin was there to meet me at the station, the dogs howling in delight, rushing towards me as I practically skipped over the bridge towards them.

'It went well then?' Robin asked.

'Steve Reed said, and I quote: "You're pushing an open door" and I'm meeting his team next week to talk details,' I said, still buzzing.

The next week, I went back to the Home Office, this time alone, for a meeting with the lead Defra official, sitting down in a tiny cubby-hole office.

'I've been in this role for twenty years and I hate to say it, but due to the sheer volume of environmental issues, and of course vast number of other issues, it is extremely rare for a nature campaign to cut through the noise, but you have made an inarguable case. We agree that it aligns with our 2030 nature recovery targets, and you have our full support.'

His compliment made me sit back in my chair for a moment, speechless.

'So what do we do now?' I asked. 'I've never got past the pitching phase.'

The official explained that his team would discuss specific legislative options with MHCLG, so I brought up the secondary legislation option of Building Regulations, and the new and untested route of adding a swift-brick provision to the new-and-yet-to-be-finalised national development management policies (NDMPs). It was Richard Benwell and Jeff Knott who had first mentioned NDMPs as a possible option, explaining that while it wouldn't be legislative, NDMPs would have statutory weight and therefore were markedly different from the similar National Planning Policy Framework.

'If I could pick any of them, I would pick Building Regulations,' I concluded.

The official nodded, writing more notes, asking more questions, and told me he would be back in touch after meeting with the MHCLG officials.

A week later, he rang me. Shutting the kitchen door having just been feeding my dunnock, I kept an eye on the bird flitting through the leaf litter and picked up the phone.

'Good news and bad news,' the official said. 'Bad news is that Matthew Pennycook's team have said no to our request to include swift bricks in the Planning and Infrastructure Bill. But in the same breath they said the reason why they won't do that is because they are going with the Building Regulations route.'

It took me a few seconds to process what I was being told. I watched the dunnock creep and dash along to the drystone wall and cock its head, looking at me. Twenty-two months of campaigning and finally the MHCLG was on board.

'What happens next?' I asked, not wanting to jump the gun.

'My team has another meeting to confirm, and we can bring you back in for the wording and the details,' the official explained.

When Robin got home, I told him to sit down.

'I don't know for certain, but I think I will look back at this moment in a few weeks' time and realise that this is the moment where I won my campaign.'

Robin jumped up to hug me. 'I don't want to tell anyone because it's not confirmed, but I think we've done it,' I said, shaking my head in disbelief. 'I think we've bloody done it!'

I sent a message to Zac and his reply was punctuated by dozens of exclamation marks.

A few days later, at the end of September, I had the chance to celebrate a little at a Natural England parliamentary reception where

I would finally meet Gibraltar's environment minister, John Cortes. As I stood in line outside the House of Lords, it was my adopted name that I heard on the lips of the security guards.

'It's the Swift Lady!' one of them said, beaming. 'Come through,' he said, ushering me past the bigwigs.

Holding a glass of champagne, I was busy scanning the faces, looking for John Cortes. Out of the crowd Lord Robathan strode up to me and kissed my cheek. Lord Randall shook my hand and nodded in his understated way of twinkling support. New MPs introduced themselves and asked how they could help. The Labour MP for Stroud, Dr Simon Opher, spoke warmly about his local swift group and agreed to submit a Written Question to MHCLG, write a letter to Matthew Pennycook signed by as many fellow Labour MPs as possible, and submit a Ten-Minute Rule Bill (to remind the government of the broad political support in case they wavered on the decision).

'How the tables have turned,' Lord Robathan whispered, patting me on the back.

Tony Juniper hugged me and then in walked John Cortes. I ran to him, launching into a huge hug that almost knocked his glasses off.

'John. I've been told that the Ministry of Housing have said they'll add a swift-brick requirement to Building Regulations!' I said, clutching both his hands in excitement.

Shaking my hands vigorously as he congratulated me, he said, 'You must come to see the swifts flying over the passage and on to you come spring, as a way of celebration. It would be my honour to host you.'

That night we had dinner together and I listened to John describing standing on a cliff, looking out at the Strait of Gibraltar, watching thousands of swifts on their way home. As I left

Westminster, I didn't feel the joy I expected to feel when I launched the campaign, but instead a profound relief. My shoulders felt tangibly lighter, as though I could breathe easy, stepping down from the perpetual state of being in survival mode.

*

Perhaps I jinxed it by telling John, by saying the words out loud, by trusting the message I had been given – because nothing happened. Having expected to get confirmation by the start of October, the days turned into weeks. As the leaves turned brown, Simon Opher lingered at the end of divisions so he could lobby Matthew Pennycook after voting. Others did the same, including Anna Gelderd MP, a passionate nature advocate. When Simon Opher emailed me that the Whips' office had advised him to cancel his Ten-Minute Rule Bill because government action for swift bricks was being prepared, I took that as a good sign. But when November came, I started politely nagging the Defra officials. At the end of November, I finally got a reply:

> MHCLG are clear they want to use a non-legislative route, and so would prefer not to change Building Regulations which would require secondary legislation taking approx. a year to draft, review, consult, publish etc before it could come into force. Rather MHCLG are recommending that swift bricks be addressed through a National Development Management Policy (NDMP), which will come under the National Development Management Framework (NDMF). Consultation on the NDMF has now finished and is expected to be published by the end of this calendar year. The next step is to develop the associated NDMPs, and

then public consultation on them, which could take a year.
As this is a planning mechanism, it could apply to both new
builds and renovations/extensions of existing structures.
I understand MHCLG Ministers have recently received
advice from their officials to this effect.

My inbox had other emails from MPs relaying how they had spoken
to Matthew Pennycook in the lobby. The housing minister had mentioned swift bricks and hedgehog holes in the same breath and,
although he had been vague, said there was no intention of legislat-
ing. The familiar feeling of dread seeped through my body again. I
rang Zac to talk it over. In an ironic twist of fate, Zac sent a message
to Michael Gove, asking him how effective a swift-brick NDMP
could be. Gove replied immediately confirming that if the wording
stopped loopholes, an NDMP would be a powerful tool because it
had statutory weight. Gove had become a pantomime villain to me,
but his response was oddly reassuring. Discussing with Zac, then
Josie, Jeff and Jemma, wanting to sense-check everyone's views, I
replied to the Defra officials stating that a swift-brick NDMP would
only be effective if the wording stipulated three conditions about
guidance, monitoring and enforcement. I sent the email off, feeling nauseous, my body shaking as I processed the blow: the sucker
punch of a government U-turn, which I hadn't anticipated.

As Advent whirled around again, Zac invited me to a parlia-
mentary reception where Anna Gelderd relayed a brief chat with
Matthew Pennycook to us. As I listened to her talking about the
National Planning Policy Framework, I panicked.

'What did he say *exactly*?'

'That swift bricks, and hedgehog holes and bat boxes, have
been included in the new NPPF, being announced tomorrow,'
Anna replied.

The speeches started, putting our discussion on ice.

'If this is the government action we've been promised, the birds are screwed,' I whispered to Zac. 'Half the politicians in here, and most of the public, will think that this is a meaningful step but it's not even progress. It's already in the NPPF and it makes almost no difference,' I said, verging on growling. 'An NDMP is the threshold for a win.'

'We aren't going to give up,' Zac replied. 'We will push for an NDMP at the very least.'

Barry Gardiner MP came up to me after the speeches, smiling as he recognised me. Tapping the swift brick, he asked how it was all going.

'I need your help. Can you submit an Oral Question tomorrow when Matthew Pennycook announces the NPPF changes?' I asked.

'Absolutely,' Barry replied.

The next day, I watched the live Parliament TV channel, seeing Barry sit down on the green benches, having to be in the chamber at the very start of the session despite Matthew Pennycook being the third minister to speak. I sent Barry a message about the need for statutory weight, and I watched as he looked at his phone and typed a reply, the ping on my phone showing a big thumbs up. Finally, after over an hour, Matthew Pennycook came in and made a short speech that was attacked immediately by the Opposition. After being criticised and mocked in the usual gung-ho, vitriolic manner which never fails to appal me, he took questions. Barry stood up.

'My hon. Friend is a champion for the natural world, and I am aware that he is sympathetic to the need to include biodiversity measures in all new builds, such as swift bricks, which are an essential nesting habitat for the survival and recovery of cavity-nesting birds. Will he provide this much-needed boost for a declining population that has sadly been placed on the critically endangered red list? Will he ensure that these simple requirements are not only in the NPPF but are translated into the national development management policies to ensure they have statutory weight?'

Barry's delivery was perfect, his voice emphasising the words 'statutory weight' as his hand pointed towards Matthew Pennycook decisively.

Matthew Pennycook replied. 'My hon. Friend will be pleased to know that we have added text to the NPPF to encourage the incorporation of features to protect threatened species, including swifts, but also bats and hedgehogs. We will consult on the NDMPs in the spring of next year.'

I couldn't tell whether Matthew Pennycook was going to save the swifts. He had whipped in favour of Zac's amendment and we had met when he was shadow minister, but he had never replied to any meeting request or email since he had been in office. I had managed to get a bunch of flowers delivered to him that morning, asking for a meeting on the accompanying little card as the only means of direct contact. The meeting with the MHCLG was postponed, the Defra officials relaying that the MHCLG officials weren't yet ready to discuss details of NDMPs.

If the government went on to implement a swift-brick NDMP – with the right wording – then the birds had a chance and the campaign would amount to a win, but my hope had been diluted, along with my trust. It felt as if I was playing a game of snakes and ladders. Over Christmas as I socialised with friends and family, while they were merry on wine, I felt drunk on cynicism.

As 2025 began and Parliament resumed, I read a newly published paper by Defra and MHCLG entitled 'Planning Reform Working Paper: Development and Nature Recovery'. From bed, I read the summary that began with the following:

The government wants to accelerate development while going beyond simply offsetting harm to unlock the positive impact this development can have in driving nature recovery. This new approach would use funding from development to deliver environmental improvements at a scale which will have the greatest impact – moving us from an unacceptable status quo that can hold up development without improving nature, to a win-win for both.

Reading the joint statement that perfectly aligned with mandating swift bricks conjured a fresh anger inside me. I was reading a promise to create legislation to ensure a win-win for nature in the context of building houses that would go on to exclude the *only* category of wildlife that literally depended on new builds to exist. A rage spilled out of my mind and into my face, making my jaw ache and my skull throb, and then I erupted, yelling, 'WHY THE FUCK WON'T YOU JUST FUCKING MANDATE SWIFT BRICKS? WHAT THE FUCK IS WRONG WITH YOU?!'

God, it felt good to shout.

I stared blankly ahead for a few moments, embracing the anger, finally admitting to myself how livid I had become. I took a deep breath. Then I stood up, got dressed and caught the train into London for yet another meeting in the Houses of Parliament.

*

Arriving in London, I made a detour, getting off the underground at Marble Arch. With my swift brick under my arm, I walked along the edge of Hyde Park to Speakers' Corner. I hadn't been back since launching the campaign almost two and a half years before. Memories, not of being cold and nervous, but of feeling hopeful, haunted me. On the ground there is a plaque that acknowledges the origin of Speakers' Corner. It hides a horrible truth, marking the spot of the Tyburn Tree. For 650 years, this was the main location for public hangings. The condemned were encouraged to make speeches, traditionally begging for their life with emotional pleas, their words printed in pamphlets, distributed to vast crowds. I hadn't known this when I had chosen Speakers' Corner, but the place and tradition took its name from those about to die, who were encouraged to speak freely, who begged for pardons that never came. While my speech and ongoing campaign didn't mark *my* life hanging in the balance, it did mark the swifts' existence. It *is* life or death for this species and for any birds reliant on buildings who find themselves unable to breed in this country. I imagined ten thousand tiny swift coffins around my feet, their appeals unheard, and wondered how many more would be added before the government did something.

I stood for a moment before walking down the wide avenues to Westminster. I was not the spectacle that day. Apart from the pocket of oats for the pigeons, I was interchangeable with others of my kind, but above us all was a feathered kind whose sequined coats gleamed: starlings. A flock of hundreds, they pooled together in the sky, twisting into a spiral that moved like a slinky in slow motion, undulating over the roofs of Whitehall as though conducted by some invisible force. I looked around but no one else nearby saw; they were all glued to their phones. Higher the starlings flew before suddenly dropping, landing one after another in the avenue of trees a little further up the road, merging with the dark bare branches, invisible.

Each one has stars emblazoned on their chests, triumphantly frolicsome, instinctively brave, surviving despite the adversity of being our neighbours. It is their lives I am carrying in the swift brick, along with the swifts, house martins and house sparrows. And in return, the birds lift me up, lending me their technicoloured wings.

When I arrive at the Houses of Parliament, I glance up at Big Ben. The most famous clock in the world, it now feels like an hour-glass for birds and for so much of the natural world. Greeted by the security guards who welcome me back into the halls of power, I have the same, agonisingly simple plea: Mandate swift bricks to save our feathered neighbours.

The Fight to Save our Swifts

Thanks to awareness sparked by the campaign and the ongoing advocacy of the SLN, a few more local planning authorities have included swift bricks in their planning policies, and large commitments have been made by the housebuilding industry.

However, the British Trust of Ornithology still estimates rapid decline with fewer than 40,000 pairs of swifts by 2025. Mandating swift bricks through a swift-brick requirement in building regulations or a swift-brick amendment to a bill is increasingly urgent. Without swift bricks, there is no guaranteed nesting habitat for swifts anywhere in Britain. If they can't breed, they will cease to exist.

Our home is their home.

For the latest campaign updates and action requests, go to www.hannahbournetaylor.com or find me on X (formerly known as Twitter) as @WriterHannahBT and on Bluesky as @Hannah Bourne-Taylor

How YOU can help swifts now
Political
- Email and write a letter to the secretary of state for housing, communities and local government, asking them to mandate swift bricks.
- Email and write a letter to the housing minister asking them to mandate swift bricks.

- Book a surgery appointment with your own MP, asking them to help advocate for swifts. In-person meetings are much more effective than emails. To find out who your MP is and to find out their contact details go to https://members.parliament.uk
- Email and write a letter to your own MP, asking them to advocate for swift bricks.
- Get as many people as you know to do all of the above. The more people ask MPs and our government to act, the more they will consider action.
- Ask your local planning authority to include swift bricks in their local planning policies, during public consultations and through personally lobbying the planning committees.
- For more information about political action email me at thefeatherspeech@gmail.com
- Raise awareness by presenting the short animation 'A Swift Story' to your local school and local societies: https://www.youtube.com/watch?v=AJhc-vcssKc; and by showing The Feather Speech to people (age appropriate): https://www.youtube.com/watch?v=Ft8nmG3OyO0 (or by giving people this book).

A reminder of the key points outlining why the government need to mandate swift bricks that you can communicate to . . . everyone:

- Cavity-nesting habitat in buildings has been excluded from legislation and policy in the UK to date.
- There is a British Standard for swift bricks that perfectly sets up legislation.
- In 2024, The Netherlands mandated swift bricks through their equivalent to Building Regulations.

- Leaving a measure to housebuilders' voluntary and unchecked commitments is not enough, especially a measure that experts deem urgently essential to stabilise and recover Red Listed species in the UK.

- Without swift bricks there is no guaranteed cavity-nesting habitat for birds reliant on our buildings anywhere in the UK.

- The 1.5 million homes being built and the ten new towns will have zero nesting habitat for these birds without swift bricks.

- Many EU countries have year-round protective legislation for cavity-nesting habitat. The UK only has it for the breeding season.

- Guidance in the National Planning Policy Framework has not been effective.

- Local government cannot effectively implement a measure deemed urgent – the review cycles of Local Plans are five years and only nine local planning authorities out of over 400 have acted.

- Swift bricks provide nesting habitat for eight species of urban birds and therefore allow us to retain our most accessible touch point to nature.

- Four cavity-nesting birds are Red Listed (swifts, house martins, house sparrows and starlings). Common swifts fare the worst with a 60 per cent breeding-population decline between 1995 and 2020, which left an estimated 59,000 pairs. Since then, they have declined by a further 24 per cent, leaving an estimated population of fewer than 45,000 pairs in the UK in 2024, set to fall to fewer than 40,000 by 2025.

- While other biodiversity measures for new builds can provide really useful support for wildlife, swift bricks are distinct as unlike the other measures they are not supplementary but provide critical nesting habitat for birds who are reliant on buildings and have no special nesting-habitat protection.

- Gibraltar reacted to the same cavity-nesting bird declines thirty years ago by adding a planning policy on swift bricks and have stabilised their swift populations.

Practical

- Join the Swifts Local Network if you want to get involved with swift conservation at a local level, especially if you want to set up a local swift group and would like to become part of the community: send an email request to swiftslocalnetwork+owner@googlegroups.com
- Become a member of the charity House Martin Conservation www.housemartinconservation.com
- Find out if you have a local swift group through checking Action for Swifts' list https://actionforswifts.blogspot.com/p/swift-groups-on-facebook.html or by emailing swiftslocalnetwork+owner@googlegroups.com

Emergency help for swifts

If you find a grounded swift (or any bird) never ever throw it in the air.

The following Facebook groups are great at coordinating emergency swift care:

Swift & Swallow SOS – Coordinating Rescues &
    Supporting Finders
All Things Swifts

Grounded swifts will likely need expert help and not all wildlife centres will know how to look after them. Hot weather or extreme wet weather often leads to swifts on the ground. While you try to get help, put the swift on a towel in a box away from stress and noise. Handle the bird with gloves if possible to prevent damaging its all-important wing feathers. If you try to give it a drink (if you can't get expert advice), only do it using a cotton bud along the side of its bill or offer a bottle cap of water – do not put water in its mouth yourself. Swifts only eat insects, and live insects (crickets) can be bought online or at local pet store. Meat such as minced beef will keep it alive but will make its feathers fatally brittle, so do not feed meat, ever. The handling, looking after and circumstances of releasing a swift are all crucial. Seek expert advice immediately.

For commercial advice about swift bricks
I have set up a consultancy – The Feather Speech Consultancy CIC – to advise housebuilders and companies who are building: https://hannahbournetaylor.com/the_feather_speech_consultancy

Please contact me via my website for more details: http://www.hannahbournetaylor.com or my email: thefeatherspeech@gmail.com with the subject 'CIC'.

Installing swift boxes and bricks
There are loads of options online for:

- installing swift bricks in new builds
- retrofitting swift bricks
- installing external swift boxes to existing walls

I am impartial but here are some recommendations:

Swift bricks:
The S brick by Action for Swifts S Brick (actionforswifts.com). Contact becky@actionforswifts.com who will help you with your

enquiry and order. Swift bricks provide nesting habitat for: house sparrows, swifts, house martins, starlings, blue tits, great tits, nut hatches and wrens.

Swift boxes:

- WoodStone Burgos Swift Box available via various suppliers you can find by searching online (woodcrete lasts longer than wood, so is more sustainable and doesn't get as hot but they are 12 kg, so bear the weight in mind). WoodStone also make house martin cups.
- Peak Boxes do a range of wooden boxes.

For installation guidance for commercial projects, use the British Standard guidance (BS 42021:2022). Each supplier will also advise, but the basic rules are:

- Install (the right way up) under the eaves of walls so the placement is a minimum of 4 metres (the higher the better).
- Do not install on a south-facing wall (it gets too hot).
- Ideally, install on a wall that has open space directly in front of it.
- If possible, install more than one – a couple next to each other works well as all cavity-nesting birds are colony nesters.
- Play swift calls on a speaker set up very close to the new nest site to attract prospecting swifts, especially in May and July (but if using an open window, shut as much as possible as sometimes swifts will fly in).

Download the free app Swift Mapper

Swift Mapper is a conservation mapping tool – easy and free to use. Anyone can submit records of breeding swifts, building a picture of where they are nesting around the UK. This enables local conservation action for swifts to be focused in the right places. All records will be available to anyone interested in swifts and their conservation: local authority planners, architects, ecologists, developers, conservation groups and individuals who want to help their local swifts. Mapping breeding swifts helps determine where active nest sites need to be protected, and where new nesting opportunities for swifts would be best provided – the closer new potential nest sites are to existing swift colonies, the greater the chance they will be occupied.

Download Merlin App for bird sound ID – (for the love of birds).

General political advocacy for nature restoration

- Become a parish councillor, district councillor . . . or MP or/ and campaign for something you love.
- Follow the actions of Wildlife and Countryside Link: www.wcl.org.uk @WCL_News
- If you want to become a toad patroller, find out more on www.froglife.com
- To find out more about the needs of farmland birds, or to donate to Farmland Bird Aid Network, go to www.farmlandbirdaidnetwork.org

www.hannahbournetaylor.com

X and Instagram: @WriterHannahBT

Bluesky: hannahbournetaylor

Facebook: The Feather Speech

To join in with the game First Bird of My Day, find me on X.

The Feather Speech

Made by Hannah Bourne-Taylor at noon at Speakers' Corner on Saturday 5 November 2022, to launch her swift-brick petition

I stand here as a go-between for swifts to ask for your comradery because they need our help. Today I open a petition and invite you to sign it to make swift bricks compulsory in new housing across Britain. Together we can try to stop these remarkable British birds passing into legend.

Swifts are awe-inspiring and Every Bird Counts. Small enough to fit in the palms of our hands, swifts spend more time airborne than any other bird on earth. They eat, bathe, court and sleep on the wing, flying millions of miles in their lifetimes, living in the sky. They are adventurers, travelling from Britain to southern Africa, crossing the Sahara Desert twice every year, not landing like other birds ... until they come home to us. Adults return to the exact holes in our walls: to cul-de-sacs and terraces, old houses and wherever there is a space for them to rest their heads and have their feathered children. By sharing our walls with swifts, birds whose agility and speed inspired fighter-jet design, we share our homes with feathered patriots, who bring summer with them and fill our skies with joy.

But these iconic birds have been on the Red List of highest conservation concern for one year. They face national extinction, their population plummeting, hindered further by their homes being inadvertently blocked off by us.

If a swift could fight for their existence with words, they might say this:

You have not seen what I have seen. I have spiralled above clouds cloaked in the setting sun, spun through the eyes of ferocious storms, crossed deserts, oceans, continents. For generations my kind has existed, our blood line unbroken for millions of years. And we have screamed in delight at your creativity, innovation, progression. But now we are screaming for you to help us. To look up. To remember you share your home with other kinds. Feathered, furred, finned, scaled, winged. Our shared home is becoming parched of life, destroyed, flooded, licked by flames, ABLAZE. Through these shared struggles we only ask for one thing. A safe place to rest after our perilous journey home. You can help us. You can remember your walls also belong to adventurers. You can unblock the holes and make new ones. You can sign the petition to help us and we will be forever grateful. We will scream in delight at your creativity, innovation, progression.

The Feather Speech is not just a campaign aimed at the government or to the people of Britain. It is an alliance with our wild neighbours. Let the records show we care, we are connected and we will unite on behalf of the nature on our doorsteps, starting with swifts, who watch over us all.

As we prepare to welcome our feathered patriots home in the spring, let us recognise the power of our own voices. When the environmental crisis feels overwhelming, let us come together and show that Passion is a Superpower.

This petition has six months to gather 100,00 signatures to help these irreplaceable British birds. Don't sign because I ask. Sign because swifts can't. Sign because Every Bird Counts.

Acknowledgements

It turns out that a solo campaign requires many teams of people. The same is true for writing a book. Firstly, thank you to my publicist Katie Hambly and the brilliant team at Elliot & Thompson: Amy Greaves, Marianne Thorndahl, Celia Hayley, Pippa Crane and Katie Bond. Katie, thank you for your vision, patience and commitment, and for coming to The Feather Speech. Thank you to my literary agent Sophie Lambert and to Alice Hoskyn and everyone at C&W, and to Anna Stelter and the Simon & Schuster sales team. Thank you to the wonderful artist Ingrid Nilsson who created the fantastic artwork for the book cover.

Thank you to my family and my loves, Robin, Shoebill and Loony.

A huge thank you to the 109,896 people who signed my petition. This campaign belongs to you.

The rest of my thanks are to the conservation and political world. The people listed below illustrate what we can do if we unite for nature.

Swift folk:
Thank you to the founders and members of The Swifts Local Network and all the life-long swift conservationists who have spent decades creating the foundations of awareness and solutions for swifts and other cavity-nesting urban birds, here in the UK and around the world. Special mentions of thanks to Mike Priaulx, for your encyclopaedic knowledge of local planning authorities in

particular, and swift conservation in general. Your help to launch this campaign was fundamental.

Thank you to Action for Swifts – Dick Newall, Henry Kenner and Becky Ingram, and Jim. The birds are so lucky to have you and the brilliant S Brick and the countless ways in which you have fought for these iconic birds for decades!

Chris Mason and Paul Wren: you are the dream team both in terms of practical insight and emotional support. What you do for birds is remarkable, and you have helped me enormously in so many ways – thank you so much.

Stephen Fritt and Michael Oxford – your detailed expertise, dedication and persistence as well as your active support are greatly appreciated.

To all the swift rehabbers out there, especially Chet Chunago and Zoe Crealsey who have been on speed dial a few times. Thank you so much to the brilliant Margaret Aimes, Julie Baxton and Sylvia Scott.

George Candelin AKA Keeper of the Swifts – thank you for taking me under your wing. It is an honour and privilege to visit the swifts in the tower.

Nature Conservationists and NGOs:
Thank you to the conservation world – without scientists and NGOs, there would be no data that show the declines of cavity-nesting birds and the loss of nesting habitat. Thank you to all the people within the NGOs who have advised me, supported me and put their names and their organisations' names forward in active support of this campaign:

Craig Bennett, CEO of The Wildlife Trusts; Roger Mortlock, CEO CPRE; James 'Skylark' Wallace, CEO, River Action;

Ben McCarthy, Head of Nature Conservation & Restoration Ecology, National Trust; Dr Rose O'Neil, CEO, Campaign for National Parks; Nida Al-Fulaij, CEO, People's Trust for Endangered Species; Mike Childs, Head of Science, Policy and Research, Friends of the Earth ; Will Travers and Dr Mark Jones, Born Free; Chris Sherwood, CEO, RSPCA; Andy Lester, Head of Conservation, A Rocha UK; Sue Sayer MBE, Director, Seal Research Trust; Sally Hayns, CEO, Chartered Institute of Ecology and Environmental Management; Chris Luffingham, Acting Chief Executive, League Against Cruel Sports; Jo Judge, Co-Chair, IUCN National Committee UK Species Survival Working Group.

Special thanks to The British Trust for Ornithology, especially Juliet Vickery, Rob Robinson and Ieuan Evans.

Thank you very much to everyone at The Royal Society for the Protection of Birds for championing me and The Feather Speech campaign from the very start and for doing so much in so many different ways to help its progress, and especially to: Laurinda Luffman, Beccy Speight, Emma Marsh, Kate Jennings, Alice Hardiman, Katie-Jo Luxton, Guy Anderson, Chris Calow, Lucy Townsend, Luke Phillips, Gemma Cantelo, Carl Bunnage, Rafaelle Robin, Jet Woodwards and Jeff Knott.

Thank you, Wild Justice – Mark Avery, Lucy Lapwing, Chris Packham and Ruth Tingay – for coming to my aid in the final throws of the petition, and Mark for your invaluable insight as I stepped into the world of politics and lobbying.

Timo Roeke, BirdLife International, thank you for paving the way in The Netherlands and for your specific advice at policy level.

Thank you to urban ornithologists with a speciality in swifts: Anders Hedenström, Professor, Department of Biology, Lund University, and Dr Thais Martins.

Huge thanks to Richard Benwell and Wildlife&Countryside Link for your active and formal support, for contributing to the policy wording, proposals and everything in and around them.

Thank you very much to the main ecologists who helped advise, word and support the political proposals: Michael Oxford MCIEEM; Murray Davidson, Vice Chair of Local Government Ecologists and Environment and Natural Resources Manager, Hastings Borough Council; Claire Wansbury, FCIEEM FLS CEcol CMLI CEnv. AtkinsRéalis Fellow and Technical Director; Tom Docker CEcol MCIEEM, Managing Director Middlemarch.

A very big thank you to Tony Juniper, CBE, and Natural England.

Creatives:

To the original crew of The Feather Speech launch. Thank you for your creative, talented minds and for being so generous: Tim Flach and photographic team; Rewriting Extinction – Paul Goodenough, Veronika Villamil-Treit and Elisa De Pasquale; Guido Daniele; Rachel Louise Brown and your amazing students at the London College of Communication, University of the Arts, London, with extra special thanks to Goda Kraštinaitytė and Udbhav Nayak; Matt Stadlen, Paul and Alex Dickinson, The Met Police and Christian Tuckwell-Smith. Thank you so much Adam Blackmore-Heal (www.bhealmedia.co.uk) and Ben Cook (www.benjamincook.co.uk).

Thank you very much to all of you who were part of The Feather Speech, walking with me on that cold, wet day. Special thanks to my sister, Tamzin Davies, my Mummy, Kate Gates for helping so much with the logistics, as well as Leona and the Baker family, and the Dixons.

Thank you to the talented and kind artists and photographers who offered their artwork for free to help promote the petition, including Jonathan Pomroy, Mark Chivers, Claire Nuttall, Carl Bovis, Robert Booth and Holly Brodie and Ira Theobold for creating artwork especially for the campaign. Thanks to all the journalists who gave the birds airtime, especially Louise Turner, Patrick Barkham, and aptly named Henry Bird. Thank you so much to my fellow nature authors for such generous support. Big thanks to my dear friends Stacey Komolavanij and David Smith for your creative genius.

Campaign and political mentors:
Forever thanks to Dominic Dyer, James Wallace, Richard Benwell, Mary Tester. Thank you for always being there for me and the birds. You are inspirational forces for nature.

Will Dennis – thank you your support, belief and energy, for being the co-founder to The Feather Speech Consultancy CIC and for introducing me to the shining light, Josie Cadwallader-Hughes. Josie and Thakeham – thank you for showing true nature leadership.

Thank you to Neo: Jeff Knott – Jeff, you became a rock for me almost instantly. Your calmness, problem-solving ability, experience, insight and hilarious sense of humour made you such a great ally. Thank you so much for responding to my endless messages and for all the light you give me in the darkest of times.

Political champions:
To the politicians of Britain and beyond, who stood united for birds:

MPs: Robert Courts; Matt Vickers; Duncan Baker; Siobhan Baillie; Caroline Nokes; Kit Malthouse; Richard Foord; Richard Burgon; Samantha Dixon; Helen Lucy; Kerry McCarthy; Caroline Lucas, who stood united for birds at the petition parliamentary debate. You did us and the birds proud and so many people – at least 109,896 people – were extremely grateful.

Special thanks to MPs Anna Gelderd, Dr Simon Opher (aka Dr Swift!) and Barry Gardiner for so firmly establishing the swift-brick campaign in the Commons, and to the following MPs for all actively lobbying for swifts: Ellie Chowns; Phil Brickell; Olivia Blake; Abtisam Mohamed; Cat Smith; Chris Hinchcliffe; Cat Eccles; Sarah Champion; Rachael Maskell; Tonia Antoniazzi; Satvir Kaur; Neil Duncan-Jordan; Jo Platt; Steve Witherden; Will Stone; former Environment Minister and MP, George Eustice; Tim Farron; Nadia Whittome; James Naish; and my MP Sean Woodcock – and to any more who join this important bird club!

Peers: The Rt Hon. The Lord Randall of Uxbridge; The Lord Lucas; The Rt Hon. The Lord Blencathra; The Baroness Bennett of Manor Castle; The Baroness Hoey; The Baroness Taylor of Stevenage OBE. Your speeches in the House of Lords in support of Lord Goldsmith of Richmond Park's swift brick amendment became legendary instantly. Thank you so much for your leadership and support.

Thank you too, to: The Baroness Jones of Moulsecoomb; The Rt Hon. The Lord Benyon; The Lord Moylan; The Baroness Hayman of Ullock; The Rt Hon. The Lord Robathan for your help, support, advice and actions along the way.

Thank you, Caroline Lucas, for inspiring me before I launched my campaign, and to Cath Miller and the team, for supporting throughout the campaign.

Thank you to Sam Hall, CEO of CEN, and the Defra officials who have worked on behalf of cavity-nesting birds: Edward Barker, Michael Sigsworth and the rest of the team.

Extra special thanks to three politicians who have been fundamental to the campaign: Kit Malthouse MP; Professor John

Cortes, MBE, MP, JP, Ministry for Education, the Environment, Sustainability, Climate Change, Heritage, Technical Services and Transport, HM Government Gibraltar; and The Rt Hon. The Lord Randall of Uxbridge. Thank you so much for your counsel and advocacy. This campaign would not have got this far without you.

Thank you very much Ben Goldsmith, Chair of the Conservative Environment Network, nature advocate extraordinaire.

Thank you to Secretary of State Steve Reed for your support.

My final thank you goes to mine and the birds' ace card, Zac Goldsmith. Thank you for being the wings of the campaign. Our wild neighbours are so lucky to have you by their side.